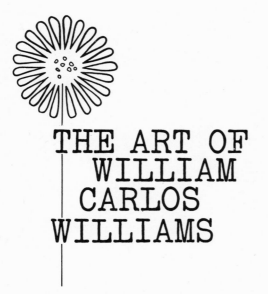

THE ART OF WILLIAM CARLOS WILLIAMS

UNIVERSITY OF ILLINOIS PRESS URBANA · CHICAGO · LONDON 1968

THE ART OF

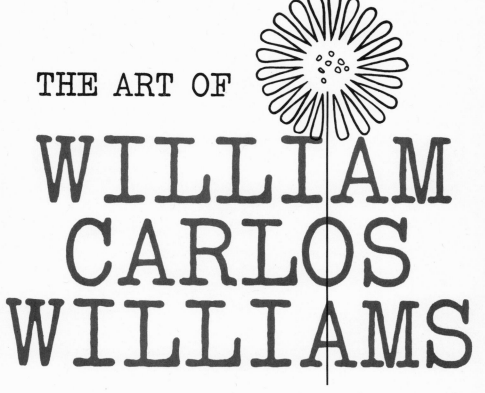

WILLIAM CARLOS WILLIAMS

A Discovery and Possession of America

JAMES GUIMOND

©1968 by the Board of Trustees of the University of Illinois
Manufactured in the United States of America
Library of Congress Catalog Card No. 68-11028

252-72449-6

ACKNOWLEDGMENTS

For insights into Dr. Williams' life and personality I wish to thank Mrs. Florence Williams, Mr. James Laughlin, and the late Mr. Charles Sheeler and his wife Musya—all of whom were kind enough to grant me interviews in 1963 and 1964.

I was aided in my research on Mr. Sheeler and Charles Demuth by the staff of the Whitney Museum of American Art and by a travel grant from the English Department of the University of Illinois. I am indebted to Mr. David Posner and Mr. Donald Gallup for permission to study the collections of Dr. Williams' papers and works in the Lockwood Memorial Library Poetry Collection, State University of New York at Buffalo, and in the American Literature Collection, Yale University. Permission to quote from unpublished works in these collections was granted by Mrs. Florence Williams, the State University of New York at Buffalo, and Yale University.

Finally, I wish to acknowledge that much of the quality of this book is due to the aid I have received from three persons. I am indebted to my daughter Laura for her patience; I am indebted to my wife for her industry, intuitions, and criticisms. Most of all, I am indebted to Professor Sherman Paul for directing my Doctoral thesis on William Carlos Williams and, afterward, for continuing to give me the benefit of his encouragement, his insights, and his extremely valuable skills and experience as a scholar and writer.

ABBREVIATIONS

Abbreviations for William Carlos Williams' works and sources which are most frequently cited in this study. For permission to quote from these and Dr. Williams' other works, I am indebted to Mrs. Florence Williams and New Directions Publishing Corporation.

Autobiography   *The Autobiography of William Carlos Williams* (New York: Random House, 1951).

Buffalo Collection   Dr. Williams' papers and manuscripts in the Poetry Collection of the Lockwood Memorial Library, State University of New York at Buffalo.

CEP   *The Collected Earlier Poems of William Carlos Williams* (Norfolk, Conn.: New Directions, 1951. Copyright 1938, 1951 by William Carlos Williams).

CLP   *The Collected Later Poems of William Carlos Williams,* rev. ed. (Norfolk, Conn.: New Directions, 1963. Copyright 1944, 1948, 1950 by William Carlos Williams).

FD   *The Farmers' Daughters* (Norfolk, Conn.: New Directions, 1961).

GAN   *The Great American Novel* in *Great American Short Novels,* ed. R. P. Blackmur (New York: Thomas Y. Crowell Co., 1960).

IAG   *In the American Grain* (Norfolk, Conn.: New Directions, 1956).

IWW   *I Wanted to Write a Poem,* ed. Edith Heal (Boston: Beacon Press, 1958).

Kora *Kora in Hell: Improvisations* (San Francisco: City Lights Books, 1957).

ML *Many Loves and Other Plays* (Norfolk, Conn.: New Directions, 1961).

Money *In the Money* (Norfolk, Conn.: New Directions, 1940).

ND 16 "The Lost Poems of William Carlos Williams," ed. John C. Thirlwall in *New Directions 16* (New York: New Directions, 1957).

ND 17 Dr. Williams' comments and manuscripts quoted in John C. Thirlwall's "William Carlos Williams' 'Paterson,'" *New Directions 17* (New York: New Directions, 1961).

Pagany *A Voyage to Pagany* (New York: The Macaulay Co., 1928).

Paterson *Paterson* I-V (Norfolk, Conn.: New Directions, 1963. Copyright 1946, 1948, 1949, 1951, ©1958 by William Carlos Williams).

Pictures *Pictures from Brueghel and Other Poems* (New York: New Directions, 1962. Copyright 1949, 1955, 1959, 1962 by William Carlos Williams).

SAA *Spring and All* (Dijon: Contact Publishing Co., 1923).

SE *Selected Essays* (New York: Random House, 1954).

SL *The Selected Letters of William Carlos Williams,* ed. John C. Thirwall (New York: McDowell, Obolensky, 1957. Copyright 1957 by William Carlos Williams). Excerpts reprinted by permission of New Directions, agents for Mrs. William Carlos Williams.

WM *White Mule* (Norfolk, Conn.: New Directions, 1937).

Yale Collection Dr. Williams' manuscripts, letters, and papers in the Collection of American Literature, Yale University Library.

Quotations from T. S. Eliot's *The Waste Land* are taken from *Collected Poems, 1909-1962* (New York: Harcourt, Brace & World, Inc., 1963). Reprinted by permission of the publishers.

CONTENTS

Chapter One 1

Chapter Two 29

Chapter Three 65

Chapter Four 93

Chapter Five 127

Chapter Six 153

Chapter Seven 175

Chapter Eight 201

Bibliography 245

Index 253

CHAPTER | ONE

A poem can be made of anything.
  Kora in Hell

Would it disturb you if I said
you have no other speech than poetry?
  "Writer's Prologue to a Play in Verse"

William Carlos Williams found subjects for his art everywhere in the life around him. Weeds, wild flowers, slums, and subway signs, his encounters with his patients and their babies, the aphorisms of his Puerto Rican mother, the medieval tapestries at the Cloisters museum, and chance conversations at neighborhood bars—all of these things were fit for his poems, novels, plays, and short stories. "There is nothing to eat, / seek it where you will," he wrote in a late poem, "but the body of the Lord" (*Pictures*, 93). Moreover, he was convinced that the "poetry" of his subjects was not foreign to them, not a transcendental symbol nor an intellectual form imposed upon material reality. Poetry existed, he wrote in his *Autobiography*, in the very language "to which we have been listening all our lives," in "the actual words, as we hear them spoken under all circumstances. . . . It is actually there, in the life before us, every minute that we are listening, a rarest element—not in our imaginations but there, there in fact" (*Autobiography*, 361, 362).

But though this "rarest element" is omnipresent in life, it is always hidden there and the circumstances of its presence are

never familiar. Men cannot rely upon past revelations to discover and live by the "poem" of their lives. They must discover
the underlying meaning of their existences from the immediate
language they speak, "as realistically as we recover metal out of
ore," for

one of the characteristics of this rare presence is that it is jealous of
exposure. . . . Its face is a particular face, it is likely to appear under
the most unlikely disguises. You cannot recognize it from past appearances—in fact it is always a new face. . . . It will not use the same
appearance for any new materialization. And it is our very life. It is
we ourselves, at our rarest moments, but inarticulate for the most part
except when in the poem one man, every five or six hundred years,
escapes to formulate a few gifted sentences (*Autobiography*, 362).

Evil, destruction, and waste occur inevitably whenever the
language of men's imaginations becomes incapable of appre-
hending this "rare presence" within its new and unfamiliar disguises. Then, when it confronts the new, the mind contracts in
fear and instead of nurturing and articulating new life it maims
or destroys the promise which always accompanies it. And without the "word" of poetry nothing in life has value, for then men
cannot recognize or preserve what is valuable in the world or
themselves. Without poetry life becomes totally destructive, a
"war" which "eats its young . . . creates only to mutilate and
swallow its own offspring" (*SE*, 245). Men, women, and all their
works are lost in the ravenous, self-destructive violence of the
"sea of blood" Williams described in *Paterson IV:* "the perverse
confusions that come of a failure to untangle the language and
make it our own as both man and woman are carried helplessly
toward the sea (of blood) which, by their failure of speech,
awaits them. The poet alone in this world holds the key to their
final rescue" (*ND 17*, 254).

The poet—the person possessing the word of the creative
imagination—exists in many forms in Williams' works. He—or
she—may be a painter like Charles Sheeler (*Autobiography*,
333), a Negro porter on the Erie Railroad (*IAG*, 210), an ex-
plorer like Columbus in *In the American Grain*,[1] or a scientist

[1]"Salt puts his own faith in a naive gentleness to the test . . . showing
Columbus to have been the poet that he was—or he never could have held
the tiller so unfailingly and for so long. A practical man would have turned

like Madam Curie in *Paterson IV*. But no matter what the poet's particular identity might be, in Williams' mind his function was constant. Only he can divert the energies of life from destruction to creation. Only he can rescue men by giving them the language through which they can possess the land where life grows and fulfills itself. "The ocean of savage lusts in which the wounded shark gnashes at his own tail is not our home," Williams wrote about *Paterson IV*, "It is the seed that floats to shore, one word, one tiny, even microscopic word, is that which can alone save us" (*SL*, 292).

Throughout his long career, Williams sought a "redeeming language" to communicate all the manifestations of this "rarest element" which are present in the life around us. "The thing has been with me to work the language in order to find what new may be done with it," he wrote in what is probably his best description of his career as a writer.

Not merely does one chase after newness for the sake of sensation or abandon the old because it is stale. There is a necessity to reinvestigate our means of expression in every age. . . . Unless every age claims the world for its own and makes it so by its own efforts in its own day . . . no one can be said to have lived. . . . These pieces show my own efforts to possess my world. . . .
Rutherford, N.J.
June 14, 1942[2]

The world William Carlos Williams possessed began in Rutherford, a northern New Jersey suburb where he was born on September 17, 1883. After attending schools in Switzerland and Paris and the Horace Mann School in New York City, he passed a special examination and entered the University of Pennsylvania Medical School in 1902. He received his degree in 1906 and spent the next four years in internships in New York City and in travel and postgraduate study abroad. After returning to Rutherford in 1910, he began the medical practice which lasted until he was incapacitated by strokes in 1951.

He married Florence (Flossie) Herman in 1913. In the same year he bought a house at 9 Ridge Road in Rutherford and pub-

---

back." "Introduction" to Sidney Salt, *Christopher Columbus and Other Poems* (Boston, 1937), p. 8.

[2]Williams' introduction to "Some Flower Studies" in *This Is My Best*, ed. Whit Burnett (Cleveland, 1945), p. 641.

lished his first book of serious poems, *The Tempers*. During the next fifty years, until his death in 1963, Williams lived with his wife in this house and managed a full literary career, writing poems, short stories, plays, novels, history, critical essays, an auto-biography, making translations, and carrying on a large personal correspondence.

When he was a boy, Williams later recalled, Rutherford was a rural community with a population of 3,000.[3] "It was an un-conscious triumph," he later wrote, ". . . to just be able to get out of doors and into my personal wild world. . . . flowers and trees were my peculiar interest. To touch a tree . . . to know the flowers was all I wanted" (*Autobiography*, 20). It was the world he described in his short story "Old Doc Rivers": "The horses trotted up the Plank Road. Past the railroad cut. It was a dark spring night. The cherry blossoms were out on the McGee property. Past the nurseries. Down the steep hill by the swamp. The turn. By the Cadmus farm. The County Bridge; clattering over the boards. Over the creek. The creek was flowing swiftly, an outgoing tide, a few lights streaking it, a few sounds rising, a faint ripple and a cool air" (*FD*, 79).

During Williams' lifetime, virtually all of this pastoralism was lost. During the twentieth century, northern New Jersey became one of the ugliest, least "poetic" places in the world. An epit-ome of the environment is Paterson, the "thrashing, breeding / . debased city" which Williams described in his poem *Paterson*:

> reversed in the mirror of its
> own squalor, debased by the divorce from learning,
> . . . .
> —flowers uprooted, columbine, yellow and red,
> strewn upon the path; dogwoods in full flower,
> the trees dismembered; its women
> shallow, its men steadfastly refusing—at
> the best
>
> (II, iii, 99-100)

Williams' prose and poetry are filled with images of waste, abuse, decay, and destruction. The invention of "the bomb" did not surprise him greatly; he seems to have considered it another

---

[3]"Seventy Years Deep," *Holiday*, XVI (Nov., 1954), 54.

example of man's long warfare against life. "Waste, waste!" he cries in a late poem, "dominates the world."

> . . . the witchcraft trials at Salem
>> to the latest
>>> book burnings
> are confessions
>> that the bomb
>>> has entered our lives
> to destroy us.
>> ("Asphodel," *Pictures,* 168)

The relationship between man and nature in Williams' environment is too often, as he entitled one of his poems, a "Defective Record" of senseless exploitation, ignorance, and destruction.

> Cut the bank for the fill.
> Dump sand
> pumped out of the river
> into the old swale
>
> killing whatever was
> there before—including
> even the muskrats. . . .
>> *(CEP, 420)*

Once there were many natural springs in the region, and some of them were "kept up beautifully." But now there are none because "the people that went there . . . actually shat in it, stole the pipe, killed the fish, dumped garbage, tramped the grass, the usual thing" *(Autobiography,* 393).

The men and women of the region destroy one another and themselves as thoroughly and crassly as they exploit their environment. In Williams' works, particularly his prose, this destruction is often brutal and violent. But he was equally alert to the consequences of cultural decay and economic deprivation: the slow waste and erosion of men's abilities for living ably and creatively. Contrasting the subjects of two of his short stories— "Ancient Gentility" and "The Girl with the Pimply Face"— Williams lamented: "Where had the refinement originated, the infinite gentleness alongside the criminal vulgarity, to [the?] total indifference to refinement which surrounded them . . . these were two old people [in "Ancient Gentility"] who in 2 generations had been so unrecognizably deformed. . . . I never [knew] when I would be confronted . . . with a marvel. Either

it would be a relic from a remote past . . . or something in-
credibly crass, betraying such ignorance, perhaps idiocy. . . .[4]

Williams was particularly sensitive to the fates of the women
of his region. He wrote of a waitress' "momentary beauty to be
enjoyed by / none of us. Neither by you, certainly, / nor by me"
(*CEP*, 446). And he described their tragedies with great sympathy in his play *Many Loves* and short stories like "The Farmers' Daughters." The fates of the region's men in Williams'
works are no better. Usually their "male excellence" of daring
and creativity is lost as surely as their women's beauty is wasted.
Some—like Sam Patch in *Paterson* and Dago Schultz in "An
Old Time Raid"—destroy themselves in their violent searches
for adventure. Others like Old Doc Rivers and Joe Stecher in
the *White Mule* trilogy waste themselves in the sordid competi-
tiveness of the professional and business worlds.

Since Williams was convinced that "in language is anchored
most of all the wisdom and follies of our lives,"[5] he believed
that the waste and decay around him were both caused by and
reflected in a breakdown in language and communication. In
Paterson II, his persona Mr. Paterson complains that the language of his locality is "worn out" and therefore unfit for poetry
(II, iii, 103). "For everything we know and do is tied up with
words," Williams wrote in 1934, "with the phrases words make,
with the grammar which stultifies, the prose or poetical rhythms
which bind us to our pet indolences and medievalisms." Therefore men could not "even begin to think straight" until they get
back to the words of pure experience, "words washed clean"
(*SE*, 163).

Once, perhaps sometime in the past, Williams believed, language was fresh or "clean." It had communicated realities precisely, sensitively. But now, like everything else, it was abused
and corrupted. "Language is in its January," he wrote in 1929.
"Language, which is the hope of man, is by this enslaved,
forced, raped, made a whore" [by academicians and philoso-
phers] (*SE*, 96). In his poem "The End of the Parade," Williams

---

[4]"The Short Stories of William Carlos Williams," pp. 16-17. Unpublished
introduction for an edition of his short stories in the Yale Collection. ZA
223.

[5]"How to Write" in Linda W. Wagner, *The Poems of William Carlos
Williams* (Middletown, Conn., 1964), p. 147. See also *SE*, p. 163. "How to
Write" was originally published in *New Directions 1936* (Norfolk, Conn.,
1936), n.p.

wrote that language which had once been fit for "song" had degenerated until it could only convey coercions, crude "percussion / strokes."[6] In another poem he compared poetry with a house which had been soundly built, but then there had been "neglect-tastelessness—," a "decay of the senses," "the descent into ugliness" (*CLP*, 116). As a consequence, the very material of the poet's art was apt to be repugnant and unreliable. "Meanings have been dulled," Williams wrote in 1929, "then lost, then perverted by their connotations (which have grown over them) until their effect on the mind is no longer what it was when they were fresh, but grows rotten as *poi*—though we may get to like *poi*" (*SE*, 89-90).

Several of the people whom Williams most loved and respected rejected the world in which he had chosen to live and be a poet, and this must have aggravated his doubts and anxieties about his "age" and his environment. Williams' mother was born in Puerto Rico. Her brother sent her to Paris to study painting and music, and then, when the family's money was lost, she was forced to return to Puerto Rico, leaving "everything behind to go back to that country where there was nothing" (*GAN*, 323). But after she moved to New Jersey, Puerto Rico seemed a paradise to her—"a / clean air, high up, unoffended / by gross odors."[7] Two of Williams' closest friends, Ezra Pound and Robert McAlmon, became expatriates. Williams defended himself against Pound's violent ridicule of "murica" and anyone who chose to live there, but in *Paterson* he confessed that he envied the men who could escape to the "peripheries."

> to other centers, direct—
> for clarity (if
> they found it)
>   loveliness and
> authority in the world—
>
> a sort of springtime
> toward which their minds aspired
> but which he saw,
> within himself—ice bound
>   (I, iii, 48)

[6]*CLP*, p. 45. The inspiration for this poem is possibly derived from Charles Demuth's painting of the same title which Williams owned. In Demuth's painting, a triumphant, sooty industrialism fills the world; so perhaps Williams' poem is a similar indictment of industrialism.

[7]"All the Fancy Things," *CEP*, p. 321. See also *CEP*, pp. 324, 375-378.

And later, in the poem, he consoled himself with the bleak realization that because the world's decay and degradation were universal there was no need for him to "move from this place" where he was born. He would despair anywhere (II, ii, 93).

Set against this awareness of the ugliness and waste around him was Williams' elemental faith that something valuable could somehow be made of his world. In his poem "Morning" he portrayed himself

> . . . with a stick,
> scratching within the littered field—
> old plaster, bits of brick—to find what
> coming? In God's name! Washed out, worn
> out, scavengered and rescavengered—
>
> Spirit of place rise from these ashes
> repeating secretly an obscure refrain:
>
> This is my house and here I live.
> Here I was born and this is my office—
>
> —passionately leans examining, stirring
> with the stick, a child following.
> Roots, salads? Medicinal, stomachic?
>
> (*CEP*, 395)

In 1950, when he had just written the grimmest, most despairing poetry of his career—*Paterson IV*—Williams was asked if poetry sprang from an attitude which was "essentially sad or unhappy, basically in disagreement with the state of affairs contemporary with the poet . . . a feeling of unhappiness, such as social discontent, personal frustration, &c?" He replied that poets were actually happy men because

basic faith in the world, and actual love for the world . . . is the basic ground of a poet's makeup. . . . He makes something out of his poems. That comes from a desire to build something useful—an affection for his fellow men. . . . I think that is where the modern poet, in the best sense, differs from his romantic, despairing confrères of the past. We know that we have a big job to do. . . . Therefore, let the hopeful artist manufacture of the materials of his art something—altho it may not be recognized by the ordinary person—which will be an organization of materials on a better basis than it had been before . . . he only does that if he feels that it's worth doing, and therefore he's an optimist. He believes in his world, he believes in his people, and that's the reason he's a poet.[8]

[8]"Symposium on Writing," *The Golden Goose*, Series 3, No. 2 (Autumn, 1951), p. 92.

Williams' "basic faith in the world" was the corollary of his belief in renewal, his conviction that decay, disorder, and death give birth to new life. For him "January" was both an "Invocation and Conclusion," because it was "the beginning of all things! / Sprung from the old burning nest / upward in the flame!" (*CEP*, 105). His mind was filled with an awareness of beginnings and endings; as a poet and as a physician he was concerned above all with life and death, the newborn and the very old. He could write of winters of his land and spirit which "are the desolate, dark weeks / when nature in its barrenness / equals the stupidity of man" (*CEP*, 433). And he could write some of the best poems about spring ever written.

> The birches are mad with green points
> the wood's edge is burning with their green,
> burning, seething—No, no, no.
> The birches are opening their leaves one
> by one. Their delicate leaves unfold cold
> and separate, one by one. Slender tassels
> hang swaying from the delicate branch tips—
> Oh, I cannot say it. There is no word.
>   (*CEP*, 228)

> Now the grass, tomorrow
> the stiff curl of wildcarrot leaf
> One by one objects are defined—
> It quickens: clarity, outline of leaf
> But now the stark dignity of
> entrance—Still, the profound change
> has come upon them: rooted, they
> grip down and begin to awaken
>   (*CEP*, 241-242)

Williams believed that human life underwent this process of renewal when the imagination made the world "alive" to men, made them aware of its excellences. "The imagination is the transmuter," he wrote. "It is the changer. Without imagination life cannot go on, for we are left staring at the empty casings where truth lived yesterday while the creature itself has escaped behind us" (*SE*, 213).

When some part of life is threatened by decay, works of art may enable men to renew or retain possession of its best qualities. Williams explained that he wrote a book about his mother because she was about to die, and his book would be "something of her—something impressed with her mind and her spirit . . .

remaining to perpetuate her—for our profit."[9] For the artist, he wrote in *Paterson V,* can lift his images of things and persons beyond the decay and abuse which afflict them in the natural world and into a "world of art" that has survived through the ages (V, i, 244). Or art could renew life after men had wasted it by destroying it or allowing it to decay into dull tawdriness. A poem, Williams wrote in 1939, creates "a counterfoil to the vague and excessively stupid juxtapositions commonly known as 'reality,' " because its effect is "to revive the senses and force them to re-see, re-hear, re-taste, re-smell and generally revalue" the world (*SE,* 235).

Williams insisted that if an artist wishes to renew life or enable men to possess it, his art itself will have to be renewed. Art can scarcely make anything new if its forms are stale and derivative. "Times change," he wrote in 1937, "and forms and their meanings alter. Thus new poems are necessary. Their forms must be discovered in the spoken, the living language of their day, or old forms, embodying exploded concepts, will tyrannize over the imagination, depriving us of its [the poem's] greatest benefits. In the forms of new poems will lie embedded the essences of future enlightenment."[10]

But a new art must obey the law of all created things. New forms, "consonant" with the artist's day, can only be created out of the chaos, out of the maelstrom of vulgar, destructive, tawdry life which surrounds the artist. Both the artist's fertility and the forms of his art, Williams wrote in 1946,

arise from the society about him of which he is (if he is to be fed) a part—the fecundating men and women about him who have given him birth. Let me insist, the poet's very life but also his forms originate in the political, social and economic maelstrom on which he rides.

The greatest creations, like those of the past in every case, arise from the close tie between the poet and the upsurging (or down surging) forms of his immediate world.[11]

[9]*Yes, Mrs. Williams: A Personal Record of My Mother* (New York, 1959), p. 24.

[10]"A Note on Poetry" in *The Oxford Anthology of American Literature,* eds. William Rose Benet and Norman Holmes Pearson (New York, 1938), p. 1314. "The mutability of the truth, Ibsen said it. Jefferson said it. We should have a revolution of some sort in America every ten years. The truth has to be redressed, re-examined, reaffirmed in a new mode. There has to be new poetry." *SE,* p. 217. See also *SE,* pp. 179, 202.

[11]"Letter to an Australian Editor," *Briarcliff Quarterly,* III, 11 (Oct., 1946), 208.

Williams arrived at these ideas about poetry very early in his career, but he did not arrive at them automatically. When he started writing poetry in the early 1900's, the Genteel Tradition underpropped the "official" poetry of the United States. New Jersey's most important and successful poets were Henry Van Dyke and Richard Watson Gilder, whose poems describe the bucolic aspects of rural and suburban New Jersey.

Everything tends to be idealized, including the landscape; but the very lack of passion and depth and reality speaks of suburbia—a pleasant, protected, ornamental refuge. . . .

This of course was the basic vision of the Genteel School as a whole. Poetry was not to deal with all of life, but with a part of it, the higher octaves only—love, nature, God, culture. As technically the key word is "finish," so emotionally the key word is "idealism." It was a world of visions rather than of reality that they hoped to present.[12]

Williams' first book of poems, published in 1909, was as visionary as anything in the Genteel Tradition. He strained unsuccessfully to reproduce the Genteel poets' mellifluous "finish," and his subjects were eminently idealistic: love, God, truth, beauty, and friendship. "Look at the titles in the early 1909 book," he later remarked, "' Hymn to the Spirit of Fraternal Love'—my but I was high falutin'—'Hymn to Perfection'—I *would* have to write a hymn on perfection" (*IWW*, 13-14).

But in the early 1900's there was a growing discontent with the glossy "perfections" of the Genteel Tradition. There was a growing conviction among artists throughout Europe and America that some form of new art should arise from the confused, brutal, and yet vital common life around them. The spirit of the new art was expressed by the Irish poet John Synge when he wrote that the "poetry of exultation" would always be the highest form,

but when men lose their poetic feeling for ordinary life, and cannot write poetry of ordinary things, their exalted poetry is likely to lose its strength of exaltation. . . .

In these days poetry is usually a flower of evil or good; but it is the timber of poetry that wears most surely, and there is no timber that has not strong roots among the clay and worms.

Even if we grant that exalted poetry can be kept successful by itself, the strong things of life are needed in poetry also, to show that what is

[12]Nathaniel Burt, "Henry Van Dyke and Richard Watson Gilder: The Garden Poets" in *The Literary Heritage of New Jersey*, eds. Richard M. Huber and Wheaton J. Lane (Princeton, 1964), pp. 60-61.

exalted and tender is not made by feeble blood. It may almost be said that before verse can be human again it must learn to be brutal.[13]

Among American artists, the revolution began among the painters. In 1908 a group of eight American artists, among them Robert Henri and John Sloan, rebelled against the National Academy and organized an exhibition in the Macbeth Gallery. Their paintings completely ignored stereotyped, Genteel themes and dealt with industrial and urban subjects drawn from the slums and factories of contemporary America.[14]

The poets were close behind the painters. Magazines—some with appropriate names like *Glebe* and *The Soil*—were founded to publish a rebellious, "new poetry." Orrick Johns—one of Williams' closest friends during this period—wrote that in 1915 Alfred Kreymborg, the editor of *Glebe* and *Others,* enthusiastically read to him "passages of Sandburg, Masters, and Lindsay. He told me that as a reader for the Bonis he had learned that people all over the country, and in London and Paris, were writing a new, strange, vital kind of poetry. They were taking the substance for the form, but [were] working out new forms too. It was a spontaneous uprising, a rebellion against the trite old rhymes, images and expressions of English verse."[15]

A number of American critics perceived the vitality of the new art. Van Wyck Brooks attacked "Highbrow" American culture in 1915 and argued that mysticism was fine, "but, on the other hand, one cannot have enough good human mud for ballast." The previous generation had "generally assumed that the only hope for American society lay in somehow lifting the 'Lowbrow' elements to the level of the 'Highbrow.' " But it was now plain that when idealistic ethics and culture were left to themselves they produced "a glassy inflexible priggishness . . . that paralyzes life." And it was equally plain, Brooks concluded, that the lower levels of life possessed "a certain humanity, flexibility, tangibility which are indispensable."[16] "If it comes to a choice between the art of vitality and sensation and the art of

[13]John M. Synge, *Poems and Translations* (Dublin, 1911), pp. 3-4.
[14]John I. H. Baur, *Revolution and Tradition in Modern American Art* (Cambridge, Mass., 1951), p. 13.
[15]Orrick Johns, *The Time of Our Lives* (New York, 1937), p. 222.
[16]Van Wyck Brooks, *America's Coming-of-Age,* rev. ed. (Garden City, N.Y., 1958), pp. 83, 15-16.

subtlety and intellect," James Oppenheim editorialized in *The Seven Arts* a year later,

> perhaps the raw appetite is wiser than "fine taste." If one must choose, there is much to be said for the street and the mill and the saloon, and all places where life is a hot flame, and not the curling wisp of incense.
>
> The truth of the matter is that great art was never *pure*. It was the expression of the whole man, and not merely his sublimated upper layer. He never separated soul from body. . . .
>
> Extremely significant for our future, then, is the emergence in America of the so-called "new poetry." From the older, the New England standpoint, it lacks refinement, gracefulness and respectability. But it is a vital growth from below upwards.[17]

Williams was one of the earliest and most passionate of these rebels. A Don Quixote in a Model T—as Alfred Kreymborg described him in *Troubadour*—he visited Grantwood, the artists' colony at Ridgefield, New Jersey, and the Greenwich Village parties where he met the modernist painters Marsden Hartley, Marcel Duchamp, Man Ray, and Charles Sheeler as well as Kreymborg, Orrick Johns, Wallace Stevens, Marianne Moore, Mina Loy, and the other partisans of the new poetry. He was immensely stimulated by this intense experimentation in the arts and immediately related it to his own ambitions and concerns. "Here was my chance," he later wrote, "that was all I knew. There had been a break somewhere, we were streaming through. . . ." Suddenly each artist had a chance to realize "his own designs" and objectives. As for himself, Williams recalled, this breakthrough meant that he would be able to make a "local assertion" to use the place he knew best as the material for his art (*Autobiography*, 138).

Williams proclaimed his "local assertion" in the first poem of *Al Que Quiere* (1917) in which he called for a band of "grotesque fellows" who would have his earthy tastes and go with him "poking into negro houses / with their gloom and smell! / in among children / leaping around a dead dog!"[18]

[17]James Oppenheim, "Editorials," *The Seven Arts*, I (Dec., 1916), 154, 155-156.

[18]*CEP*, pp. 117-118. See also *IWW*, p. 21. "A younger culture," Williams wrote in a 1929 defense of Joyce, "or one at its beginning, in full vigor, wishes for a fusion of the spirit with life as it exists here on earth in mud and slime today." *SE*, p. 87.

But the deeper significance of his "germination" as a poet is contained in his early poem "The Wanderer." It is in this poem, first published in 1914, that many of the responses which shaped Williams' development first appear.[19]

In "Advent," the first section of the poem, Williams appears as a young poet aboard a ferry crossing the Hudson—very much like Whitman on the Brooklyn ferry. He wonders self-consciously, "How shall I be a mirror to this modernity?" and immediately receives the answer through his apprehension of a spirit or daemon who personifies the free, powerful, and creative forces of his environment.

> When lo! in a rush, dragging
> A blunt boat on the yielding river—
> Suddenly I saw her! And she waved me
> From the white wet in midst of her playing!
> She cried me, "Haia! Here I am, son!
> See how strong my little finger is!
> Can I not swim well?
> I can fly too!" And with that a great sea-gull
> Went to the left, vanishing with a wild cry—
> But in my mind all the persons of godhead
> Followed after.
>
> *(CEP, 3)*

Williams' desire to be a "mirror to this modernity" dramatizes his renunciation of a poetic attitude which was an implicit rejection of his locality. In most of the poetry which he published before "The Wanderer," in *Poems* (1909) and *The Tempers* (1913), Williams avoided using vernacular language. These poems, he later recalled, were "full of inversions of phrase, the rhymes inaccurate, the forms stereotype" (*Autobiography*, 107). Their content expressed the withdrawal which characterized his mother's attitude toward their environment. "I was personifying

---

[19]"The Wanderer," *CEP*, pp. 3-12. The earliest version of the poem appeared in *The Egoist*, I, 6 (March, 1914), 109-111. The present, received text appeared in *The Catholic Anthology* (London, 1915). Both *The Egoist* and *The Catholic Anthology* were edited by Pound. The only substantial difference between these two versions of "The Wanderer" is that in *The Egoist* the old woman is referred to as a prostitute and the young poet's initiation is obviously sexual. Williams probably deleted these lines in the 1915 version—when he realized that the old woman symbolized his grandmother. See *ND 17*, p. 257; *Autobiography*, pp. 60-61; "The Three Letters," *Contact III* (1921), 10-13; *ND 16*, pp. 18-19.

her, her detachment from the world of Rutherford," he said later of the poems in *The Tempers*. ". . . her ordeal as a woman and as a foreigner in this country . . . remote from me, detached, looking down on an area in which I happened to live" (*IWW*, 16).

Sometime about 1908 Williams began to write a narrative poem, in imitation of Keats's *Endymion*, which would have been the epitome of his mother's attitude. It dealt with the wanderings of a noble, sensitive Prince in a debased landscape whose brutal inhabitants do not speak his language. But then, Williams recalled later, he became disgusted with his own "heroics" and burnt the poem. *"The Wanderer*, featuring my grandmother, [and] the river, the Passaic River, took its place—my first 'long' poem, which in turn led to *Paterson*. It was the 'line' that was the key—a study in the line itself, which challenged me" (*Autobiography*, 60-61).

Williams' reference to "the line" refers to his wholehearted adoption of American vernacular speech which began with "The Wanderer." His poems published in *Al Que Quiere*, he later commented, were "written in conversational language, as spoken, but rhythmical. . . . From this time on you can see the struggle to get a form without deforming the language" (*IWW*, 22-23). His reference to his maternal grandmother, Emily Wellcome, is equally significant. Unlike Williams' mother, she did not withdraw from the world around her. "She grubbed this earth with her own hands," Williams wrote about the shack where she lived on the Connecticut shore.

> . . . defended
> herself . . . against thieves,
> storms, sun, fire,
> against flies, against girls
> that came smelling about, against
> drought, against weeds, storm-tides,
> neighbors, weasels that stole her chickens,
> against the weakness of her own hands,
> against the growing strength of
> the boys, against wind, against
> the stones, against trespassers,
> against rents, against her own mind.[20]

---

[20]*CEP*, pp. 171-172. For other references to Williams' Grandmother Wellcome and her way of life, see "From: A Folded Skyscraper," *The American Caravan*, ed. Alfred Kreymborg *et al.* (New York, 1927), p. 217; "The Last

In "Clarity," the second part of "The Wanderer," Williams broadened the significance of the poem by identifying the old woman (his grandmother), who is the spirit of his environment, with the Goddess Demeter in the Homeric "Hymn to Demeter" and the myth of Kora.

> . . . I have seen her at last, this day,
> In whom age in age is united—
> Indifferent, out of sequence, marvelously!
> Saving alone that one sequence
> Which is the beauty of all the world. . . .
> . . . .
> It is she of whom I told you, old
> Forgiveless, unreconcilable;
> That high wanderer of by-ways
> Walking imperious in beggary!
>
> (*CEP,* 4)

Demeter is the goddess of grain and the earth's fertility. Her daughter Kora (or Core) represents beauty and springtime. In the myth, Kora is abducted by Hades who takes her to the underworld where, renamed Persephone, she becomes his queen. Demeter wanders disconsolately through the world searching for her daughter, "disfiguring her form for many days she went among the cities and rich fields of men . . . in fashion she was like an ancient crone who knows no more of childbearing. . . ."[21]

Williams knew the myth of Demeter well. He entitled his fourth book *Kora in Hell* (1920), and Ezra Pound dedicated *Ripostes* to him in 1912 with an inscription from Propertius: "To William Carlos Williams *'Quos ego Persephonae maxima dona feram.'* " His description of the old woman as uniting all the ages of the world, "Saving alone that one sequence / Which is the beauty of all the world," refers to the time of Demeter's wandering when Kora (springtime) was lost to the world and Demeter (the earth) disguised her beauty, fertility, and power.

Williams' description of the old woman as Demeter expresses his feelings about his local environment. She exists in filth and

---

Words of My English Grandmother," *CEP,* pp. 443-444; "A Descendant of Kings," *FD,* pp. 58-68.

[21]*The Homeric Hymns,* trans. Andrew Lang (New York, 1900), pp. 188-189.

beggary, yet she signifies "all the persons of godhead" to the poet: " 'It is she / The mighty, recreating the whole world' " (*CEP,* 4). In fact, Williams described Elsa von Freytag Loringhoven, the same sort of old woman, as "America personified in the filth of its own imagination."[22]

In the myth Demeter disguises herself as an ugly, barren crone to mourn the loss of Kora, but she remains a powerful goddess capable of conferring great benefits upon mankind—just as winter "disguises" the earth's fruitfulness but contains the seeds of spring. Similarly Williams was convinced that, beneath its growing ugliness and squalor, his environment possessed as much potential significance and beauty as any age or locale. He wrote in *The Great American Novel* that "the good of the past is the same good of the present. That the power that lived then lives today. That we too possess it" (*GAN,* 334). In *Kora in Hell* he claimed that his townspeople were

Giants in the dirt. The gods, the Greek gods, smothered in filth and ignorance. The race is scattered over the world. Where is its home? Find it if you've the genius. Here [is] Hebe with a sick jaw and a cruel husband . . . Herakles [*sic*] rowing boats on Berry's Creek! Zeus is a country doctor without a taste for coin jingling. . . . The ground lifts and out sally the heroes of Sophocles, of Aeschylus. . . . It's all of the gods, there's nothing else worth writing of. They are the same men they always were—but fallen. Do they dance now, they that danced beside Helicon? They dance much as they did then, only, few have an eye for it, through the dirt and fumes (*Kora,* 50-51).

In the next three sections of "The Wanderer"—"Broadway," "The Strike," and "Abroad"—Williams enters the modern world which he wishes to "mirror" and whose potential divinity he has perceived in the person of the old woman.

First he goes to "Broadway," the main business street of Paterson—though this could also refer to the famous street in Manhattan. What he sees shocks him: "crowds walking—men as visions / With expressionless, animate faces; / Empty men with shell-thin bodies / Jostling close above the gutter, / Hasting—nowhere!" (*CEP,* 5). It is the crass, dehumanized modern metropolis, the "city of dreadful day" populated by automatons whom Eliot described in *The Waste Land* and whom Williams described later in *Paterson.*

[22]"The Three Letters," 11. See n. 19 above.

> Unreal City,
> Under the brown fog of a winter dawn,
> A crowd flowed over London Bridge, so many,
> I had not thought death had undone so many.
>
> (*The Waste Land* I.60-63)

> Who because they
> neither know their sources nor the sills of their
> disappointments walk outside their bodies aimlessly
> for the most part,
> locked and forgot in their desires—unroused.
>
> (I, i, 14)

Since the old woman embodies the world's condition for the poet of "The Wanderer," her form and condition change to express the repugnance which the city arouses: "then for the first time / I really saw her, really scented the sweat / Of her presence and—fell back sickened!" (*CEP*, 5).

However, the young poet is only briefly repulsed by his environment. He quickly recovers and dedicates himself to the task of renewing his environment and its citizens by making them aware of the old woman's—i.e., the world's—true presence. His newly vowed dedication to his environment is more deeply shaken in "The Strike," the next section of the poem. He goes to the city's slums where he sees the 1913 Paterson strikers waiting in the bread lines. Though he admits that he has failed them in some way, he is more revolted by the strikers' debased condition than he is sympathetic to it. Years later Williams used lines from this section of "The Wanderer" in *Paterson* to signify "the aesthetic shock occasioned by the rise of the masses upon the artist."[23]

> Can it be anything but brutality?
> On that at least they're united! That at least
> Is their bean soup, their calm bread and a few luxuries!
> . . . .
> "Faces all knotted up like burls on oaks,
> Grasping, fox-snouted, thick-lipped,
> Sagging breasts and protruding stomachs,
> Rasping voices, filthy habits with the hands.
> Nowhere you! Everywhere the electric!
>
> (*CEP*, 7)

[23] *SL*, p. 259. The lines from "The Wanderer" which Williams used in *Paterson* appear on II, i, 58. John C. Thirlwall places a different interpretation on the significance of "The Strike" and its relation to *Paterson* in *ND 17*, pp. 256-261.

He discovers none of the earth's divinity in the city's poor ("Nowhere you!"). The "electric" shocks of their brutal physical appearance and habits threaten the very sensitivity which he must possess to be a poet: "Ugly, venomous, gigantic! / Tossing me as a great father his helpless / Infant till it shriek with ecstasy / And its eyes roll and its tongue hangs out!–" (CEP, 7).

Williams always insisted that nothing was too "low" to be poetry. The poet's function, he wrote in 1937, was "to lift, by use of his imagination and the language he hears, the material conditions and appearances of his environment to the sphere of the intelligence. . . . Thus anything that the poet can effectively lift . . . becomes his material. Anything. The commonplace, the tawdry, the sordid all have their poetic uses. . . ."[24] But like other poets who used commonplace or tawdry subjects, Williams had his saturation point, the point at which he needed to have some distance between himself and his subjects so that his imagination could raise them to the "sphere of the intelligence." Don't "fall into the machine," he advised a young poet, "do not become involved, too intimately involved, in your subject" (SL, 319). In Paterson Williams depicted his persona Mr. Paterson as nearly losing himself in the unconscious, abused humanity and nature he sees around him in the Garrett Mountain Park:

> he sees squirming roots trampled
> under the foliage of his mind by the holiday
> crowds as by the feet of the straining
> minister. From his eyes sparrows start and
> sing. His ears are toadstools, his fingers have
> begun to sprout leaves (his voice is drowned
> under the falls)
>
> (II, iii, 101-102)

Similarly in "Song of Myself," even Whitman is forced to admit that there are limits to his power to

> Embody all presences outlaw'd or suffering,
> See myself in prison shaped like another man,
> And feel the dull unintermitted pain.
> . . . .
> Enough! enough! enough!
> Somehow I have been stunn'd. Stand back!
> Give me a little time beyond my cuff'd head, slumbers,
>   dreams, gaping,
> I discover myself on the verge of a usual mistake.
>
> (Sections 37-38)

24"A Note on Poetry," p. 1313.

And Wordsworth complains in *The Prelude* that in London the "whole creative powers of man" are asleep (VII,681) and the love which makes poetry possible cannot "thrive with ease / Among the close and overcrowded haunts / Of cities, where the human heart is sick, / And the eye feeds it not, and cannot feed" (XIII, 202-205).

In "Abroad," the next section of the poem, Williams portrayed himself as achieving sufficient distance between himself and his environment in the same way that Wordsworth did—by retreating to the country: "The patch of road between the steep bramble banks; / The tree in the wind, the white house there, the sky!" (*CEP*, 8). The old woman takes the young poet on a flight over the New Jersey mountains. There, she tells him, he will be "safe." She then renews his vow to serve her by acquainting men with the true meaning of the world around them. The young poet eagerly accepts her command and shouts:

> "Waken! my people, to the boughs green
> With ripening fruit within you!
> Waken to the myriad cinquefoil
> In the waving grass of your minds!
> Waken to the silent phoebe nest
> Under the eaves of your spirit!"
>
> (*CEP*, 8)

The old woman immediately challenges him. The people below, she says, will be unable to respond to the poet's message because they are "bowed by their passions / Crushed down. . . . The weight of the sky is upon them" (*CEP*, 8-9).

This middle section of "The Wanderer"—"Broadway," "The Strike," and "Abroad"—expresses a problem that troubled Williams throughout his career: how does the poet actually live in the tawdry decaying world which he must renew? Williams was fully aware of how damaging the world could be. "Like all young men or women of intelligence," he wrote to a young Indian poet in 1950,

coming from an environment which in its common aspect is dreadfully backward, you enjoy being away from it. The horrors of some of the phases of India must sicken you. You are young. You are glad to have escaped (temporarily) from the necessity for doing something about that country. . . .

. . . You want, like all the young, to live the thrilling intellectual and emotional life you crave. You don't want to be bothered to have to give that up and throw yourself into that ancient maelstrom. For it may very well be the end of you. Truly it may. For it is not at all certain that you will succeed in doing anything, even with the greatest wit and intelligence. You may not even be wanted. They may be better off without you. That's a hard thought.[25]

And yet as he grew more aware of his responsibilities as a poet to his locality, Williams came to consider it more and more despicable for an artist to deny his origins, his age, or any aspect of his local environment. Again and again in his criticism Williams insists that the American artist must conceive "the possibility, the sullen, volcanic inevitability of the *place*" and be willing "to go down and wrestle with its conditions" (*IAG*, 225). No matter how degraded, vulgar, and grotesque the artist's *"place"* might be, he still had to deal with the totality of life around him. "What shall we say more of the verse that is to be left behind by the age we live in," Williams wrote in 1952, "if it does not have some of the marks the age has made upon us, its poets? The traumas of today, God knows, are plain enough upon our minds . . . yet our poems must show how we have struggled with them to measure and control them. And we must SUCCEED even while we succumb...." (*SL*, 315-316).

For Williams was convinced that only by having and maintaining roots in a locality, no matter how risky this might be, could an artist produce excellent work for a substantial period of time. A poet like Pound may "live for a time on a gathered hoard of skills"; but, Williams insisted, "the greatest creations, like those of the past . . . arise from the close tie between the poet and the upsurging (or down surging) forms of his immediate world."[26] Therefore the artist must first expose himself to his immediate world and *then* hope that it will not destroy him or his art. "Some exposure to the sharp edge of the mechanics of living" is necessary to the poet, he wrote in 1940. "It doesn't matter what the form is, these [dire necessities] are all of a class, to give the poet his sense of precision in the appreciation of

[25]*SL*, p. 289. In a rough draft of *Paterson* in the Yale Collection, Williams wrote:
  "The real world, the daily world, continues its assault to the intelligence's environment, that tends to fly off after the unattached—leaving the smells
    —and bandies mostly the past but
  for no reason than that the past is free. . . ."
[26]"Letter to an Australian Editor," 208.

values, what is commonly spoken of as 'reality' " (*SE*, 238). But, Williams went on to emphasize, none of these sharp edges of life were themselves poetry. No matter how driven by "death, disease or economic pressures" poets may be, they must never "permit themselves to be caught in the snare of their ˅⁓ lives and let that affect their decisions touching their worl ᴖᴖ̣ship. . . . It is a balance as to the push of reality's either stimulating them to excellence or killing them outright . . ." (*SE*, 239).

In the last part of "The Wanderer"—the sections entitled "Soothsay" and "St. James' Grove"—Williams depicts himself taking this risk. He submits himself to his environment by allowing the old woman to immerse him in the "filthy Passaic," the sewage-filled river which is the epitome of his environment's degradation, so that he will indeed be a "mirror" to the modern world around him.

> Then she, leaping up with a fierce cry:
> "Enter, youth, into this bulk!
> Enter, river, into this young man!"
> Then the river began to enter my heart,
> Eddying back cool and limpid
> Into the crystal beginning of its days.
> But with the rebound it leaped forward:
> Muddy, then black and shrunken
> Till I felt the utter depth of its rottenness
> The vile breadth of its degradation
> And dropped down knowing this was me now.
>   (*CEP*, 11)

There is an essentially similar immersion in the myth of Demeter. During her wanderings in search of Kora, Demeter is taken into the house of King Celeus as a nurse for his son Demophoön. Demeter holds Demophoön in the hearthfire to make him immortal, but she is interrupted and cries: "I would have made thy dear child deathless and exempt from age for ever, and would have given him glory imperishable. But now in nowise may he escape the Fates and death, yet glory imperishable will ever be his, since he has lain on my knees and slept within my arms. . . ."[27] Demeter then reveals to Celeus and his sons the arts of husbandry and the Eleusinian rites which will guarantee the earth's fruitfulness for men.

Her act is the archetypal pattern of renewal through immersion in a destructive element; other examples are baptism and

[27] *The Homeric Hymns*, p. 198.

ordeal rituals. "Any form whatever," according to Mircea
Eliade, "by the mere fact that it exists as such and endures,
necessarily loses vigor and becomes worn; to recover vigor, it
must be reabsorbed into the formless if only for an instant; it
must be restored to the primordial unity from which it issued;
in other words, it must return to 'chaos' (on the cosmic plane),
to 'orgy' (on the social plane), to 'darkness' (for seed), to 'water'
(baptism on the human plane, Atlantis on the plane of history,
and so on)."[28] In the myths and rituals based on this pattern,
men accept, or at least risk, the fate of nature—decay, formlessness, death—and are rewarded with the renewal of being which
characterizes natural life. "Verily, verily, I say unto you, Except
a corn of wheat fall into the ground and die, it abideth alone:
but if it die, it bringeth forth much fruit" (John xii.24).

Williams alluded specifically to the rebirth theme in the myth
of Demeter in several poems written before "The Wanderer."
Fire and water immerse an unnamed being in "The Ordeal"
(CEP, 23). "Portent" is even more explicit; it could be about
Demophoön: "Red cradle of the night, / In you / The dusky
child / Sleeps fast till his might / Shall be piled / Sinew on
sinew" (CEP, 27).

When he wrote "The Wanderer," Williams adapted this rebirth theme to his environment and the context of the poem. In
"Soothsay" the old woman prophesies the benefits of the poet's
acceptance of nature's condition.

> And she—"Behold yourself old!
> Sustained in strength, wielding might in gript surges!
> . . . .
> A vine among oaks—to the thin tops:
> Leaving the leafless leaved,
> Bearing purple clusters! Behold
> Yourself old! birds are behind you.
> You are the wind coming that stills birds,
> Shakes the leaves in booming polyphone—
> . . . .
> Linking all lions, all twitterings
> To make them nothing! Behold yourself old!"
>   (CEP, 9-10)

[28]Mircea Eliade, Cosmos and History: The Myth of the Eternal Return,
trans. Willard R. Trask (New York, 1959), p. 88. Eliade's "Myth of the
Eternal Return" can be applied to many of Williams' works, particularly A
Dream of Love, Paterson I-V, and "Asphodel." See Chapter Eight below. See
also C. G. Jung and C. Kerényi, Essays on a Science of Mythology, trans. R.
F. C. Hull (New York, 1963).

By growing "old," by accepting the decline of vigor and the
death which is the fate of natural things, the poet will also
receive nature's strength and combine its forces in the "wind" of
his voice or poetry.

Williams seems to describe this experience in general terms in
a letter to Marianne Moore written in 1934. After strongly
agreeing with her observation that he possessed an "inner security" Williams went on to comment that this feeling was the
consequence of an intense feeling of formless-selflessness, "something which occurred once when I was about twenty, a sudden
resignation to existence, a despair—if you wish to call it that,
but a despair which made everything a unit and at the same
time a part of myself. . . . Things have no names for me and
places have no significance. As a reward for this anonymity I feel
as much a part of things as trees and stones."[29]

Williams depicts his immersion and rebirth—his despairing
"resignation to existence" and consequent oneness with the
world around him—in "St. James' Grove," the last section of
"The Wanderer." Instead of fire, the destructive element is the
sewage-filled water of the Passaic River.

> . . . she lifted me and the water took a new tide
> Again into the older experiences,
> And so, backward and forward,
> It tortured itself within me
> Until time had been washed finally under,
> And the river had found its level
> And its last motion had ceased
> And I knew all—it became me.
> And I knew this for double certain
> For there, whitely, I saw myself
> Being borne off under the water!
>
> (*CEP*, 11-12)

As a result of his "death," the poet's relationship with his world
is renewed. Earlier in the poem he begged for "a new grip"
upon the reality around him, "up and out of terror, / Up from
before the death living around me . . ." (*CEP*, 6). After his
immersion at the conclusion of the poem, the old woman does

---

[29]*SL*, p. 147. This "despair" was the negative aspect of Williams' immersion in the objective reality around him. He described its positive force in
his *Autobiography* (pp. 356-357) and in his poem "Lear," *CLP*, p. 237. J.
Hillis Miller has an excellent discussion of this aspect of Williams' art in
Chapter VII of *Poets of Reality* (Cambridge, Mass., 1965).

grant the young poet this wish, but in a rather limited and oblique way. His relationship with nature will be timeless— "immemorial"—and some portion of it will be preserved from decay for his happiness.

> "For him and for me, river, the wandering,
> But by you I leave for [his?] happiness
> Deep foliage, the thickest beeches—
> Though elsewhere they are all dying—
> Tallest oaks and yellow birches
> That dip their leaves in you, mourning,
> As now I dip my hair, immemorial
> Of me, immemorial of him. . . ."
>
> *(CEP, 12)*

Williams maintained the conviction throughout his career that the artist and his art must spring from the totality of existence—including the "filthy Passaic," the repugnant, chaotic, and "anti-poetic" elements of reality both inside and outside of himself. In 1917—in what is probably his first critical article— Williams asserted that freedom of subject matter was even more important than freedom of form to the American artist. American poetry, he wrote, must have new forms, but "even more than that it must be free in that it is free to include all temperaments, all phases of our environment, physical as well as spiritual, mental and moral."[30] The artist, he wrote in 1939, "attacks, constantly toward a full possession of life by himself as a man" (*SE*, 199). "The poem to me," he said in a letter a decade later,

. . . is an attempt, an experiment, a failing experiment, toward assertion . . . of a new and total culture, the lifting of an environment to expression. . . . It embraces everything we are.
The poem . . . is the assertion that we are alive as ourselves—as much of the environment as it can grasp: exactly as Hellas lived in the *Iliad* (*SL*, 286).

To be fully alive and creative, therefore, men must be open and receptive to everything around them. They cannot ignore any of the natural forces inside or outside themselves, no matter how alien or destructive these forces may seem. For "disorder (a chaos)" also feeds the tree of art (*CEP*, 460).

---

[30]"America, Whitman, and the Art of Poetry," *The Poetry Journal*, VIII (Nov., 1917), 29.

Williams agreed fully with the idea that art must tap the dark anarchistic elements of the self. The artist must not reply in kind when he is criticized by the orderly minded; instead he must go on composing in a condition which is "a sort of night . . . except to himself where, within, there burns a fiery light, too fiery for logical statement."[31] He also believed that the artist must contact the chaotic or alien instinctual forces outside as well as inside of himself—the social or environmental equivalents of his unconscious psychic powers. Poetry, he wrote in 1929, does not require any "special soil" or "civilization" to protect it. "It lives where life is hardest, hottest, most subject to jailing, infringements and whatever it may be that groups of citizens oppose to danger."[32] In *In the American Grain* the American Indians represent such instinctual beings, and Williams judges his subjects in terms of their response to them. "The Puritan," he argued, "finding one thing like another in a world destined for blossom only in 'Eternity,' all soul, all 'emptiness' then here, was precluded from SEEING the Indian. They never realized the Indian in the least save as an unformed PURITAN. The *immorality* of such a concept, the inhumanity, the brutalizing effect upon their own minds, on their SPIRITS —they never suspected."[33] In Williams' other works the child, Negro, and the "poor" often fulfill approximately the same function that the Indian does in *In the American Grain*. They are the free, natural, *new* beings whose vitality the artist must recognize and contact if his art is to maintain its vitality. For the word is revealed in them, and the artist or society that fails to recognize their "measure" must suffer for this ignorance (*SE*, 270-271; *Pictures*, 167-168).

But new beings and instinctual drives are extremely inarticulate. Discovering their presences and values is only the first of the artist's responsibilities. He must still fulfill and communicate them by enabling them to realize their true, unique forms. To do this, Williams believed, the artist must possess technical skill. "The senseless / unarrangement of wild things—," Wil-

[31]*SL*, p. 239. See also "How to Write," p. 145 and "Seventy Years Deep," 78.

[32]"A Note on the Art of Poetry," *Blues*, I, 4 (May, 1929), 77-78.

[33]*IAG*, p. 113. See Chapter Three below and also Louis Martz, "The Unicorn in Paterson," *Thought*, XXXV (Winter, 1960), 545-548.

liams believed, is "the stupidest rime of all—" (*CEP,* 330); and therefore it is the artist who is a pioneer—who uses primitive, autochthonous materials—that needs most to be a good craftsman and develop the techniques which will renew his art and his world.

Williams often emphasized in his critical comments that the artist began with the instinctual. He never felt that simply speaking for the "dregs" or a "primitive profundity of personality" made a man a good artist. "I threw it aside in complete disgust when I saw how Evangelical he had become," he wrote about a book by Kenneth Patchen.

I think Patchen is obsessed by a divinity streak. He thinks he is God and that everything he says is good. He isn't self-critical enough—unless he really thinks he is John the Baptist. That won't do. It's all right to give the subconscious play but not *carte blanche. . . .* We let it go to see what it will turn up, but everything it turns up isn't equally valuable and significant. That's why we have developed a conscious brain (*SL,* 193-194).

In the same way, Williams praised Carl Sandburg for recognizing that "the report of the people" is "the basis of all art and of everything that is alive with regenerative power"; but he immediately condemned Sandburg for failing to

see that the terms the people use are so often the very thing that defeats them. It is by his invention of new terms that the artist uniquely serves. The process is much more complex than Sandburg realizes. . . .

The poet in himself, tormented by the things which Sandburg evinces, dissatisfied with mere repeated statement, over and over reiterated but undeveloped, digests that powerful incentive and puts it out as imaginative design, a new thing that embodies all their timeless agonies. It may not seem as effective to the active tormented man as the direct outcry—of an Okie in the desert, as Sandburg envisions him—but it has far more carrying power (*SE,* 276).

Williams stated the purpose which guided his career as an American poet in a talk which was printed in *Poetry* (1919). "To each thing its special quality, its special value that will enable it to stand alone. When each poem has achieved its particular form, unlike any other, when it shall stand alone— then we have achieved our language." He was already aware that this would not be an easy achievement. "I must write," he said in the same talk, "I must strive to express myself. I must study my technique, as a Puritan did his Bible. . . ."[34] But Williams never lost faith in the necessity of this achievement. "It is difficult / to get the news from poems," he wrote in one of his last poems, "yet men die miserably every day / for lack / of what is found there. / Hear me out / for I too am concerned . . ." (*Pictures*, 161-162).

During his long career as a writer, Williams always strove not only to discover the "words" of his contemporary environment, but also to increase his technical skill and invent new forms. "Such a poem as 'The Yachts' was written right off," he remarked in a 1950 interview,

without changing a word; some other poems I have jotted down, rejected them and returned to them as late as a year or two afterward and completed them. Sometimes I become completely stuck and . . . reject them. . . . In general, the most spontaneous bits of poems are written right off, quickly, from a sob-conscious [*sic*] or unconscious self and it just does actually pour out without the knowledge of the man who writes it. But, the better artist he is, the better he's able to recognize what is good and *why* it's good—and how to organize it into a satisfactory poem.

If your interest is in theory . . . and your mind is alive and you're trying to improve your poems technically, you will produce the work, and will never cease to produce it. In fact, I hope that with my last breath I shall make an addition to my technical equipment so that I will feel a little more satisfied to think of myself than I have been in the past.[35]

[34]"Notes from a Talk on Poetry," *Poetry*, XIV (July, 1919), 213, 216.
[35]"Symposium on Writing," pp. 94, 91.

CHAPTER | TWO

Williams' early development as a poet was influenced by two major concerns which can be discerned in many of his poems and critical remarks published between "The Wanderer" and the late 1920's.

First, he was determined that his poetry should reveal a "contact with experience" which he believed was essential to good writing (*SE*, 32). The artist must continually be in touch—no matter how imaginatively or circuitously—with his "locality," "an immediate objective world of actual experience" (*SE*, 33-34). Poetry must never be an escape from reality into prettiness or literary conventions, "empty nonsense having no relation to the place or the time they were written in."[1] In 1919 Williams praised Emanuel Carnevali, a young Italian poet living in America, because his poetry was a vivid expression of reality rather than poetic conventions. "What do I care," Williams exclaimed, "if Carnevali has not written three poems I can thoroughly admire? Who can write a poem complete in every part surrounded by this mess we live in?—His poems will not be constructed, they cannot be. He is wide open! . . . —We older can compose, we seek the seclusion of a style, of a technique, we make replicas of the world we live in and we live in them and not in the world."[2] And a few years later he began *Spring and All* with the contention that nearly all previous art had been "especially designed" to keep up a barrier between the senses

[1]"Four Foreigners," *Little Review*, VI, 5 (Sept., 1919), 36.
[2]Quoted in Paul Rosenfeld, *By Way of Art* (New York, 1928), p. 197.

and the moment of immediate experience. The intention of his own writing, Williams asserted, was to destroy this "constant barrier between the reader and his consciousness of immediate contact with the world," and to "refine, to clarify, to intensify that eternal moment in which we alone live" (*SAA*, 1, 3).

Williams' second great concern is best expressed in the term possession. He believed that it was not enough for an artist simply to exist in a locale, passively recording what he contacted. He insisted over and over that art was a form of action, not a substitute for it. The artist must possess his world, live in it, take responsibility for it, and use it for his imaginative pleasure. Human life was valuable, Williams wrote, "when completed by the imagination. And then only" (*SAA*, 30). Only in the "seriousness of a work of art" could men find a solution for the "continuous confusion and barrenness" which life imposes on the man who will not create his own, autonomous aesthetic reality (*SE*, 109). Therefore art must never be a "plagiarism after nature" (*SAA*, 35), an "imitation of the senseless / unarrangement of wild things— / the stupidest rime of all—" (*CEP*, 330). Instead art should be an "addition to nature," an imaginative construction of the artist's locality whose form and vitality both parallel and improve upon the reality from which it springs (*SAA*, 50-51). "Have I added," Williams wrote in a 1927 work-note, "some dignity, cogency, potency, interest, exhileration [*sic*] reason to this place—not to this microscopic banality, this suburb, this vacancy—but to this *place*—then I will have written."[3]

Williams knew that his poetic goals were ambitious, and that he could not attain them working in isolation. In a 1922 *Contact* editorial he emphasized that devotion to a locale was not synonomous with parochialism. "We have not stated," he wrote, "that an American in order to be an American must shut his mind in a corncrib. . . . We see no advantage in being ill informed when one might be well informed. We see every advantage to a man in up-to-date information made his own through experience of its significance in his own environment" (*SE*, 32). A year earlier, in his first *Contact* editorial, he argued that America would cease to be an "artistic desert" only when there

---

[3]This work-note is written on a rough draft of "Notes in Diary Form" which is dated December 13, 1927 and which is contained in the Buffalo Collection.

was an "interchange of ideas in our country," a "sense of mutual contact" among serious American artists (*SE*, 29).

Fortunately for Williams, all the "mutual contact" that he could desire was readily available to him. He had met Ezra Pound and H.D. at the University of Pennsylvania, and he had kept in touch with them through visits and correspondence after they became expatriates. Moreover, his home in Rutherford was only half an hour away from Greenwich Village. "I could attend a literary gathering most any week night and get home without missing an appointment," he later recalled,

and on Sundays I could spend the day exchanging thoughts with the promising "intellectuals" of the times. These meetings always included such people as Malcolm Cowley, Maxwell Bodenheim, Marsden Hartley, Marianne Moore, Charles Demuth and Charles Sheeler. . . . There were "the little magazines," *The Dial, Contact, The Criterion, The Soil* . . . and *Others*. . . . Most of these efforts were short-lived. The important part was knowing the people who contributed to them. These people were stimulating, and to them I owe much.[4]

Two of these groups of artists and artistic movements were particularly pertinent to Williams' early development as a poet: the Imagist-free verse movement and the Precisionist school of American painters, particularly Charles Demuth and Charles Sheeler who were his close friends.

In March, 1913, *Poetry* published an article containing the "three principles" which H.D., Pound, F. S. Flint, and Richard Aldington considered the basic tenets of their new school of poetry, the *Imagistes*.

1. Direct treatment of the "thing" whether subjective or objective.
2. To use absolutely no word that does not contribute to the presentation.
3. As regarding rhythm: to compose in the sequence of the musical phrase, not in sequence of a metronome.[5]

Rule 1 means that the poet should not intrude himself into the poem. Images are assumed to be intrinsically "poetic" in themselves, since, as Pound insisted, "the natural object is always the *adequate* symbol."[6] The poet therefore should present these images and not use them, in the symbolistic fashion, as representations of something higher. Rule 3 applies to language. The Imagist poet must use free, or "musical," lines of verse rather than

---

[4]"Seventy Years Deep," *Holiday*, XVI (Nov., 1954), 55.
[5]"A Retrospect," *Pavannes and Divisions* (New York, 1918), p. 95.
[6]*Ibid.*, p. 97.

counted meters. Rule 2 states a general principal which underlies rules 1 and 3. The Imagist's treatment of language and his subjects must be as precise and economical as possible. Gratuitous emotions and ideas cannot be used to make a subject poetic. Redundant words and inversions cannot be used to pad out meters and complete rhymes.

Williams agreed enthusiastically with these principles. By following them he was able to achieve the poetry without barriers he desired. "We had followed Pound's instructions," he later recalled, "his famous 'Don't,' eschewing inversions of the phrase, the putting down of what to our senses was tautological . . . merely to fill out a standard form" *(Autobiography,* 148). In 1929 he specified "what those [poets] of 1914 and thereabouts" won that was of definite value.

> At least inversions of the sentence seem finished. At least "poetic" diction should not be tolerated. We have at least learned to speak plainly in verse. At least one can say clearly what he means without necklaces of adjectives to halt us with their "nuances." Lofty thoughts certainly ought to be finished now as material for a poem.[7]

Some of Williams' early poems are unfortunately good examples of the worst sort of poetic diction. One written about 1909 begins:

> I've fond anticipation of a day
> O'erfilled with pure diversion presently,
> For I must read a lady poesie
> The while we glide by many a leafy bay.
> *(ND 16, 5)*

The language is so distorted to fit the metrical pattern that its qualities are lost. Some of Williams' other early poems have no pattern at all. For example, "To the Outer World," published in 1914, is not composed "in the sequence of a metronome."

> At peace here—I feel you about me.
> Do not think that I disdain your fine clothing,
> The distinctions of your robes clinging about the shoulders.
> *(ND 16, 10)*

The language is natural and undistorted, but it lacks distinction or precise identity. No attempt has been made to discover a "musical phrase" or emphasize any natural speech patterns. The poems in *The Tempers* (1913) are a mixture of these two tend-

7"For a New Magazine," *Blues,* I, 2 (March, 1929), 31.

encies, formlessness and stiff poetic diction. "Some . . . continue
to be mélanges of repetitive devices and techniques; in others,
however, Williams used innovations leading to the colloquial
speech line. This collection is representative of much poetry
written around 1912—reacting against restrictive traditions,
poets were giving imagination full play, almost despairingly."[8]

"The Wanderer" is technically the most successful of Williams' early poems. Its long, colloquial lines with their biblical
cadences are vigorous and flexible. But shortly after he wrote
"The Wanderer," Williams decided that loose, Whitmanesque
lines were too undisciplined. "American verse of today," he
wrote in a 1917 article, "must have a certain quality of freedom.
. . . and yet it must be governed." He went on to conclude that
Whitman was the "rock," the "first primitive" for modern
American poets. They could not "advance" until they had
"grasped Whitman and then built upon him."[9]

Approximately a year earlier, in 1915, Williams had already
begun to reform his poetic language by the Imagist-free verse
criterion of composition "in the sequence of the musical
phrase." "Danse Russe," published in the December, 1916 *Others,* is a good example of Williams' free but governed style of
poetry.

> If when my wife is sleeping
> and the baby and Kathleen
> are sleeping
> and the sun is a flame-white disc
> 5   in silken mists
> above shining trees,—
> if I in my north room
> dance naked, grotesquely
> before my mirror
> 10   waving my shirt round my head
> and singing softly to myself:
> "I am lonely, lonely.
> I was born to be lonely,
> I am best so!"
>
> *(CEP,* 148)

Several definite but discreet patterns make the "music" of the

---

[8]Linda W. Wagner, *The Poems of William Carlos Williams* (Middletown,
Conn., 1964), p. 13.

[9]"America, Whitman, and the Art of Poetry," *The Poetry Journal,* VIII
(Nov., 1917), 29, 31.

poem's language more perceptible. For example, the concentration of i vowels in lines 4-6 draws attention to the smooth sibilance of "shining" and "silken mists." Or, six of the seven lines 5-11 are composed of or end with prepositional phrases and have an anapestic quality—two or more unstressed or lightly stressed syllables in a crescendo to the final, stressed noun. These contrast with the more rapidly, frequently stressed lines 12-14 so that the qualities of both types of stress pattern are more clearly accentuated than they are in normal speech. Here is Pound's composition by "the musical phrase, not in sequence of a metronome." As a result the words of the poem exist in their own right, each with its own qualities more clearly perceptible. They have, as Williams wrote later about Gertrude Stein's writings, "a curious immediate quality quite apart from their meaning, much as in music different notes are dropped, so to speak, into repeated chords . . . for themselves alone" (SE, 114).

About 1917 Williams began to apply the Imagist principle of "direct treatment of the thing" fairly rigorously. He frequently explains the significance of his subjects or states his attitude toward them directly in his poems in Al Que Quiere, most of which were published in Others in 1916. "The Old Men," for example, concludes with Williams' direct expression of sympathy for the "Old men cut from touch" (CEP, 158). In other poems like "Chicory and Daisies" or two of his poems entitled "Pastoral," Williams concludes the poems with explicit assertions of the significance of his subjects (CEP, 121, 122, 124). Several other poems in Al Que Quiere—"Tract," "Riposte," and "Gulls"—are harangues in which Williams expounds his theories of life, death, and poetry to his townspeople.

Williams presents his subjects more objectively and asserts himself more discreetly in most of the poems in Sour Grapes. He was particularly careful to communicate the significance of his subjects through metaphors rather than explicit statements in the book's flower poems—"Great Mullen," "Daisy," "Primrose," and "Queen-Ann's Lace." The yellow of the primrose, for example, possesses all the exuberant vigor of summer and its sun:

> Clear yellow!
> It is a piece of blue paper
> in the grass or a threecluster of

> green walnuts swaying, children
> playing croquet . . .
>
> *(CEP,* 209)

The flower is not yellow *like* the sun; it is a sun in itself—when seen as truly and vividly as its nature deserves.

Also in *Sour Grapes* Williams often expresses the emotional power of his subjects through the use of exclamation points or phrases like "Oya!" and "Ha!"—rather than explicit praise. This practice corresponds closely to the *kana,* a Japanese particle used by Zen poets in their *haiku* poems. The *kana,* which is often translated by an exclamation point, can be attached to a noun, adjective, or adverb to signify "a certain feeling of admiration or praise or sorrow or joy." It expresses an eloquent silence during which the poet refuses to verbalize or intellectualize a sensual experience because he is "intoxicated" with a feeling that can only be exclaimed "in an unutterable, inaudible cry."[10] Williams' exclamations seem to convey the same meaning as the *kana.* They indicate that he has experienced his subjects with intense emotion. But he refuses to articulate or identify this emotion further, since this verbalization would dilute the subject by shifting the reader's attention from the concrete object.

Sometimes in *Sour Grapes* Williams uses his own feelings as the subjects of his poems. But when he does this, his feelings are more "objectified" than they are in *Al Que Quiere.* "To Waken an Old Lady" is, like "The Old Men," an expression of sympathy with the old. However, Williams defines the woman's condition entirely in terms of an "objective," natural metaphor.

> Old age is
> a flight of small
> cheeping birds
> skimming
> bare trees
> above a snow glaze.
> Gaining and failing
> they are buffeted
> by a dark wind—
>
> *(CEP,* 200)

[10]D. T. Suzuki, "Lectures on Zen Buddhism" in *Zen Buddhism and Psychoanalysis* (New York, 1960), pp. 2, 4.

By avoiding the conventional simile in line one, by not making her condition "like" the birds', Williams makes it an objective equivalent of their winter flight rather than a poet's subjective comparison.[11]

In the second half of the poem, Williams sympathizes with the old woman's condition. He describes those details of the birds' flight which express his desire that she enjoy the pleasures which are possible for her.

> But what?
> On harsh weedstalks
> the flock has rested,
> the snow
> is covered with broken
> seedhusks
> and the wind tempered
> by a shrill
> piping of plenty.

Williams conveys this emotion precisely even though he does not state it directly. His sympathy for the old woman does not mitigate his awareness of her condition, for the weedstalks are "harsh" and the wind is only "tempered" by the birds' enjoyment of their "plenty."

By keeping himself "out of the picture" (*IWW*, 21), Williams achieved the precise, "direct treatment of the 'thing' whether subjective or objective" which Pound and the other Imagists desired. His poetry had not yet attained the tense, elliptical austerity which characterized his work of the 1930's, but it shows that he was already moving toward his Objectivist ideal of a poetry which "doesn't declaim or explain; it presents."[12]

As William Pratt has commented, there have been "few other kinds of poets in the twentieth century" than the Imagists. Their principles have been so all-pervasive that they "have been carried forward in the mature poetry of nearly every one of the major poets of our time."[13] What was unique about Williams'

---

[11]"I have always had a feeling of identity with nature, but not assertive; I have always believed in keeping myself out of the picture. When I spoke of flowers, I *was* a flower. . . ." *IWW*, p. 21.

[12]"A Note on Poetry" in *The Oxford Anthology of American Literature*, eds. William Rose Benet and Norman Holmes Pearson (New York, 1938), p. 1313. See also Kenneth Burke, "Heaven's First Law," *The Dial*, LXXII (Feb., 1922), 197, 199, 200.

[13]William Pratt, "Introduction," *The Imagist Poem* (New York, 1963), p. 38.

development as an Imagist was his determination to apply the movement's principles to local, modern, colloquial subject matter and language—the "filthy Passaic" of contemporary life of which he had vowed to speak in "The Wanderer." " 'I've always wanted to fit poetry into the life around us,' " he said in 1956. ". . . I'm not the type of poet who looks only at the rare thing. I want to use the words we speak and to describe the things we see, as far as it can be done. I abandoned the rare world of H.D. and Ezra Pound. Poetry should be brought into the world where we live and not be so recondite, so removed from the people" (ND 17, 253).

The other Imagists usually derived their images and language from worlds of "rare things"—worlds where language, feelings, and objects are so intrinsically musical, significant, and beautiful that they would be poetic no matter how barely or directly they might be presented. Some of the Imagists, H.D. and Richard Aldington, for example, found this type of world in the pristine landscapes and delicate emotions of the Greek Anthology. Others like Pound and Eliot adopted for their norms great ages of past art—archaic Greece, medieval Ravenna, seventeenth-century England—"some epoch, some golden age . . . when the Image, the intuited, creative reality, was habitually known and respected."[14]

Williams, however, kept his poetry firmly anchored in the world around him. He analyzed the consequences of his decision to use primarily American speech and images in an article on Gertrude Stein. The American writer, he asserted, could not rely upon his material to be musical or poetic in itself. It was filled with "senseless repetitions, the endless multiplications of toneless words" (SE, 119). Nor could he retreat to the private world of his emotions and copy them for his subjects; they were likely to be as confused as the environment (SE, 119-120). Faced with these handicaps, how, he asked, could American writing "compete with excellence elsewhere and in other times . . . be at once objective (true to fact) intellectually searching, subtle and instinct with powerful additions to our lives?" Such a goal would be impossible, he decided, "without invention of some

[14]Frank Kermode, "Disassociation of Sensibility" in *Modern Criticism: Theory and Practice,* eds. Walter Sutton and Richard Foster (New York, 1963), p. 310.

sort, for the very good reason that observation about us engenders the very opposite of what we seek: triviality, crassness and intellectual bankruptcy. And yet what we do see can in no way be excluded. Satire and flight are two possibilities but Miss Stein has chosen otherwise" (*SE,* 118).

Williams too had chosen neither to flee from American subject matter nor to satirize it. His early poetry reveals three distinct types of "invention" which enabled him to use local materials, to possess his world, and yet to meet the extremely high standards which he had learned from the Imagists.

The earliest and simplest of these techniques is Williams' careful selection of local materials which could be presented in a bare concise manner. He praised Laforgue for his "building upon the basis of . . . what is of value to the man in the welter as he found it, and a rigid exclusion of everything else" (*SE,* 36). A few years later he praised Poe for having a "lean style, rapid as a hunter and with an aim as sure" instead of wallowing in "nameless rapture" over the " 'excessively opportune,' " obviously attractive natural beauties of America. Williams' critical standards fuse with Poe's as he lapses from the past tense to the present in discussing American literature: "It is a fight . . . to *borrow nothing* from the scene, but to put all the weight of effort into the WRITING. Put aside the GRAND scene and get to work to express yourself" (*IAG,* 227).

Williams states the principle of his selectivity in his early poem "Apology." Why does he write?

> The beauty of
> the terrible faces
> of our nonentities
> stirs me to it:
>
> colored women
> day workers—
> . . . .
> in cast off clothing
> faces like
> old Florentine oak.
> (*CEP,* 131)

Such persons, he explains in *Spring and All,* make up the vital class in society. They possess "the energizing force of imagination." Like magnets, they attract "particles" of experience which adhere to them and therefore there is an immediate affinity between them and the artist. "Among artists, or as they are sometimes called 'men of imagination' 'creators', etc. this force is recognized in a pure state—All this can be used to show the relationships between genius, hand labor, religion . . ." *(SAA,* 70).

In his earlier poems, particularly those in *Al Que Quiere,* all of Williams' human subjects are earthy, vital, and lower class: Negroes, children, workmen, his grandmother Wellcome, a drunkard who proudly proclaims that he is a penniless rumsoak and that the "stuff" of his life "is the feel of good legs / and a broad pelvis" *(CEP,* 140). Their language, actions, and appearances are intrinsically unique, candid, and picturesque. Having selected these subjects, Williams only has to describe them or transcribe their speech and add line divisions to make them into poems.

The natural images in Williams' early poems have the same vitality and picturesqueness. Wild flowers and weeds, a single "ancient star" shining alone in the sunrise, a "crooked black tree warped passionately to one side" in its eagerness to grow—each possesses an intrinsically dramatic, vivid identity which is communicated by Williams' bare, tonic descriptions.

There is a similar vitality and simplicity in Williams' poems about himself in *Al Que Quiere.* He writes about his moods either early in the morning or late at night—when his sensitivity is at its height and when his mind is free from the stifling affairs of his middle-class townspeople.

Two of the best examples of this mode of possession are "January Morning" and "Dedication for a Plot of Ground" which are two of the longest poems in *Al Que Quiere.* The quality of both poems depends almost entirely on Williams' skillful selection of details. "January Morning" is devoted to a single mood and "Dedication" to a single subject, Williams' grandmother Wellcome, but in both poems he achieves unity by keeping very closely to his subjects and not introducing any alien or irrelevant images. The structural qualities of the poems are minimal—bare, chronological enumeration and nothing more. Both are excellent examples of what Kenneth Rexroth has described as Williams' "way of keeping / Still about the world"[15]—his gift for recognizing that certain things are poems all by themselves and that they need

[15]Kenneth Rexroth, "A Letter to William Carlos Williams," *The Signature of All Things* (New York, n.d.), p. 48.

as little as possible said *about* them by the poet. Williams never lost this restraint, and throughout his career he was able to realize that sometimes a poem could be made of the sight of a cat climbing over a jam closet *(CEP,* 340) or the words on a note telling his wife that he'd eaten the plums in the icebox which she had saved for breakfast *(CEP,* 354).

But though Williams never lost his taste for these simple, vital subjects he was also committed to creating a poetry which would "include all temperaments, all phases of our environment." He was fully aware that there were parts of his world which demanded more subtle and difficult poetic techniques if he was to realize their qualities in his art.

The 1927 work-note—included with the manuscript of "The Descent of Winter" in the Buffalo Collection—contains this brief but relevant guide to Williams' poetic ambitions during the 1920's: "Have I added some dignity, cogency, potency, interest, exhileration [*sic*] reason to this place . . . then I will have written." Many of his best poems written during the 1920's can be classified as responses to one of two challenges. First, there were the American subjects which challenged Williams because of their drabness and dullness. "The thing, the United States," he raged in an essay, "the unmitigated stupidity, the drab tediousness of the democracy, the overwhelming number of the offensively ignorant, the dull nerve . . . cannot be escaped" *(SE,* 119). It was to these subjects that Williams sought to give exhilaration, interest, and potency.

Second, there were the American subjects which were much more than simply picturesque or vital in themselves. Certain subjects in any locality, Williams believed, were essentially beautiful or "artistocratic" in nature *(IAG,* 224). They were potentially "classic" or "universal" in their intrinsic excellence —if this excellence could be realized in works of art which would add the proper "dignity" and "cogency" to them. By 1926 when he received the *Dial* award Williams consciously desired to write poems "celebrating the local material . . . in a dignified way," using "only the material that concerned the locale that I occupied . . . to have no connection with the European world, but to be purely American" *(ND 17,* 307). During his 1924 European trip Williams had seen classical works of art which possessed this excellence. But he was frightened by these works because he feared that their perfections were so much greater than those of the reality around him that he would become estranged from life. He wandered lost between "the stonelike reality of ancient excellence and the pulpy worthlessness of every day" (*Pagany*, 157). Yet little more than a decade later he wrote confidently about the subject of one of his poems: "there is a dignity in this girl quite comparable to that of the Venus. . . . Why not imagine this girl Venus? Venus lives! . . . [my poem] presents a simple image in the same sort of light that the Athenian placed the Venus—only in not the same context."[16]

The poetic techniques which Williams used to add significance and exhilaration to his subjects closely resemble the stylistic qualities of paintings by Charles Sheeler and Charles Demuth, two members of the Precisionist school of American painting who were his contemporaries and close personal friends.[17]

During the early 1920's, as Williams later recalled, the painters and poets were closely allied. The principles of "impressionism, dadaism, surrealism applied to both painting and the poem" (*Autobiography*, 148). Williams' development at this stage in his career was very similar to Demuth's and Sheeler's. They were the same age—all three were born in 1883—and had all begun their careers under the influence of the Genteel Tra-

[16]"The So-Called So-Called," *The Patroon*, I, 1 (May, 1937), 37-38, 40. See also Chapter XVIII of *A Voyage to Pagany* (New York, 1928).

[17]The best source of information about the Precisionist painters is Martin L. Friedman, *The Precisionist View in American Art* (Minneapolis, 1960). Two good general studies are Milton W. Brown, *American Painting from the Armory Show to the Depression* (Princeton, 1955) and John I. H. Baur, *Revolution and Tradition in Modern American Art* (Cambridge, Mass., 1951). There are two excellent books on Sheeler: Lillian Dochterman, *The Quest of Charles Sheeler* (Iowa City, 1963) and Constance Rourke, *Charles Sheeler: Artist in the American Tradition* (New York, 1938). No comparable study of Demuth exists, but Andrew Ritchie, *Charles Demuth* (New York, 1950) and Paul Rosenfeld, "Charles Demuth," *The Nation*, CXXXIII (Oct. 7, 1931), 371-373 are helpful.

My summary of Sheeler's and Demuth's early careers is largely indebted to Dochterman, pp. 38-40. Reproductions of Demuth's and Sheeler's works, which are referred to later in this chapter, are available in Friedman, Dochterman, and Rourke.

dition. Sheeler and Demuth were studying at the Philadelphia Academy of Fine Arts at about the same time that Williams was writing his *Endymion*-imitation and the poems which appeared in his 1909 *Poems* and *The Tempers*. During the period between 1910 and 1914 all three rejected their early work and began to deal with their subjects in a relatively broad, naturalistic way: Sheeler's Fauvist landscapes, Demuth's vaudeville water colors, Williams' "The Wanderer" and some of the poems in *Al Que Quiere*. Between 1912 and 1915, they became acquainted with international art movements—Cubism and Imagism— whose techniques they skillfully adapted to American conditions during the late 1910's. All three were on the fringe of the group which Alfred Stieglitz gathered around him at his galleries—first at 291 and later at An American Place.

It is difficult and not too relevant to know exactly how much overt stylistic influence Sheeler's and Demuth's paintings had upon Williams' poetry. The chief reason for the stylistic similarities between his work and theirs was probably due to certain temperamental affinities. Williams was writing poems very much like his friends' work at a time when no direct influence was possible. For example, his poems "To a Solitary Disciple" and "Ballet" are remarkably like Demuth's "white architecture" series. The former poem even has the "ray lines" which Demuth adopted from Futurism: "See how the converging lines / of the hexagonal spire / escape upward—" (*CEP*, 167). However, Demuth developed this style of architectural-landscape painting during a trip to Bermuda in 1917; Williams' poems were published in *Others* in 1916. Similarly, Williams' "Good Night" (*CEP*, 145-146) shows the same meticulously precise and understated perception of the ordinary artifacts of American life which characterizes Sheeler's still-life interiors; yet this poem was published in *Others* in 1916, seven years before Williams met Sheeler or knew of his work.

Both Demuth and Sheeler "brought out" something in Williams himself. Each man expressed in his art and his way of life certain developing qualities which were parallel or comparable to certain qualities that were developing in Williams. Therefore he was interested in Demuth and Sheeler both as men and as artists. It is for this reason that his writing is often similar to their paintings in ways which are expressive of the developments of all three men.

Williams referred to Demuth on several occasions in which he spoke of art as a lively, imaginative, essentially aristocratic activity. Demuth had once told him, Williams wrote in his Prologue to *Kora in Hell,* that the virtue of art "is in an opening of the doors, though some rooms of course will be empty, a break with banality, the continual hardening which habit enforces" (*SE,* 26). Demuth's art and his attitude toward life—sophisticated, sharp-witted, and irreverent—corresponded to Williams' taste for "something new. . . . Something to enliven our lives by its invention, some breadth of understanding, some lightness of touch. . . ."[18] On the other hand, Sheeler's work and attitudes corresponded to one of the most serious elements in Williams' personality, his desire to see and experience life with absolute clarity. Constance Rourke has described Williams' and Sheeler's first meeting.

Sheeler had read portions of "In the American Grain" published in *Broom,* was warmly enthusiastic about them, and exclaimed when he met Williams at the [Matthew] Josephsons', "Here is the man I've been looking for all my life!" And Williams, who knew some of Sheeler's work, felt that he had "looked at things directly, truly. It was a bond. We both had become aware of a fresh currency in expression, and as we talked we found that we both meant to lead a life which meant direct association and communication with immediate things."[19]

Williams was immensely impressed by Sheeler's ability to see and present these "immediate things" entirely, in terms of both their unique and their general or universal identities (*SE,* 233).

Among the Precisionist painters, Demuth was the great enemy of what Williams called the "unmitigated stupidity, the drab tediousness" of American life (*SE,* 119). Something of a dandy, a close friend of Marcel Duchamp, Demuth was—to use Wallace Stevens' term—a "Connoisseur of Chaos" and a master of the witty title. His painting of a glum water tower and chimney is entitled "Aucassin et Nicolette." Commonplace reality is Demuth's subject, but in his paintings it exists as it does in circus and vaudeville—two of Demuth's favorite pastimes—lively, hard, and vivid, very much under the direction of an Impresario of the Real. In contrast, Sheeler is the man of integrity, full of

[18]"For a New Magazine," 31. For other references by Williams to Demuth see "America, Whitman, and the Art of Poetry," 34; *SAA,* p. 16; *Autobiography,* pp. 151-152; *SE,* p. 26.

[19]Quoted in Rourke, *Charles Sheeler,* pp. 49-50.

respect for the commonplace, which he clarifies and organizes so that each object's identity is based upon a fresh perception of its unique qualities, its denotations, rather than its utilitarian or sentimental connotations.

Both Sheeler and Demuth used local materials, but in far different ways. Demuth decorated barns near Lancaster with Pennsylvania Dutch hex signs; one of Sheeler's best works is his tempera and crayon "Bucks County Barns," an exquisitely precise rendition of contrasting native materials, weathered grey wood and sandy yellow stone. The presence of both these attitudes in Williams is well illustrated by Sheeler's and Demuth's respective portraits of him. Sheeler's photograph, one of his few portraits, shows Williams soberly contemplative, sitting by a tree in a forest or garden. Demuth's "poster-portrait" is based on Williams' poem "The Great Figure."[20] Entitled "I Saw the Figure 5 in Gold," it expressionistically symbolizes Williams as an abstract, scarlet fire engine racing through the streets of New York.

Williams achieves the same cold precision and nervous speed that characterizes many of Demuth's paintings in poems like "Flight to the City," "Young Love," "Rapid Transit," and "The Agonized Spires"—all published in *Spring and All,* which was dedicated to Demuth. All of these poems use deliberately commonplace, even drab, urban imagery. But, like Demuth's paintings, their effect is artificially, theatrically rapid, vivid, and forceful. The most frequent punctuation mark is the dash—used more to indicate gasps for breath rather than pauses. Williams used as few periods as possible, and his syntax is minimal. The lines are extremely short, often single words. Images, situations, phrases of conversation—all are wrenched out of the context of daily life and deftly inserted into the torrential aesthetic reality of the poems.

"Struggle of Wings," first published in 1926, is one of Williams' most direct statements of this style in which commonplace materials are used in a deliberately uncommon, almost abstract or surrealistic way.

[20]*CEP,* p. 230. For Williams' comments on Demuth's painting, see *SL,* pp. 97-98. Sheeler's portrait photograph of Williams is reproduced facing p. 208 of *Briarcliff Quarterly,* III, 11 (Oct., 1946).

And it is Innes on the meadows and fruit is
yellow ripening in windows every minute
growing brighter in the bulblight by the
cabbages and spuds—

. . . .

up and down the Rio Grand the sand is sand
on every hand (Grand chorus and finale)
                                        (. . . . .

Out of such drab trash as this
by a metamorphosis
bright as wallpaper or crayon
or where the sun casts ray on ray on
flowers in a dish, you shall weave
for Poesy a gaudy sleeve
a scarf, a cap and find him gloves
whiter than the backs of doves[21]

The process, Williams explained in a prose passage in *Spring and All,* is to use real "things with which he [the onlooker] is familiar, simple things—at the same time to detach them from ordinary experience to the imagination" (*SAA, 34*).

Williams' need for this "metamorphosis" can be deduced from several of his writings of the 1920's, but it is *A Voyage to Pagany* which is most revealing. Evans, the autobiographical protagonist of the novel, is obsessed by the drabness in life which is caused by frustration and decay, his inability to satisfy his desires or to preserve what he loves. A physician and scientist, he is too ruthlessly intelligent to accept the rationales for these losses which are offered by traditional religion.

When he would read of birds extinct, the wood pigeon, when he beheld manners decaying, when he saw the worn cheeks of the school girls oppressed by an insistent lack of peace—the wearing cheek, the darkening eye, the lips losing their outline and the seamy neck—for what? Against what? And religion, that childish horror of misapplication, the stewing and stewing of that stale sauce [an afterlife?], into which the scraps of the last guest are thrown mechanically again each day. . . . He knew all kinds of people intimately in their lesser phases. He longed through an iron mesh always—through which nobody broke *(Pagany,* 152-153).

[21]*CEP,* pp. 292-293. The first ellipsis is mine; the second is Williams'. "Struggle of Wings" was first published in a slightly different version in *The Dial,* LXXXI (July, 1926), 22-24.

He believes that art, the art of Europe's great cathedrals, was the only true relief from frustrations that men have created. Men and women love God, he implies, because they have never been able to solve the difficulty of loving one another satisfactorily. Cathedrals are "the lack of [this] solution" hardened into a form, "everything made static" into a beautiful form (*Pagany*, 50-51). Then, when Evans' own desires are painfully frustrated, he temporarily gives up all human contact and creates his own, secular cathedral out of the nature around him.

> He forgot the train. . . . The sea, a fusion of metals, zanthrochromic sea.—Now, never dropping back to feeling, he was all eyes. The world existed in his eyes, recognized itself ecstatically there. This then was real: all he saw—but not in man. Therefore never could he look long into the eyes of anyone. . . . Elsewhere, everywhere he saw reality, split, creviced, multiplied. The brilliant hardness of the world, clear, full of color and outline, depth, shadow, reaffirming light, filled him with security and contentment (*Pagany*, 119).

Later in Vienna Evans discovers another sort of "hard" art which enables men to endure the loss and ugliness caused by disease. He arrives in Vienna in 1924, at the depth of Austria's depression, to do postgraduate work at a great clinic. The patients are "the most miserable, the most dejected he had ever beheld." The clinics are an "inferno," but both "fat butcher-like" doctors and the deformed patients are transformed by the desire for truth which makes medicine an art and religion. The doctors are artist-priests "presiding over a world of the maimed, living in the hospital, pondering and dreaming—[creating] a great sense of beauty over this sordid world" (*Pagany*, 199, 206). When the pathologists finish their lectures, "nothing remained that was not seen, described and—a clarity put upon it. . . ." Evans "was caught by this wonder of abandon to the pursuit of knowledge. The beauty of it took him again and again" (*Pagany*, 207).

The art of the cathedral or clinic uses "organic" materials—men's bodies and lusts—but it freezes them into an inorganic pattern which is an aesthetically satisfying antithesis to the decay, frustration, and ugliness of organic life. It "detaches" the materials of life from organic nature and makes them parts of permanent orders—the aesthetic order of the cathedrals, the beautifully logical order of the doctors' diagnoses.

In his chapter on Poe in *In the American Grain*, Williams explains precisely how such an artificial, logical art could nevertheless be an indigenous product of a squalid, disordered locality. The America of Poe's time was an "UNFORMED LUMP, the *'monstrum, horrendum, informe, ingens, cui lumen ademptum.'* " The instinctive reaction of a sensitive man to such an environment would be an exaggerated desire for reason and order—exactly because he found so little of it around him. Therefore,

what Hawthorne *loses* by his willing closeness to the life of his locality in its vague humors; his lifelike copying of the New England melancholy; his reposeful closeness to the town pump—Poe *gains* by abhorring; flying to the ends of the earth for "original" material—
    By such a simple, logical twist does Poe succeed in being the more American, heeding more the local necessities, the harder structural imperatives . . . (*IAG*, 228).

Williams uses this detached style in many of his early poems to add excitement and vivid action to the "UNFORMED LUMP" of the life around him. In "Overture to a Dance of Locomotives" he makes images evoking the excitement and movement of a train trip perform before the reader. Dull routine is shattered by unexpected glimpses of beauty and rapid visual and auditory rhythms.

> The rubbing feet
> of those coming to be carried quicken a
> grey pavement into soft light that rocks
> to and fro, under the domed ceiling,
> across and across from pale
> earthcolored walls of bare limestone.
>
> . . . .
>
> Gliding windows. Colored cooks sweating
> in a small kitchen. Taillights—
> In time: twofour!
> In time: twoeight!
>
> (*CEP*, 194-195)

Similarly, he turns a suburban drive in the rain into a surrealistic fantasia in "Romance Moderne."

> Lean forward. Punch the steersman
> behind the ear. Twirl the wheel!
> Over the edge! Screams! Crash!
> The end. I sit above my head—
> a little removed—or
> a thin wash of rain on the roadway
> —I am never afraid when he is driving,—
>
> (*CEP*, 182)

Williams uses this style more ambitiously in some of his other 1920's poems not only to enliven but also to give force and vivid speed to his local materials. The technique of these poems closely resembles Demuth's coldly precise industrial paintings like "Paquebot Paris" (1921) and his other urban scenes painted during the 1920's. Williams' images in these poems are deliberately "flattened" by an absence of development in the same way that Demuth—and also John Marin and Stuart Davis—used city walls as flat planes which they assembled like theatrical flats. Williams injects clichés, advertising slogans, and banalities into his poems in the same way that Demuth and Davis used signs, words, and sharp, fragmentary images of urban objects. Finally, Williams' short lines resemble the flashy precision of Marin and Demuth's water color brushwork in poems like "The Agonized Spires," "At the Faucet of June," "Flight to the City," "Rapid Transit," and "Young Love."

> O "Kiki"
> O Miss Margaret Jarvis
> The backhandspring
> I: clean
>   clean
>   clean: yes . . New York
>
> Wrigley's, appendicitis, John Marin:
> skyscraper soup—
> (CEP, 253)

However, this poem, "Young Love," ends on a different note:

> but I merely
> caressed you curiously
> fifteen years ago and you still
> go about the city, they say
> patching up sick school children
> (CEP, 255)

This is one of Demuth's favorite techniques: dramatically juxtaposing images of a world he values against an exciting, tawdry environment which encroaches upon it. Factories and water towers subdue and drown out eighteenth-century buildings in Demuth's architectural landscape paintings in the same way that the carnival of the city infringes upon Williams' emotion for the woman he "merely / caressed."

When Williams—particularly in the 1920's—or Demuth dealt with subjects they admired such as flowers, their reaction was to take them entirely out of life where they could decay and disappoint. Both Demuth's flower paintings and Williams' flower poems present their subjects as timeless, richly abstract, beautiful designs. The flowers are beautiful, valuable; therefore the poet or painter "saves" them by lifting them out of the sooty world of time and decay and into his aristocratic, aesthetic vision. Sometimes in these poems Williams speaks of his subjects as if they were impervious to change: "to engage roses / becomes a geometry— / . . . . Somewhere the sense / makes copper roses / steel roses" (CEP, 249) or a "white butterfly / . . . fragile among the red / trumpeted petunias, / is ribbed with steel / wired to the sun" (CEP, 425). At other times Williams achieves a similarly static effect by beginning his poems with rather loose, subjective descriptions which he abruptly halts to arrest his subjects' development in time or in the reader's emotions:

> A grace of petals skirting
> the tight-whorled cone
>
> Come to generous abandon—
> to the mind as to the eye
>
> Wide! Wider!
> Wide as if panting, until
>
> the gold hawk's-eye speaks once
> coldly its perfection
>
> (CEP, 369)

But despite the "perfection," there is a despairing, implicit criticism beyond this technique: only the artist in his moments of aristocratic vision will allow an object to exist in its full purity and integrity. "Poetry is imposed on an age by men . . . whose primary cleanliness of mind makes them automatically first rate," Williams wrote in 1929. "Filth finally swallows all."[22] Or, as he wrote near the end of "Struggle of Wings": clothe Poesy "richly, those who loathe him / will besmirch him fast enough" (CEP, 293).

Williams wrote few of these extremely rapid, hard, vivid poems after the 1920's, chiefly because his conception of poetry changed radically in the early 1930's. He became convinced at that time that poetry should be serious and difficult rather than entertaining. He also became a staunch advocate of an "anti-

---

[22]"A Note on the Art of Poetry," Blues, I, 4 (May, 1929), 79.

poetic" theory of beauty whose chief tenet was that beauty and ugliness were parts of a single whole. Nothing beautiful—like a flower—could exist without its "soil" of ugly, drab antecedents, and therefore Williams ceased presenting his beautiful subjects in splendid, static isolation from time and the world around them.

There was one major legacy of Williams' hard style of the 1920's in his later poetry. During the 1930's and 40's he wrote many works, culminating in *Paterson,* which are ruthlessly hard and objective "autopsies" of the world around him. His technique in these poems has certain affinities with the ironic methods that Demuth used in his urban landscape paintings.

The Precisionists, like most modern painters, almost never moralized or editorialized their subjects. Their extremely "immaculate" styles and emphasis on abstract design has caused some critics to consider them apologists for modern urban and industrial life.[23] Only Demuth was an exception to this tendency among the Precisionists. He was never in any way a "socially conscious" artist, yet he was able to imply a critical attitude toward his urban and industrial subjects while treating them in an entirely objective, modernist manner. Demuth's industrial landscapes give the impression that he might have read Whitman's warning that the "largeness of nature or the nation were monstrous without a corresponding largeness and generosity of the spirit of the citizen. Not nature nor swarming states nor streets and steamships nor prosperous business nor farms . . . may suffice for the ideal of man"[24]—and then decided to treat the theme comically. Ironically and wittily he compares the gigantic physical size and power of his urban or industrial subjects with their imaginative blankness and emptiness. The grain elevators of "My Egypt," for example, do not merely fill the canvas, they loom over the spectator like a steamboat bearing down on him. Enormous force has obviously gone into their construction, but no sensitivity or imagination. Swollen with grain, they are more faceless and inhuman than the Sphinx. In another painting swirls of smoke and soot cascade from the triumphantly thrusting smoke stacks and towers of dark, anonymous factories. This, the title informs us, is "Incense from a

[23]Friedman, *The Precisionist View,* pp. 28-29.
[24]"Preface" to 1855 edition of *Leaves of Grass.*

New Church." In both paintings there is no appeal to the emotions; there is only the dry irony of the titles to reveal the absurd difference between the wealth and power of American society and its drabness and insensitivity.

This type of precise yet entirely implicit criticism was very close to the sort of critical art which Williams prescribed. "Contempt for the age won't help anyone," he wrote in a 1937 article, "Nor will running from it help. All that will help is to nail [down?] its stupidity and its craven sordidness. The artist might do this if he had the courage, the wit, the lively intelligence for it—"[25] Because of his allegiance to "the Objective method," which "doesn't declaim or explain; it presents," Williams could not editorialize or even explain his subjects; he needed wit and intelligence like Demuth's to communicate his diagnosis of his age.

Williams' "It Is a Living Coral" is an early example of this sort of comic diagnosis. In the first third of the poem Williams describes the engineering of the Capitol in Washington. Its dome weighs eight million pounds and is constructed of iron plates. Yet it is able to "expand / and contract with / variations / of temperature." Because of its brilliant engineering, the structure functions beautifully, as sensitively as "the folding / and unfolding of a lily" (*CEP,* 325). Then in the rest of the poem Williams ironically contrasts the "lily" of the Capitol's construction with the aesthetic and intellectual stupidity expressed by the building's murals: "Baptism of Poca- / hontas / with a little card / hanging / under it to tell / the persons."

Williams' diagnoses of his age became harsher during the depression. His vision of his society's flaws are still as subtle and objective as Demuth's, but there is the additional awareness that these failings cause suffering. "The Yachts" ends with the tragic awareness that men's allegiance to "all that in the mind is fleckless, free and / naturally to be desired" makes them totally indifferent to humanity—"Arms with hands grasping seek to clutch at the prows. / Bodies thrown recklessly in the way are cut aside" (*CEP,* 106-107).

Some of Williams' other poems and his short stories of the 1930's are more oblique than "The Yachts" but are equally acute. Williams intended them to be what he entitled his first

[25]"The So-Called So-Called," 38.

book of short stories, *The Knife of the Times,* the surgeon's scalpel which would expose the "cancers" of sloth, ignorance, and indifference which maim humanity.[26]

"A Bastard Peace," for example, seems—if read superficially— to be an entirely neutral description of an urban landscape. Williams' cryptically contemptuous title is his only warning that he disapproves of his subject. However, when the intentions of the objects Williams describes are contrasted with their actual effect, then the poem becomes a criticism of industrial society. A "heavy / woven-wire fence / topped with jagged ends" blocks people from the river and guards the rights of private property —"a long cinder-field" (*CEP,* 414). The parched grass, a dandelion in bloom, and a butterfly are the only signs of beauty. Nature has been destroyed for an industrial progress that produces such bounties as "Three cracked houses— / a willow, two chickens." The only traffic is a small boy with a homemade cart. The noon whistle blows but no workers enter or leave, "nobody goes / other than the kids from school." The people of the landscape are cut off from nature by an industrialism which gives them nothing in return but unemployment and poverty. The peace of the title is "bastard" because it is based not on fulfillment and satisfaction but on waste and impoverishment. The development of the poem resembles the structure of Demuth's satirical landscapes in that it is based on the ironic discrepancy between its subject's intended, "normal" function and its actual performance or being.

Yet the poem remains totally hard and objective. Its vision is so precise and sensitive in itself that—like the Viennese doctors' autopsies or Demuth's paintings—it both reveals and alleviates the despair which its message could arouse. "It is a contrast," as Williams wrote about a passage in *Paterson II,* between his subject and "the fineness, the aristocracy of the metrical arrangement of the verse. I do have measure here, but the very subject hides it from the uninitiated . . . the vulgarity is lifted to distinction by being treated with the very greatest in art which I can conceive" (*ND 17,* 276-277).

It is illuminating to contrast Demuth's and Williams' ironic

[26]Williams himself used this metaphor in an article endorsing Major Douglas' Social Credit theories: "A Social Diagnosis for Surgery," *New Democracy,* VI, 2 (April, 1936), 26-27.

structural techniques with those of Pound and Eliot. In *The Cantos* and *The Waste Land* meaning is often derived from the ironic juxtaposition of a partial, brutalized present and a fuller, more sensitive past age:

> When lovely woman stoops to folly and
> Paces about her room again, alone,
> She smoothes her hair with automatic hand,
> And puts a record on the gramophone.
> *(The Waste Land* III.253-256)

Thus the present is seen as an ironic diminuation of past excellence. In Demuth's paintings and Williams' poems the present image is—aesthetically—an ironic diminuation of its own potentiality. Morally, the ironic contrast is between actual men's works and their powers or responsibilities. Or as Webster's puts it, "irony . . . a result that is the opposite of what might be expected or considered appropriate" (*New World* ed.).

In Demuth's ironic paintings—and in Williams' poems which resemble them—there is always the sense that the artist has happened to his materials or subject. They have experienced him. It is because of his personal qualities, as an artist, that they have achieved the form which they possess in the work.

This was only one of Williams' attitudes toward his subjects. Another, equally significant attitude can be seen by comparing his works with those of Charles Sheeler.

Sheeler's paintings are as personal as Demuth's in the sense that he has very thoroughly composed them. But his method of composition is completely lacking in self-assertion. Sheeler's forms always give the effect that they have been chosen to realize his subject's intrinsic qualities—not his own emotional mood or technical virtuosity. His paintings give the impression that his subjects have happened to him: he has experienced them, meditated upon them, lived with them until he has been able to find the form which expresses their reality more truly than their original, natural shapes. Gradually, as Sheeler said of Holbein's "Goldsmith," reality has been *distilled* until the "subject in nature, if we could see it, would seem only a feeble approximation of the picture," for in the painting there "are no adulterants of its basic reality."[27]

[27]Quoted in Rourke, *Charles Sheeler*, p. 181.

According to Constance Rourke, Williams once asked Sheeler
how he found his subjects: " 'Do you go out for them, seize
them?' " Sheeler replied that he could not "go out and find something to paint. Something seen keeps recurring in memory with
an insistence increasingly vivid and with attributes added which
escaped observation on first acquaintance. Gradually a mental
image is built up which takes on a personal identity. . . . Since
the value of the mental picture can be determined only by the
degree of response it arouses in other persons it must be restated
in physical terms—hence the painting."[28]
Both Sheeler and Williams were convinced that this "basic
reality" or "personal identity" of a subject could only be realized through a "classical" approach. By this term they did not
mean any form of neoclassicism, any duplication of past designs
or materials. "I feel that the language of the arts should be in
keeping with the spirit of the age," Sheeler wrote. And according to Constance Rourke, his exploration of early American
architecture and crafts had convinced him that "the classic in
this country may still be found in many places if it is sought
without prepossessions of magnitude or grandeur. It has often
been overlooked; one surmises that much of it still remains to
be discovered . . . it cannot be copied or imported, but is the
outgrowth of a special mode of life and feeling."[29] Similarly, in
a 1937 article Williams argued that if the aesthetic virtues which
existed in the classics were truly timeless, then they had to be
operative "in the conditions of our own lives." "All that is
necessary is to discover in today conditions and aspects comparable to those which were used excellently in the past and to
invent a means for using them as new and excellent in our days
as were the inventions of other days."[30]
The mark of this classicism, Williams believed, was that it
gave the local subject a universal significance or validity. "From
the shapes of men's lives," he wrote, "imparted by the places
where they have experience, good writing springs. . . . One has
to learn what the meaning of the local is, for universal purposes.
The local is the only thing that is universal. . . . The classic is
the local fully realized, words marked by a place" (SE, 132).

[28]Quoted in ibid., pp. 167-168.
[29]Quoted in ibid., pp. 77, 184.
[30]"The So-Called So-Called," 37.

Williams derived the vocabulary for this conception from John Dewey. Dewey emphasized in *Democracy and Education* that culture was an interaction of men with their environments in the form of "preconceived connections." If a connection between a man and his environment is of high enough quality, other men will adopt it. Then it will have a universal significance linking "up the net results of the experience of the group and even the race with the immediate experience of an individual."[31] Dewey applied this theory to American literature in a 1920 article in *The Dial* which he wrote in response to a call from James Oppenheim for a "national poetry." American poets, Dewey argued, had to become better acquainted with their local environments before they would achieve a universally valid art, national or otherwise. "We are discovering," Dewey wrote, "that the locality is the only universal. Even the suns and stars have their own times as well as their own places. . . . When the discovery sinks a little deeper, the novelist and dramatist will discover the localities of America as they are, and no one will need to worry about the future of American art."[32] It is not certain whether Williams read *Democracy and Education*. He quoted the dictum from Dewey's *Dial* article that "the locality is the only universal" in *Contact*, and he used this terminology for the rest of his career as a rationale for the intense locality of his materials.[33]

Sheeler was the American artist whom Williams most specifically praised for realizing his local materials in a universal way. In his *Autobiography* and his essays on Sheeler, Williams used his friend as the example of what an American artist could achieve if he knew and used his materials well enough.

[31]John Dewey, *Democracy and Education* (New York, 1916), p. 255.

[32]Dewey, "Americanism and Localism," *The Dial*, LXVIII (June, 1920), 687-688.

[33]Dewey's phrase is quoted out of context in *Contact II* (Jan., 1921), p. 7. Years later Williams wrote: "In fact, there can be no general culture unless it is bedded . . . in a locality—something I have been saying for a generation: that there is no universal except in the local. I myself took it from Dewey." *SL*, p. 224. Williams also was indebted to Count Hermann Keyserling, whom he referred to in his *Autobiography*, p. 391 and his story "Under the Greenwood Tree," *FD*, p. 225. Presumably he read *America Set Free* (New York, 1929) in which Keyserling argues that "increasing provincialism" is America's only hope for an authentic culture, since "localism alone can lead to culture." P. 51.

Driving down for illumination into the local, Sheeler has had his Welsh blood to set him on. There is a Sheelerville, Pa., up in the old mining district. The Shakers express the same feeling in maple, pine and birch, pieces which Sheeler out of admiration for what they could do with those materials keeps about him.

It is this eye for the thing that most distinguishes Charles Sheeler—and along with it to know that every hair on every body, now or then, in its minute distinctiveness is the same hair, on every body anywhere, at any time, changed as it may be to feather, quill or scale.

The local is the universal (*SE,* 232, 233).

Williams and Sheeler used several techniques to give their subjects universal significance, their total, "classical" identities.

First, they used metaphor and allusion to relate the local, American scene to broadened frames of reference, other societies, or other realms of being. Williams' poem "Composition," for example, begins with a completely ordinary useful object, a bright red paper box lined with imitation leather. It is divided into small trays and is, apparently, constructed very neatly and precisely; therefore it is a "composition" itself. Williams compares it to the sun, which is also bright, and "the table / with dinner / on it for / these are the same," i.e., also a composition. He sees it fancifully as a miniature aerodrome with "engineers" in its "twoinch trays" who convey glue to model airplanes. He admits that the object does have its practical uses—it can hold paper clips, and sewing supplies—but he ends the poem with two bold metaphors asserting the box's universal significance. Because it is a "composition," it is related to two other orderly compositions by the human mind:

> for this is eternity
> through its
> dial we discover
> transparent tissue
> on a spool
>
> But the stars
> are round
> cardboard
> . . . . . .
> (*CEP,* 260-261)

In his poem "At the Ball Game" Williams used the same technique to present an American crowd as possessing the qualities of all crowds. They laugh "seriously" but "without thought." They wish only to be amused by the action before them, "all the exciting detail / of the chase / and the escape, the error / the flash of genius." Their desire for amusement is amoral. Like the crowds who enjoyed "the Inquisition, the / Revolution," they are willing to be amused by life and death as well as sports. Therefore, they are "venomous," dangerous, willing to turn on anyone who will amuse them with exciting details "of the escape, the error / the flash of genius."

> it smiles grimly
> its words cut—
>
> The flashy female with her
> mother, gets it—
>
> The Jew gets it straight—it
> is deadly, terrifying—
> > (*CEP*, 284-285)

Or, Williams could see the "drivers for grocers or taxidrivers" in his neighborhood as "satyrs" because of the "two horned lilac blossoms / in their caps" (*CEP*, 273).

Sheeler used allusion in much the same way in some of his industrial landscapes. Soaring cranes and girders are entitled "Totems in Steel" to indicate that they too represent the impulses and ideals of a community. The geometrically precise flow of an aqueduct, interrupted by vertical "falls" of pumping stations, is entitled simply "Water." A view of grain elevators, railroad tracks, and chimneys is a "Classic Landscape," because the buildings possess the same well-proportioned simplicity as classical Greek architecture.

A second, more oblique means of universalizing local materials is described by Williams in a 1934 letter. Commenting on the role of " 'Simply physical or external realism' " in American art, he writes: "it is quite true that the photographic camera will not help us. We can though, if we are able to[,] *see* general relationships in local setting, set them down verbatim with a view to penetration. And there is a cleanliness about this method which if it can be well handled makes a fascinating project in which every bit of subtlety and experience one is possessed of may be utilized" (*SL*, 146). Using this technique, Williams and Sheeler assemble a number of subjects that seem—at first glance—to possess nothing in common beyond the fact that they come from the same locality. Actually, however, the

objects share some common trait or principle—a "general relationship"—which possesses universal significance.

In the American Grain is one of the first and best examples of
Williams' use of this technique. By narrating and quoting the
activities of a heterogeneous group of American heroes, he man-
ages to reveal several consistent, "classic" principles of national
behavior which have existed throughout American history. Similarly, though less spectacularly, Sheeler constructed interiors
composed of artifacts from different American eras and locales
in order to reveal the principles of design or spirit which they
shared in common.

In these works Williams violently, and Sheeler gently, negate
certain conceptions of time or history. They deny that the present is a dim copy of past excellence or that it is a crude re-
hearsal for a progressively more ideal future. The excellence of
the "classics," they felt, may be recovered from the past or
perpetuated into the future. It is always potentially present.

In other works, Williams and Sheeler deny the conception
that man and nature have little in common essentially, that
nature exists primarily only to be enjoyed, used, or scientifically
known by men. The structure of many of their poems and
paintings is based on their affirmations of the organic, formal
connections which can exist between the human and the natural. They insist that harmonies as well as distinctions can exist
between the human personality and the world of "beasts and
trees" (*Pictures,* 151). One of their great ambitions was, as Williams phrased it, "through metaphor to reconcile / the people
and the stones" (*CLP,* 7).

In their poems and paintings, Williams and Sheeler sought to
reconcile the natural and the artificial by insisting on the essential sameness of the laws of form which governed them. "I
would arrive at the picture which I hope eventually to paint,"
Sheeler once remarked, "through form that is architectural,
whether the subject is buildings or flowers. . . ."[34] Sheeler's still
life "Cactus," for example, compares the plant with his studio
lamps that light it. The nature of the peculiarly bulbous structure is discovered by comparing it with the roundness of the
metal lamp shades. Or in his crayon drawing "Timothy,"
Sheeler compares the linear plant stalks to the slender, cylindri-

[34]Quoted in Rourke, *Charles Sheeler,* p. 98.

cal vase in which they are placed. The delicately curved and fluted leaves of the plant serve to counterpoint the straightness of both vase and stalks; the simple, rectangular line of the table corner contrasts delicately with their verticality.

Similarly Williams often constructed his poems upon metaphors, analogies, and contrasts which stressed the formal relationships possible between nature and the human or artificial. Some of the first examples of these poems appear in "The Descent of Winter."

> Dahlias—
>   What a red
>   and yellow and white
>   mirror to the sun, round
>   and petaled
>   is this she holds?
>   with a red face
> all in black
>   and grey hair
>   sticking out
>   from under the bonnet brim
>   (*CEP*, 304)

The poem's structure is simple and effective. Two bare, unexplained images are juxtaposed to make us aware of their unexpected similarity.

In other poems Williams stressed the contrasts between the human and the natural which could be created by the same, bare, unexplained juxtapositions of images. The poem entitled "10/21" in "The Descent of Winter," for example, dramatically contrasts the destructive power of a fire burning up trash with a conservative human emotion, pity for the old. The verbs signifying the natures of the two forces, the natural and the emotional, are balanced in the poem to define one another. The flames stream and wave; they are streaked and stained with purple and flamepoints; the smoke "continues eastward—." These verbs describing the fire are all intransitive and express violent destruction. Those describing the old persons are passive, or verbs of being, expressing negations or static experiences.

> There are no duties for them
> no places where they may sit
> their knowledge is laughed at
> they cannot see, they cannot hear.
> . . . .

> Their feet hurt, they are weak
> they should not have to suffer
> as younger people must and do
> there should be a truce for them
> (*CEP, 300*)

Beyond this reconciliation of man and nature there is the need for a further, more profound and difficult reconciliation. Both Williams and Sheeler dedicated much of their careers to the achievement of an art which would unify these three entities: the natural; man the social, practical being who is united to nature through his use of it; and man the imaginative being who is distinct from nature because of his mental powers of abstraction and formalization. In their more ambitious and mature works Williams and Sheeler create entities which are fusions of three realities: the natural world of unconscious things—trees, rocks, soils, and minerals; the quotidian world of buildings and artifacts formed by men motivated by practical, material needs; and the third world of the mind, the world produced by men conscious of their aesthetic, philosophic, or mathematical capabilities. Williams and Sheeler attempt in these works to achieve the sort of organic totality which Williams used to describe the term "culture": "the realization of the qualities of a place in relation to the life which occupies it; embracing everything involved, climate, geographic position, relative size, history, other cultures—as well as the character of its sands, flowers, minerals and the condition of knowledge within its borders. It is the act of lifting these things into an ordered and utilized whole. . . ."[35]

Sheeler, as a painter, could achieve this totality only if he were able to effect a synthesis between the abstract world available to the modern artist's imagination and the representational world available to his immediate senses. Williams, as a poet, faced the equally difficult task of synthesizing the poetic and prosaic languages which are available to the modern, cultured person whose mind can hear the rhythms of Homer or Dante while his ears are filled with the noise of traffic and typewriters.

Sheeler began to achieve bold syntheses of the representa-

---

[35]*SE*, p. 157. See also D. H. Lawrence, "The Spirit of Place," *The Symbolic Meaning: The Uncollected Versions of Studies in Classic American Literature*, ed. Armin Arnold (New York, 1964), p. 30. Or see Lawrence, *Studies in Classic American Literature* (New York, 1964), pp. 5-6.

tional and the abstract in his mature paintings of the 1940's and 1950's. His chief stylistic device is montage, which he uses to superimpose different planes of reality upon one another. In "New England Irrelevancies" (1953), for example, he superimposes several New England structures upon one another. Each of these structures is a combination of planes soaring into a vertical ray. In the center of the painting the natural mode of this structure can be dimly seen: a stream or waterfall falling into a pool. This image exists in the painting very much as it exists in New England life—a dim, barely remembered presence. Superimposed upon it is the quotidian life of New England, the planes of factory or tenement brick walls which rise into the verticals of chimneys and fire escapes. Finally, creating yet part of all the structures, is the abstract design of the painting: planes and verticals as they exist in the mind of the artist. The entire painting is a harmonious synthesis of this particular form of reality which is present in New England—naturally, practically, and abstractly.

Or in "Midwest" (1954) Sheeler's subject is horizontality. The horizons of the land itself can be perceived in the center and background of the painting—strong, slightly sloping diagonals that are accentuated by vague masses of foliage. Above and upon them are man-made horizons of the Midwest, the blunt horizontals and diagonals formed by the walls and roofs of barns and sheds. Just as the natural horizon is only partially interrupted by the few masses of foliage, so also the horizontality of the buildings is accentuated—rather than dispelled—by cylindrical silos. Ordering all these horizons and diagonals are those which exist as the painting's abstract design. In this painting, like "New England Irrelevancies," the artist's abstract, aesthetic unity is the life-form which dominates the painting; yet it is a domination which is informed by the natural and the practical, which respects their reality and seeks to blend them harmoniously into its own vision.

As early as "The Wanderer" Williams dramatized the integration of his mental and aesthetic powers with the natural and quotidian life around him. However, the process is not very harmonious in that poem. The young poet is immersed in the "filthy Passiac," but he barely survives the experience. In the 1927 poem "Paterson" the same experience is dramatized more clearly, but it is equally traumatic. Williams' persona Mr. Paterson is instinctively aloof from his sordid environment. His motto is "no ideas but in things," but the things around him do not easily lend themselves to the "decorous and simple" poetic thoughts he wishes to have: "cheap pictures, furniture / filled silk, cardboard shoes, bad dentistry / windows that will not open, poisonous gin / scurvey, toothache—" (*CEP*, 234). Therefore he tries to go away "to rest and write" and maintain a "high decorum." This decorum is shattered by the urgency and power of the slum life around him—but it is a traumatic awakening to such realities as "The actual, florid detail of cheap carpet / amazingly upon the floor and paid for / as no portrait ever was" (*CEP*, 235).

"A Morning Imagination of Russia," first published in 1928, envisions a world in which revolution destroys the tawdriness of cities like Paterson and the fastidiousness of men like Mr. Paterson. His persona, a Russian intellectual, has become a man with "no cities / between him and his desires." His mind and emotions are therefore in harmony with nature: "When the sun rose it rose in his heart / It bathed the red cold world of / the dawn so that the chill was his own" (*CEP*, 305). He is also in harmony with his society, and his social responsibilities are honorable and rudimentary. He will "go to the soviet unshaven . . . and listen. Listen. That / was all he did, listen to them, weigh / for them" (*CEP*, 307). He welcomes the loss of his former privileges, even though this has made him "weak," because he now has "touch," the opportunity to be in organic contact with the natural and humble life of his environment.

A form of totality is achieved in the same way in all three poems. Each narrates the experiences of an imaginative, sensitive protagonist who is immersed in his natural and social environments because of a psychological or social cataclysm. Prosaic or even tawdry things become his poetic ideas. The strength and weakness of this approach lies in its reliance upon the personal experience of a persona. The poems based upon it have the clarity and drama of any intense personal experience, but they are also intensely subjective. They narrate a subjective vision *of* objective reality. They do not present the prosaic realities of the objective world in their own, prosaic language.

Accompanying the manuscript of "The Descent of Winter" in

the Buffalo Collection is the manuscript of a story or novel about Fairfield, New Jersey. This manuscript, dated 1927 and partially published as "Notes in Diary Form" (*SE*, 62-74), presents the prosaic realities of Fairfield in a radically objective form. By using a sort of environmental stream-of-consciousness—probably derived from *Finnegans Wake*—Williams was able to blend descriptions of trees and buildings with the thoughts and conversations of all the very different levels of humanity that inhabit northern New Jersey. All three levels of life—the natural, quotidian, and intellectual—exist in this work, and each has the impersonal reality of its own language—independent of the subjective vision of any individual. The price of this impersonality is formlessness. The work reads as if it were composed on a naturalist's camera and tape recorder which were set in a neighborhood bar instead of a forest. It is a random, accidental kaleiodoscope of facts which are sometimes interesting in themselves but which are confusing and boring when taken as a whole—a further example of "the senseless / unarrangement of wild things" which Williams had rejected earlier (*CEP,* 330).

During the 1930's Williams refined both of these methods of achieving totality. His Objectivist poems and short stories refine the "Wanderer"—Mr. Paterson motif by presenting the experience of a sensitive man confronting his prosaic world in a less emotional, less traumatic way. In *Many Loves* and his libretto *The First President* Williams experimented with incorporating mixtures of poetic and prosaic materials in structures that were already definitely narrative and dramatic. Finally, when he began *Paterson* in the 1940's, Williams united both of these devices in a key metaphor which enabled him to construct montages of language which are similar to Sheeler's montages of paint.

"A man like a city"—this metaphor was the key to the poem, Williams later recalled, for it enabled him to fuse his personal experiences with those of his city (*IWW*, 72-73; *Autobiography,* 391-392). The poet Paterson and the city Paterson coexist in the poem in a form which Williams referred to—in a work-note—as a "lyric drama." ". . . the spontaneous . . . conformations of language as it is *heard.* Attempt to feel and then transcribe these lyrical language patterns. The drama, the lyric drama (Lope de Vega) should be one expanded metaphor. Poetry de-

mands a different material than prose. [Yet] It uses another
facet of the same fact. . . ." Mr. Paterson, because he is "like"
the city, shares its condition. The prose passages of the poem
express the quotidian, prosaic realities of the city's past and
present; the poetic passages are imaginative "facets" or—to use
the metaphor of the book—echoes of these prosaic realities.

> .   .   a mass of detail
> to interrelate on a new ground, difficulty;
> an assonance, a homologue
>   triple piled
> pulling the disparate together to clarify
> and compress
>   (I, ii, 30)

But Mr. Paterson does not "echo" his environment unconsciously. He gradually becomes conscious of his responsibility as
a man and as a poet better "to know, to / know clearly . . .
whence / I draw my breath or how to employ it . . ." (I, ii, 31).
This growing consciousness leads Mr. Paterson to seek to improve his responses to the prosaic realities of his environment.
His progress toward a truly creative response gives a narrative
and dramatic structure to the poem's heterogeneous contents. In
this way Williams is able to signify what each "fact"—whether
mental, quotidian, or natural—signifies to the other realms of
life.

CHAPTER | THREE

During the 1920's Williams was among the writers and artists who chose to remain and work in America because of their faith in the potential cultural richness of American life. Williams became interested in the painter Marsden Hartley when he saw that Hartley seemed to be consciously ignoring the influence of modern French painting. It was as if, Williams recalled, Hartley "deliberately turned his back on Europe . . . his decision to quit Europe for Am[e]rica was a fully conscious one bred of a powerful conviction that here, more than anywhere else, [was] thet [sic] reward which he sought."[1] It is not relevant whether this was really Hartley's attitude toward French art and American life; it was certainly Williams'.

During his 1924 European trip, Williams himself saw and rejected European art and life in favor of the "reward" which he believed America offered him. He wrote the Daniel Boone chapter of *In the American Grain* on board the ship on which he returned to the United States (*Autobiography*, 233). Boone's significance for Williams was that he, like Washington, chose to live in and work with the hard "facts" of American life because his "whole soul, with greatest devotion, was given to the New World which he adored and found, in its every expression, the land of heart's desire."[2] Boone's genius, Williams wrote,

[1]"Marsden Hartley," unpublished biographical study, Yale Collection.
[2]*IAG*, p. 139. See also *SE*, pp. 140-142.

was to recognize the difficulty [of creating an American culture] as neither material nor political but one purely moral and aesthetic. Filled with the wild beauty of the New World to overbrimming so long as he had what he desired, to bathe in, to explore always more deeply, to see, to feel, to touch—his instincts were contented. Sensing a limitless fortune which daring could make his own, he sought only with primal lust to grow close to it, to understand it and to be part of its mysterious movements—like an Indian (*IAG*, 136).

Williams recognized that he could not, like Boone, escape to a Kentucky wilderness, much less become like an Indian,[3] but he was convinced that America's problems were primarily "moral and aesthetic."

Williams' early poetry reveals the aesthetic means which he used to possess and to become imaginatively responsible for his contemporary environment. His early prose works represent his attempts to achieve a "moral" possession of America, that is, to know the American past so well that he could base his actions upon the best "life style" possible for an American. "I came to write the book," he explained to Horace Gregory about *In the American Grain*, because "I felt from earliest childhood that America was the only home I could ever possibly call my own. I felt that it was expressly founded for me, personally, and that it must be my first business in life to possess it; that only by making it my own from the beginning to my own day, in detail, should I ever have a basis for knowing where I stood. I must have a basis for orienting myself formally in the beliefs which activated me from day to day" (*SL*, 185).

Other intellectuals and artists of this period were equally concerned with achieving the "moral" possession of the historical dimensions of their culture. Williams' ideas about America's condition correspond to—were probably influenced by—those of a group of writers including D. H. Lawrence and the *Seven Arts* critics—James Oppenheim, Waldo Frank, Randolph Bourne,

---

[3]Williams admired American Indian culture (*IAG*, pp. 30-36), but he did not believe that it could be reconstructed. "Tenochtitlan," he wrote in 1934, "with its curious brilliance may still legitimately be kept alive in thought not as something which *could* have been preserved but as something which was actual and was destroyed." *SE*, p. 143. He did, however, think that modern, white Americans could derive a purely "aesthetic" satisfaction from primitive American reality, "a poetic knowledge, of that ground," which might be as satisfactory as an Indian's way of life. *IAG*, p. 213.

Van Wyck Brooks, and Paul Rosenfeld.[4] All of these men, like Williams and Hartley, had *chosen* to live in America and were committed to realizing its potential richness. All sought some answer to Randolph Bourne's challenging question: "Where are the seeds of American promise?"[5]

Williams, Lawrence, and the *Seven Arts* critics shared two major premises in their diagnoses of American problems. They were convinced that America badly needed a clear, sincere expression by its artists of its national identity. They were also certain that an understanding of the nature of American experience could be gained through the creation of what Van Wyck Brooks called a "usable past."

Seven Arts Magazine was founded in 1916 to encourage national self-expression in American writing. Its motto was "An Expression of Artists for the Community." Its first editorial stated that Americans were living in a renascent period of national self-consciousness; the purpose of the *Seven Arts* was "to become a channel for the flow of these new tendencies: an expression of our American arts which shall be fundamentally an expression of our American life."[6] In the same issue Romain Rolland called even more eloquently upon American writers to ignore all past forms of artistic expression, no matter how perfect, and be free of all foreign models.

—The diverse personalities that compose your States must dare to express themselves, freely, sincerely, entirely, in art. They must avoid the false quest after originality. They must be careless of form. They must be fearless of opinion.

[4]The composition of the *Seven Arts* group is fairly well known. Two good introductions to the group's ideals and achievements are "Appendix A" of the 1929 edition of Waldo Frank's *The Re-discovery of America* (New York, 1929), and Sherman Paul's introduction to the University of Illinois edition of Paul Rosenfeld's *Port of New York* (Urbana, 1961). I have included D. H. Lawrence in this group because his attitude toward American culture was very much like that of the *Seven Arts* critics—before he moved to America and began hating the country. See the early versions of his essays, which appeared in *Studies in Classic American Literature,* in *The Symbolic Meaning,* ed. Armin Arnold (New York, 1964). See also Lawrence, "America, Listen to Your Own," *New Republic,* XXV (Dec. 15, 1920), 68-70.

[5]Randolph Bourne, "Twilight of Idols," *The Seven Arts,* II (Oct., 1917), 688.

[6]*The Seven Arts,* I (Nov., 1916), 52-53. These editorials by James Oppenheim are heavily indebted to Whitman, particularly his 1855 "Preface" to *Leaves of Grass.*

Above all, dare to see yourselves; to penetrate within yourselves—and to your very depths. Dare to see true. And then, whatever you find, dare to speak it out as you have found it.[7]

America, D. H. Lawrence wrote in 1918, was an entirely new place and the American experience was an entirely new one. The European "race *idea*" might still exist in the conscious, American mind, but the "quality of life-experience, of emotion and passion and desire . . . has changed."[8] However, except for a few exceptions, this new American "era of living" had not truly and consciously expressed itself; the American spirit therefore remained incomplete and destructive. But soon, Lawrence believed, artistic expression would begin in America, and then American life would flower.

In the same year Waldo Frank began his book *Our America* with the assertion that the "hidden treasure" of American life was concealed by a morass of lies. American life and energies had not been brought "into the play of articulate life," and so America remained a tongue-tied, "turmoiled giant." Politics and economics had been the only "drama," the only expression of life in eighteenth- and nineteenth-century America, but now "the drama of American life" had shifted to "the struggle for the assertion of life itself." Since "the utterance of life is art," America's new leaders would be artists. "Quite as naturally as the leaders of yesterday given up to physical discovery and exploitation were politicians, the leaders of to-morrow forced to spiritual discovery are men of letters."[9]

Williams, Lawrence, and the *Seven Arts* critics agreed that a major cause of America's dumbness was the Puritan tradition that prevented the individual from expressing or even experiencing the full range of his own being. "The Pilgrim Fathers," Lawrence wrote, "soon killed off in their people the spontaneous impulses and appetites of the self. By a stern discipline and a fanatic system of repression, they subdued every passion into rigid control."[10] "To the modern young person who tries to live

[7]Romain Rolland, "America and the Arts," *ibid.*, 48. See also Randolph Bourne's "Our Cultural Humility" in *The History of a Literary Radical* (New York, 1920).
[8]Lawrence, "The Spirit of Place," *The Symbolic Meaning*, pp. 17-18.
[9]Waldo Frank, *Our America* (New York, 1919), pp. 4, 8.
[10]Lawrence, "The Spirit of Place," *The Symbolic Meaning*, pp. 38-39. Antipuritanism was not confined to Lawrence, Williams, and the *Seven Arts*

well," wrote Randolph Bourne in the *Seven Arts,* there was "no type so devastating and harassing as the puritan." Each new generation found some new way of being puritanical and sacrificing its healthy desire for "growing widely and loving intensely."[11]

Williams agreed vigorously with the contention that Americans needed to express themselves more freely and originally. When he began his career as a writer, he later wrote, America was filled with a "ferment . . . a desire for conscious self-expression. We were sick of our repetitious elders and their pseudo-classicism."[12] He also believed that the puritanical tradition was one of the chief causes of America's lack of valid self-expression. "There has not yet appeared in the New World," he claimed, "any one with sufficient strength for the open assertion. . . . Nowhere the open, free assertion save in the Indian" (*IAG,* 154-155).

A second major premise which was shared by Williams, Lawrence, and the *Seven Arts* critics was the assumption that America needed a better national "personality" before it could have a genuinely richer economic, social, or cultural life. "How can one speak of progress," Van Wyck Brooks wrote in 1915, "in a people like our own that so sends up to heaven the stench of atrophied personality?"[13] A year later James Oppenheim editorialized in *The Seven Arts:* " 'Produce great persons,' said Whitman; 'the rest follows.' And so we know today that before we have the planetary community we must have great national personalities."[14]

It was further agreed that valuable information about this new, "great national personality" lay in the American past. But because of the covertness of American self-expression, this information existed in the form of hints and clues which the critic and historian had to decipher. Lawrence, in particular, believed that almost all American writers were hopeless liars, but a

---

critics. During the 1920's it degenerated into a simple-minded Puritan-baiting. See Van Wyck Brooks, *America's Coming-of-Age* (Garden City, N.Y., 1958), p. xi.

[11]Bourne, "The Puritan's Will to Power," *The Seven Arts,* I (April, 1917), 631-632.

[12]"The Advance Guard Magazine," *Contact* (second series), I, 1 (Feb., 1932), 87.

[13]Brooks, *America's Coming-of-Age,* p. 84.

[14]Oppenheim, *The Seven Arts,* I (March, 1917), 505.

"strange reverberation" of the true American personality lay in the implications, undertones, and suggestions that lurked in "the familiar American classics, of Hawthorne, Poe, Whitman, or Fenimore Cooper."[15] The *Seven Arts* critics were convinced that American history and literature had to be reinterpreted to create what Van Wyck Brooks called a "usable past"—a past which would clarify the American identity and influence Americans to change it for the better. The "issues that make the life of a society do not spring spontaneously out of the mass," Brooks wrote.

They exist in it—a thousand potential currents and cross-currents; but they have to be discovered like principles of science, they have almost to be created like works of art. A people is like a ciphered parchment that has to be held up to the fire before its hidden significances come out. Once the divisions that have ripened in a people have been discerned and articulated, its beliefs and convictions are brought into play, the real evils that have been vaguely surmised spring into the light, the real strength of what is intelligent and sound becomes a measureable entity. . . .
    . . . No serious attempt has been made [in America] to bring about the necessary contraposition of forces, to divine them, to detach them, to throw them into relief; the real goats and the real sheep have not been set apart.[16]

Randolph Bourne agreed. The American intellectual, he wrote, "will have to do what Van Wyck Brooks calls 'invent a usable past'" in order to "rescue Thoreau and Whitman and Mark Twain and try to tap through them a certain eternal human tradition of abounding vitality and moral freedom, and so build out the future."[17]

Because he was a second generation American, Williams had a strong personal motive for discovering a "usable" American past. In 1939 he said that he had written *In the American Grain* because only by possessing America, by making it his own "from the beginning to my own day, in detail," could he orient himself in the beliefs which activated him (*SL*, 185). He believed

[15]Lawrence, "The Spirit of Place," *The Symbolic Meaning*, p. 16.

[16]Brooks, *America's Coming-of-Age*, pp. 85-86.

[17]Bourne, "The History of a Literary Radical," *The Yale Review*, VIII, 3 [n.s.] (April, 1919), 484. This essay is reprinted in *The History of a Literary Radical* and *The War and the Intellectuals*, ed. Carl Resek (New York, 1964).

that it was absolutely necessary for all Americans similarly to learn of their nation's origins because "what has been morally, aesthetically worth while in America has rested upon peculiar and discoverable ground . . . —and that aesthetically, morally we are deformed unless we read" (*IAG,* 109).

Like Bourne, Williams believed that the American past had to be "rescued" and made "usable" to have its proper, vitalizing effect. Writing about Aaron Burr, he defends the unconventionality of his views on the grounds that "what Burr stood for . . . is lost sight of in the calumny that surrounds his name," and therefore the truth has to be discovered, dug up and named (*IAG,* 196). "As with all else in America," he writes about Poe, "the value of Poe's genius TO OURSELVES must be *uncovered* from our droppings" (*IAG,* 219).

Most of Williams' early prose can be considered representative of his and his contemporaries' wish for either a "usable" American past or free expression in American literature. His earliest prose works, *Kora in Hell* and the prose sections of *Spring and All,* represent his first attempts to express himself in a uniquely American way, free from the traditional restraints of Puritan, genteel, or foreign influences. *In the American Grain* is his contribution to the search for a "usable" past. *The Great American Novel* is a mixture of these two intentions. Its form is essentially the free sort of "improvisation" that Williams used in *Kora,* but many passages are "preliminary sketches of characters and ideas" that appeared in *In the American Grain.*[18]

Kora in Hell is Williams' first, most violent attack upon the "sly, covert," Puritanical form of self-expression which he so hated (*IAG,* 154). The book was written under conditions that guaranteed that it would be an "open assertion" of his raw experiences. He wrote something every day without any plan: "anything that came into my head. . . . Not a word was to be changed" (*Autobiography,* 158). This sort of dadaesque, automatic writing gave him the freedom he believed characterized the "anarchical phase of writing" when the writer takes anything handy and "begins to put down the words after the de-

---

[18]Benjamin T. Spencer, "Dr. Williams' American Grain," *Tennessee Studies in Literature,* VIII (1963), 6.

sired expression in mind" without any rules or restrictions so that "every form of resistance to a complete release" is abandoned.[19]

In *Kora* Williams strenuously ignores the restrictions of his Puritan culture. On the first page he describes "Jacob Louslinger, white haired, stinking, dirty bearded, cross eyed, stammer tongued . . . mucous faced—deathling,—found lying in the weeds 'up there by the cemetery' " (*Kora,* 9). Throughout *Kora* he is particularly free and vigorous about sex. "Then there's that miller's daughter of 'buttocks broad and breastes high'. Something of Nietzsche, something of the good Samaritan, something of the devil himself,—can cut a caper of a fashion, my fashion! Hey you, the dance! Squat. Leap. . . . Stand up, stand up *ma bonne!* you'll break my backbone" (*Kora,* 44-45).[20] But Williams does not limit himself to being "shocking" about sex in *Kora;* he also vigorously ignores most of the restrictions of conventional ethical and logical distinctions.

Damn me I feel sorry for them. Yet syphilis is no more than a wild pink in the rock's cleft. I know that. Radicals and capitalists doing a can-can tread the ground clean. Luck to the feet then. Bring a Russian to put a fringe to the rhythm. What's the odds? Commiseration cannot solve calculus. Calculus is a stone. Frost'll crack it *(Kora,* 76).

In the text of *Kora,* Williams defends the chaotic quality of his "improvisations" on the grounds that *"there is neither beginning nor end to the imagination but it delights in its own seasons reversing the usual order at will"* and *"to say that a man has no imagination is to say nearly that he is blind or deaf."*[21] However, in his prologue, which was written after the rest of the book, he adds a further defense, the need for freedom of expression in American literature. He defends the unconventionality

---

[19]"How to Write" in Linda W. Wagner, *The Poems of William Carlos Williams* (Middletown, Conn., 1964), p. 145.

[20]Alfred Kreymborg claimed that Williams' frankness in his early writings caused him to receive "almost unanimous ridicule." "Shy though Bill was in person," Kreymborg wrote, "blank paper let loose anything he felt about everything, and he frankly and fearlessly undressed himself down to the ground. Not since the days of old Walt [Whitman] had an American gone quite so far, and readers were shocked all over again." *Troubadour: An Autobiography* (New York, 1925), p. 242. Actually the sales of Williams' first books were so small that it is doubtful if any great numbers of readers were shocked.

[21]*Kora,* pp. 15, 49. See also "How to Write" and *SE,* pp. 268-271.

of his work on the grounds that "nothing is good save the new" (*SE*, 21), because only the new in literature can achieve "freshness of presentation, novelty, freedom, [a] break with banality" (*SE*, 7). He then attacks Pound and Eliot as "men content with the connotations of their masters," plagiarists whose work was "rehash" and "repetition" of European poetry (*SE*, 21). Modern European poets, he remarks sarcastically, would "be more than slightly abashed to find parodies of the middle ages, Dante and *langue d'oc* foisted upon it as the best in United States poetry" (*SE*, 23-24).

In *Spring and All* and *In the American Grain* Williams identified his "improvisations" with his conception of America as a new world and American writing as a new form of literature. He tentatively stated in *Spring and All* that "the virtue of the improvisations is their placement in a world of new values—" and that they had made him discover "there is work to be done in the creation of new forms, new names for experience" (*SAA*, 44). He definitely identified American experimental writing, like *Kora*, with the means of founding a national literature in the Poe chapter of *In the American Grain*. "With Poe, words were not hung by usage with [past or European] associations, the pleasing wraiths of former masteries . . . he carried over only the most elemental qualities [of language] to his new purpose; which was, to find a way to tell his soul. Sometimes he used words so playfully his sentences seem to fly away from sense . . ." (*IAG*, 221).

The prose sections of *Spring and All* sometimes soar into fantasies like those in *Kora*, but many of them are similar in purpose and content to that book's prologue—aggressive defenses of an experimental, radically "new" American literature. The book begins with a long harangue about "the annihilation of every human creature on the face of the earth" (*SAA*, 5). Then he suddenly announces that, miraculously, "It is spring!"

In fact now, for the first time, everything IS new. Now at last the perfect effect is being witlessly discovered. The terms "veracity" "actuality" "real" "natural" "sincere" are being discussed at length, every word in the discussion being evolved from an identical discussion which took place the day before yesterday.

Yes, the imagination, drunk with prohibitions, has destroyed and recreated everything afresh in the likeness of that which it was. Now indeed men look about in amazement at each other with a full realization of the meaning of "art" (*SAA*, 9).

Williams continues his tirade about spring, art, and destruction for two more pages and then triumphantly presents his poem "By the Road to the Contagious Hospital" as an example of a newly created, spring world:

> All along the road the reddish
> purplish, forked, upstanding, twiggy
> stuff of bushes and small trees
> with dead, brown leaves under them
> leafless vines—
>
> Lifeless in appearance, sluggish
> dazed spring approaches—
>
> (*CEP*, 241)

Just as the spring plants must struggle against the cold wind and dead leaves to live, so also the new art must struggle against enemies to realize itself. It has reawakened hope "once more in men's hearts," and they cry: "IT IS THE NEW! Let us go forward!" But its appearance also causes "terrific confusion," and as mankind presses forward the enemies of the new art seize the opportunity. "THE TRADITIONALISTS OF PLAGIARISM try to get hold of the mob. They seize those nearest them and shout into their ears: Tradition! The solidarity of life!" (*SAA*, 15).

Williams includes in his category of "plagiarists" both those writers who escape from reality by plagiarizing from other literature, and those who plagiarize from nature by unimaginatively copying from it. His conception of true poetry is opposed to both kinds of plagiarism: words which communicate an imaginatively constructed reality. Whatever he writes that will be of value, will, Williams proclaims, be "an escape from crude symbolism, the annihilation of strained associations, complicated ritualistic forms designed to separate the work from 'reality'— such as rhyme, meter as meter and not as the essential of the work. . . ." "The word must be put down for itself, not as a symbol of nature but a part, cognisant of the whole . . ." (*SAA*, 22).

Williams further developed this theme of a quest for "pure" words—a totally imaginative, nonderivative literature—in *The Great American Novel*, which was published in the same year as *Spring and All*.

As the book's title indicates, Williams presents this quest as a specifically American literary problem. *The Great American Novel* begins as a literary joke—the entire work which is "written incidentally while the author searches for an opening sentence."[22] "Yet to have a novel—," cries Williams, "Oh catch up a dozen good smelly names and find some reason for murder, it will do. But can you not see, can you not taste, can you not smell, can you not hear, can you not touch—words? It is words that must progress."[23]

But Williams' "struggle" to begin his "Great American Novel" quickly becomes a metaphor for all "beginnings"—all attempts by men to create anew and all attempts of new things to realize themselves.

New! I'm new, said the quartz crystal on the parlor table—like glass— Mr. Tiffany bought a car load of them. Like water or white rock candy—I'm new, said the mist rising from the duck pond. . . . Electricity has been discovered for ever. I'm new, says the great dynamo. I am progress. I make a word. Listen! UMMMMMMMMMMMMM—

Ummmmmmmmmmmmm—Turned into the wrong street at three A.M. lost in the fog, listening, searching—Waaaa! said the baby. I'm new. A boy! A what? Boy. Shit, said the father of two other sons. Listen here. This is no place to talk that way. What a word to use. I'm new, said the sudden word (*GAN,* 309).

As in *Spring and All,* new beings face great odds. *The Great American Novel* is filled with examples of persons and things whose development is aborted by ignorance or malice. "Aaron my dear, dear boy," cries Mrs. Burr in one of Williams' satirical historical sketches, "life has not yet begun. All is new and untouched in the world waiting, like the pear on the tree, for you to pluck it. Everyone loves you and will wait on you. For you everything is possible. Bing! and Hamilton lies dead" (*GAN,* 325).

Many of these failed beginnings in *The Great American Novel* are symptoms of a greater failure which Williams considered the cause of most of America's problems—the American inability to create a valid, indigenous culture. A "portrait" of a

---

[22]Kenneth Burke, "The Methods of William Carlos Williams," *The Dial,* LXXXII (Feb., 1927), 98.

[23]*GAN,* pp. 308, 311. For Williams, like Stein, the term "words" signified a communication of the total sensuous reality of both the referents of words and their sounds. See his critical comments on Joyce and Stein in *SE,* pp. 75-90, 113-120, and 162-166. The term "the language" which he used later in his career has approximately the same meaning.

typical American cultural event would be, Williams writes, "*Lohengrin* in ITALIAN, SUNG AT MANHATTAN—San Carlo Company Revives Wagner Opera, with Anna Fitziu as Elsa" (*GAN*, 317).

The cause of this "cuddle muddle," Williams believed, was that America was a new world—a "Nuevo Mundo" as Columbus' sailors cried—but no new *words* have been discovered by American artists so that the nation will name its own experiences and possess its own identity. "America is a mass of pulp," he exclaims,

a jelly, a sensitive plate ready to take whatever print you want to put on it. . . .
Europe we must—We have no words. Every word we get must be broken off from the European mass. Every word we get placed over again by some delicate hand. Piece by piece we must loosen what we want. . . .
I touch the words and they baffle me. I turn them over in my mind and look at them but they mean little that is clean. They are plastered with muck out of the [European?] cities.—(*GAN*, 316).

"What are we coming to," Williams cries, "we in this country? Are we doomed? Must we be another Europe or another Japan with our coats copied from China, another bastard country in a world of bastards? Is this our doom or will we ever amount to anything?" (*GAN*, 317).

Williams attacks this problem with a vigorous and imaginative but frequently confusing variety of approaches in *The Great American Novel*.

Sometimes—as in the passage quoted above—he writes half-serious polemics about the state of American culture and his remedies for it. In these passages Williams demands that artists invent new forms, new uniquely American "words." "Americans have never recognized themselves," he wrote in *In the American Grain*, "How can they? It is impossible until someone invent the ORIGINAL terms. As long as we are content to be called by somebody's else terms, we are incapable of being anything but our own dupes."[24] He stresses in *The Great American Novel* that it is not enough for American artists to be "modern" or

---

[24]*IAG*, p. 226. "Until your artists have conceived you," he wrote in 1947, "in your unique and supreme form you can never conceive yourselves, *and have not, in fact, existed.*" "An Approach to the Poem," *English Institute Essays, 1947* (New York, 1948), p. 60.

revolutionary; even the most radical innovations are valueless if they are not uniquely and purely American. "In other words it comes after Joyce, therefore it is no good, of no use but a secondary local usefulness like the Madison Square Garden tower copied from Seville—It is of no absolute good. It is not NEW. It is not an invention" (*GAN*, 312).

Williams supplements his polemics with parodies of some of the cultural and critical prescriptions which were being urged for America. He also satirizes various styles and themes in American art and writing which he considers false and stale usages of the "words" of American experience. Chapter 18, for example, is a dazzling mixture of parodies of regionalism, business correspondence, advertising, and journalism.

Mixed with these parodies of false American "words" are Williams' more serious efforts to find true expressions for American experience. "The background of America is not Europe but America" (*GAN*, 327); therefore, Williams reasons, pure or real American experience may lie in the "American background" beneath the shoddy realities of modern life. Twenty years later Williams wrote that every new being possessed a word-seed of its original being, and that it somehow retained some trace of that original "revelation" no matter how warped its later growth might be (*SE*, 270). Similarly in *The Great American Novel* his novelist wonders if some "words" of the New World's original being may be discovered despite the deformations imposed upon it by European conquerors.

What a new world they had made of it with their Cortezes, their Pizarros yes and their Lord Howes, their Washingtons even. The Declaration of Independence. I wonder, he said, whether it could be possible that the influence of the climate—I wonder if the seed, the sperm of that, existed in Columbus. Was it authentic? Is there a word to be found there? Could it be that in those men who had crossed, in the Norse as well as the Mongols [i.e., the American Indians], something spontaneous could not have been implanted out of the air? Or was the declaration to be put to the credit of that German George? Was it only the result of local conditions?[25]

But—to use Williams' own metaphor—the seed of this idea only germinates in *The Great American Novel*. He rarely stud-

[25]*GAN*, p. 320. Williams may have derived this idea from Lawrence's "The Spirit of Place," *The Symbolic Meaning*, pp. 21-22. See also *IAG*, p. 230.

ies and presents the experiences of past Americans in their own right as "words" of pure American experience. Instead he usually uses them as materials for his improvised parodies with the result that they are lost amidst the book's chaotic satires and polemics. In *In the American Grain,* however, Williams controlled his talents for improvisation and devoted his full attention to cleansing the "words" of American experience so that they would constitute the "usable past" which he and his contemporaries desired.[26]

Williams was convinced when he wrote *In the American Grain* that pure or true "words" of uniquely American experiences could be derived from the nation's past records. There was, he believed, "a source IN AMERICA for everything we think or do" and therefore the basis for an American education lay in the American past, in the "intelligent investigation of the changes worked upon the early comers here, to the New World, the books, the records . . . that what has been morally, aesthetically worth while in America has rested upon peculiar and discoverable ground" (*IAG,* 109). He assumed that the essential qualities of life in the New World were expressed not by the accepted, historical identities of his subjects but by the actual language of these "early comers here." In these studies, he wrote, "I have sought to re-name the things seen, now lost in [a] chaos of borrowed titles, many of them inappropriate, under which the true character lies hid. In letters, in journals, reports of happenings I have recognized new contours suggested by old words so that new names were constituted."[27]

As a historian, as well as poet, Williams assumed that the true names of things could only be discovered by the closest possible contact with them. His plan, he later recalled, "was to try to get

[26]The book remains, however, a highly personal and emotional one. Williams keeps his subjective responses focused on his subject and uses these responses more to illuminate his subjects than to express his own personality. See Chapter Four below on his development of this technique.

[27]This comment was on the dust jacket of the first edition. It is printed as a headnote to later editions. Williams' intention, wrote Kenneth Burke, was to enable the reader "to see beyond the label . . . to replace 'Columbus discovered America in 1492' with excerpts from Columbus's diary which show what it was like to be approaching America at the turn of that century and to see a continent not as land, but in terms of seaweed, of river birds heard passing in the night. . . ." "Subjective History," *Books* (March 14, 1926), p. 7.

inside the heads of some of the American founders or 'heroes'
. . . by examining their original records. I wanted nothing to
get between me and what they themselves had recorded" (*Autobiography,* 178). Since he wished his readers to have the same
immediate contact with his subjects, Williams made the book "a
study in styles of writing" and "tried to write each chapter in
the style most germane to its sources or at least the style which
seemed . . . appropriate to the material" (*SL,* 187). Sometimes
he used and copied his subjects' writings "with malice afore-
thought to prove the truth of the book, since the originals fitted
into it without effort" (*SL,* 187). According to Joseph E. Slate,
Williams' use of this technique exemplified his "belief that if
the emotionally charged past is allowed to speak directly to the
present, its emotion will enable the sensitive modern mind to
grasp what is important in the event."[28]

However—just to make sure that the past spoke "correctly" to
the present—Williams edited, commented upon, and organized
his materials throughout *In the American Grain* in order to
create a "usable past." The first two chapters of the book, those
on Columbus and the Norsemen, are good examples of his techniques.

By making Eric the Red the narrator of the first chapter,
Williams was able to represent the Norsemen as crude and barbaric—foils to the more sensitive Columbus. Eric, as characterized by Williams, is simply a man driven from Europe by Chris-
tianity, a faith which condemns all his deepest instincts. Even
though his son Leif discovers America, Eric has no vision of it as
a New World which possesses new things. He desires only a
place, any place, where he can remain his old, "barbaric" self
and carry on his feuds. The other Norsemen are no better, and
Eric's illegitimate daughter Freydis is even worse. She seizes the
opportunities the New World offers her for pillage, treachery,
and violence—and nothing else.

Williams did not rely upon the violent actions of the Ice-
landic sagas to convey this meaning by themselves. Instead of
their grave, sonorous style he used "a style that was barbaric and
primitive" as he believed Eric to be (*IWW,* 42). The chapter is

[28]Joseph Evans Slate, "William Carlos Williams, Hart Crane and 'The
Virtue of History,'" *Texas Studies in Literature and Language,* VI (Winter,
1965), 499.

full of tense, disjointed, terse sentences. Every word is used to communicate the violent emotions and actions, the complicated plots and treacheries, which obsessed Eric and Freydis. There are virtually no descriptions in the chapter. Places and names are mentioned but Eric never describes them, for the unique qualities of places and persons were irrelevant to him. Naturally, there are no long rhythms of *contemplative* description. Because Eric and the Norsemen never saw America as a place-in-itself with its own unique qualities, they never truly discovered it at all.

There is, however, at least one passage in Williams' source which has a glimpse of the discovery of the richness and wonder of a New World. When Leif, Eric's son, arrived at Vinland, he and his companions "went ashore and looked about them, the weather being fine, and they observed that there was dew upon the grass, and it so happened that they touched the dew with their hands, and touched their hands to their mouths, and it seemed to them that they had never before tasted anything so sweet as this."[29] But by making the chapter Eric's experience, not Leif's, Williams was able to delete this passage in the interest of creating a greater contrast between the Norsemen and Columbus.

For Williams, Columbus was the only true discoverer of America because he experienced it as a *New* World. Only because he was essentially a poet did Columbus possess the "naive faith" needed first to discover America and then to comprehend the significance of this discovery. His story, Williams believed, should be retold again and again because "in the Columbus legend lies the one opportunity all Americans can have to feel together as brothers. We together are the New World and there can never be another."[30] By himself Columbus wanders upon the beach at Santo Domingo at the moment of discovery which Williams used to conclude the chapter. All the richly descriptive

[29]*The Voyages of the Northmen* in *The Northmen, Columbus, and Cabot: 985-1503*, eds. J. E. Olson and E. G. Bourne (New York, 1906), pp. 51-52. Since Williams probably took the materials for both the Eric and Columbus chapters from this source there is a possibility that he deliberately ignored the similarity between this passage and the one from Columbus' diary which he used in *IAG*, p. 26.

[30]"Introduction" to Sidney Salt's *Christopher Columbus and Other Poems* (Boston, 1937), p. 8.

and contemplative stylistic qualities of his journal are emphasized by Williams so that the reader will understand that the
experience of discovery should be filled with a sense of awe and
wonder which is religious in its intensity and simplicity.

> I saw many trees very unlike those of our country. Branches growing
> in different ways and all from one trunk; one twig is one form and
> another is a different shape and so unlike that it is the greatest wonder
> in the world to see the diversity. . . . The fish so unlike ours that it is
> wonderful. Some are the shape of dories and of the finest colors, so
> bright that there is not a man who would not be astounded, and
> would not take great delight in seeing them. . . .
> On shore I sent the people for water, some with arms, and others
> with casks; and as it was some little distance, I waited two hours for
> them.
> During that time I walked among the trees which was the most
> beautiful thing which I had ever seen....[31]

The rest of *In the American Grain* is organized around this
opening theme of the ways men experience new worlds;
throughout the book Williams evaluates, compares, and contrasts his subjects in terms of their responses to the new.

Benjamin Spencer has noted that in *In the American Grain*
Williams actually "emerged not with one 'America' but . . .
three: a kind of Platonic idea of America historically expressed
in the American dream; a covert America intuited by poets like
Poe and Whitman; and finally an existential America, vulgar
and recalcitrant in its temporal pursuits." Similarly, as one
reads *In the American Grain,* there gradually emerge three types
of American "heroes" or "representative men"—each of which
creates and exemplifies one of these Americas.[32]

One type of American who appears throughout the book is
the destroyer of the new. He is the "new breed" of man whom
Williams defined as possessing two characteristics: "terrific
energy," and "terror before the NEW" (*IAG*, 156). The destructive Americans are represented in the early chapters by the con-

---

[31]*IAG*, p. 26. "Beautiful Thing" is the name Williams gives the young
woman who is the heroine of *Paterson III*.

[32]Spencer, "Dr. Williams' American Grain," 6-7. These three "types" are
not rigid ones. Only a few of Williams' subjects are unalloyed examples of
one type of American experience. Columbus and Burr are both lovers and
idealists of America. Poe is destructive as well as idealistic; but Williams still
approves of his destructiveness since it was directed at the false America
created by the Puritans.

quistadors Cortez and De Leon who destroyed the New World and its culture which they discovered in Tenochtitlan and the West Indies. Other destructive Americans in *In the American Grain* include Benjamin Franklin, Alexander Hamilton, and the Americans described in the "Jacataqua" chapter who have prevented a new, "great flowering" of the American spirit (*IAG,* 174), because of their fears of nature, democracy, and sexuality. The epitome of American destructiveness in *In the American Grain* is the Puritan, who both destroyed Indian culture and "keeps his frightened grip upon the throat of the world" so that no new American culture can begin (*IAG,* 67).

"There are two ways," D. H. Lawrence wrote in his review of *In the American Grain,*

of being American; and the chief, says Mr. Williams, is by recoiling into individual smallness and insentience, and gutting the great continent in frenzies of mean fear. It is the Puritan way. The other is by *touch;* touch America as she is; dare to touch her! And this is the heroic way.

And this, this sensitive touch upon the unseen America, is to be the really great adventure in the New World.[33]

Contrasted to the Puritans are Williams' heroes, the men who dare to "touch America as she is." These are the men like Daniel Boone, Père Sebastian Rasles, Aaron Burr, and Audubon in *Paterson V,* "men intact—with all their senses waking" (*IAG,* 206), who dared to discover, accept, and embrace new worlds: the American wilderness, the Indian way of life, democracy. Because they were willing to immerse themselves in America, these American heroes are able—like Boone—to enjoy a New World which is their "land of heart's desire" (*IAG,* 139).

The idealists are the third type of Americans in *In the American Grain.* These are the men like Poe, De Soto, and Raleigh who love and discover America but never enjoy it as "a land of heart's desire." The America which they love exists in their imaginations as a "Platonic idea of America" or an "American Dream," which is embodied in "the conception of the New World as a woman" (*IAG,* 220).

Williams' idealists possess enormous energy and dedication. They struggle against enormous odds to realize the potential

[33]D. H. Lawrence, "American Heroes," *The Nation,* CXII (April 14, 1926), 413.

beauty, richness, or greatness of America. But some—like Raleigh, de Champlain, and De Soto—are infatuated with a vision of the New World which is not attuned to American reality. Others—like Burr, Columbus, and Poe—are defeated by the ingratitude and treachery of their followers and country-men, "the frightened hogs or scared birds feeding on the corn" (*IAG*, 219), who have no ideals about America and hate anyone who does.

Williams does more than catalog these types of American experience in *In the American Grain*. He strives throughout the book to make his subjects into a "usable past," to assert their contemporary relevance, to discover how their modes of behavior were reborn in the past and may yet be reborn again in the present.[34]

American destructiveness began with the conquistadors. A man like Columbus among the early explorers was so rare, Williams believed, that "history begins for us with murder and enslavement, not with discovery" (*IAG*, 39). This destructive-ness was at first relatively crude and almost innocent. Spain could not be blamed, Williams argued, for the crassness of the conquistadors. They were "deafened and blinded" by "the re-creative New [World] unfolding itself miraculously before them" and therefore "bitter as the thought may be that Tenochtitlan . . . should have been crushed out because of the awkward names men give their emptiness, yet it was no man's fault" (*IAG*, 27).

The Puritans' destructiveness was far more malignant because their emptiness was sanctioned by the inverted morality of their religion. Instead of growing in America, they "looked black at the world and damning its perfections praised a zero in them-selves" (*IAG*, 65). They saw the New World as a "squallid [*sic*], horrid American Dessart [*sic*]" and prided themselves on their alienation from it (*IAG*, 82). Their religion was so "spirit-

---

[34]Williams stated his conception of the hero's rebirth with considerable clarity in his 1951 review of Ford Madox Ford's *Parade's End:* "This is not the 'last Tory' but the first in the new enlightenment of the Englishman—at his best, or the most typical Englishman. The sort of English that fought for and won Magna Carta, having undergone successive mutations through the ages, has reappeared in another form. . . . *Parade's End* then is for me a tremendous and favorable study of the transition of England's most worthy type." *SE*, p. 323. See also *ibid.*, p. 208.

ual," so "concise, bare, PURE" that they were able to mash all natural beings—the child, the woman, the Indian—"into one *safe* mold." "They must have closed all the world out," Williams claimed, ". . . Having in themselves nothing of curiosity, no wonder, for the New World . . . they knew only to keep their eyes blinded, their tongues in orderly manner . . . their ears stopped by the monotony of their hymns and their flesh covered in straight habits" (*IAG*, 112). They were "virtuously" trapped in the terrible fear and ignorance which were the inevitable effects of so total an estrangement from the nature inside and outside of themselves.

. . . spiritless, thus without grounds on which to rest their judgments of this world, fearing to touch its bounties, a fissure takes place for the natural mouth—and everything's perverse to them (*IAG*, 80).

These were the modes of a people, small in number, beset by dangers and in terror. They dared not think. If frightened by Indians or the supernatural, they shook and committed horrid atrocities in the name of their creed, the cost of emptiness (*IAG*, 112).

Like Bourne, Lawrence, and many other writers of that period, Williams believed that Puritanism did not end with the historical Puritans. It was reborn during America's colonial period in Franklin's and Hamilton's ethic of thrift and cowardice which urged Americans to suppress and exploit nature rather than enjoy it. The new nation, Williams wrote bitterly, was the offspring of "terror," "of the desire to huddle, to protect" (*IAG*, 155). The pioneer statesmen were too busy defending themselves against the wilderness to give anything of themselves to "the great New World." Yet they could not "quite leave hands off it but must TOUCH it, in a 'practical' way, that is a joking, shy, nasty way . . ." (*IAG*, 157).

And finally, Williams was convinced, Puritanism still lived—"stinking all about you . . . a kind of mermaid with a corpse for tail" (*IAG*, 115)—in the American attitude toward the freer elements of human nature, particularly the erotic. He claimed in the "Jacataqua" chapter that Puritanism's "numbing coat that cuts us off from touch" prevented all fulfillment among American women and artists (*IAG*, 178-180).

Despite his pessimism about the American tradition, Williams did not consider it hopeless. Other types of men and modes of behavior than the Puritan had existed in the American past, and he was convinced that they too could be reborn in the present. Boone, for example, was "a great voluptuary born to the American settlements against the niggardliness of the damming puritanical tradition; one who by the single logic of his passion, which he rested on the savage life about him, destroyed at its spring that spiritually withering plague . . . full of a rich regenerative violence he remains, when his history will be carefully reported, for us who have come after to call upon him" (*IAG,* 130).

Columbus was not the last man who, "possessed of that streamlike human purity of purpose" (*IAG,* 11), had been granted the experience of discovering a New World. Later Père Sebastian Rasles, a French Jesuit missionary in Maine,

recognized the New World. It stands out in all he says. It is a living flame. . . .

Here is richness, here is color, here is form. . . . Contrasted with the Protestant *acts,* dry and splitting, those of Père Rasles were striking in their tenderness, devotion, insight and detail of apprehension. This was luscious fruit. The deed was for humanity,—his passion held him a slave to the New World, he strove to sound its mettle (*IAG,* 120-121).

During America's colonial period, Aaron Burr "sought new worlds" in the growing democracy around him (*IAG,* 202), and "raised to a different level, the directness of 'common people' which reformers . . . commonly neglect, misname, misapprehend as if it were anything but to touch, to hear, to see, to smell, to taste" (*IAG,* 206). And of course there was Boone, who discovered a New World in the "wild beauty" of Kentucky—"among all the colonists, like an Indian, the ecstasy of complete possession of the new country was his alone. In Kentucky he would stand, a lineal descendant of Columbus on the beach at Santo Domingo, walking up and down with eager eyes while his men were gathering water" (*IAG,* 136-137).

Williams was convinced that even in the modern age the individual could still discover new worlds in America. True, such a man had to "descend" beneath "a field of unrelated culture stuccoed" upon the primitive reality of American life (*IAG,* 212). But Whitman, Poe, and Houston—who "took an Indian woman for his wife"—had so descended; and it was therefore possible for a modern American to possess "if not definitely a culture new in every part," at least the aesthetic satisfaction of having "the feet of his understanding on the ground, his ground, *the* ground, the only ground that he knows, that which *is* under his feet" (*IAG*, 213).

The first American idealists in *In the American Grain* are drawn to their own destructions by the immense material promise of the New World which exists in their dreams. But they receive nothing except isolation from the men surrounding them who lack ideals and visions. Columbus, claimed Williams,

saw before him the illusive bright future of a great empire founded, coupled with a fabulous conquest of heathendom by the only true church. Much had been promised him. He had succeeded in the sternest hazard, the great first step; should not the rest prove easy and natural? (*IAG*, 9).

—it was still as a man that he would bite the bitter fruit that Nature would offer him. He was poisoned and his fellows turned against him like wild beasts (*IAG*, 11).

"You will not dare to cease following me—" whispers the female "Spirit" of the New World to De Soto, "at Apalchi, at Cutifachiqui, at Mabilla, turning from the sea, facing inland. And in the end you shall receive of me, nothing—save one long caress as of a great river passing forever upon your sweet corse" (*IAG*, 45). De Soto's followers, like Columbus', turned against him. They refused to visit him or show him sympathy in his last illness, and "some were glad" when he died (*IAG*, 57). Similarly, Raleigh, who envisioned Virginia as a "perfection" of Elizabeth, lost everything—for the virgin queen and land which he never possessed.

Later during the American Revolution, the American dream was political. Burr, in particular, "saw America in his imagination, free. His spirit leaped to it—and his body followed out of a sick bed. But his spark was not preserved. He saw America, or he had seen America, as a promise of delight and it struck fine earth, that fancy" (*IAG*, 197). But the idealists like Burr who won the revolution and founded the Republic were rewarded with ingratitude and treachery. Burr himself was driven from political life. John Paul Jones was forced to win his battles with worthless ships and despite the treacherous cowardice of his subordinates. Later he had "to leave the American navy . . . to go to Russia, for release" (*IAG*, 155). Washington sacrificed and repressed almost all of his natural instincts to create and defend the Republic only to be hated by the very people whom he

served: "The minute he had secured their dung heap for them
—he had to take their dirt in the face" (*IAG*, 143).

"But his spark was not preserved." It is this phrase which
implies the fate of the American idealists in *In the American
Grain*. Williams' lovers of America, when contrasted with his
idealists, possess a certain, saving lack of ambition. Like Boone,
they desire their wilderness "land of heart's desire" and nothing
more.

Williams' idealists are much more ambitious. They want to
found or discover great empires, cities, nations, and—in the case
of Poe—national literatures. They are determined that their
vision of an ideal, beautiful America be realized as something
more than an isolated, individual experience. But their very
possession of such an idealistic vision seems virtually to guarantee that they will not realize it. Columbus, De Soto, Raleigh, de
Champlain, Washington, Jones, Burr, Poe—all desperately need
the devoted aid of their followers or their communities if they
are to realize their ideals. But instead they receive only hatred,
envy, ingratitude, and frustration.

"Bewildered, he continued," Williams wrote of Columbus,
"voyage after voyage, four times, out of his growing despair; it
seemed that finally by sheer physical effort a way must be found
—till the realization of it all at last grew firmly upon him"
(*IAG*, 11). Slowly Columbus realizes the terrible, implacable
hatred which men bear toward him: "I undertook a fresh voyage to the new Heaven and Earth . . . the most honorable and
profitable of all," Columbus recalls. He arrives in New Spain
during a storm and is immediately "forbidden to go on shore"
by the King's governor.

The tempest was terrible throughout the night, all the ships were
separated, and each one driven to the last extremity without hope of
anything but death . . . what man was ever born, not even excepting
Job, who would not have been ready to die of despair at finding
himself as I then was, in anxious fear for my own safety, and that of
my son, my brother and my friends, and yet refused permission either
to land or to put into harbor on the shores which by God's mercy I
had gained for Spain sweating blood?
And this is the thing which calls most loudly for redress and remains
inexplicable to this moment (*IAG*, 12-13).

But as one reads *In the American Grain*, Columbus' fate becomes very explicable. There is no *phthonos*, the gods' jealousy
of men's success, in *In the American Grain*. Men's jealousy is

sufficient. Again and again, Williams' idealist-discoverers are betrayed into self-destructive isolation; therefore, as he bitterly advises them in the conclusion to his chapter on de Champlain, they must be as destructive as the wildernesses they discover if they wish to survive and realize their ideals: "Rebellion, savagery; a force to leap up and wrench you from your hold and force you to be part of it; the place, the absolute new without a law but the basic blood where the savage becomes brother" (*IAG,* 74).

Poe is the consummate American idealist in *In the American Grain*—and the one Williams considered most relevant to contemporary American conditions. As a searcher for ideal beauty in America, "Poe was a new De Soto. The rest might be content with little things, not he" (*IAG,* 220). As a cultural nationalist, he transferred to literature the ideals of patriots like Burr and Washington. He was the first American writer, claimed Williams, to realize that there could be an American culture.

> He was the first to realize that the hard, sardonic, truculent mass of the New World, hot, angry—was, in fact, not a thing to paint over, to smear, to destroy. . . . That it is NOT a thing to be slighted by men. Difficult, its very difficulty was their strength. . . .
> Poe conceived the possibility, the sullen, volcanic inevitability of the *place* (*IAG,* 225).

Naturally Poe's insistence on perfection and originality alienated him from a provincial society puffed by complacency and dedicated to the borrowed, makeshift, and mediocre. It lead him to "an isolation that would naturally lead to drunkenness and death, logically and simply—by despair, as the very final evidence of a too fine seriousness and devotion" (*IAG,* 222). But this sort of aesthetic idealism, Williams believed, was exactly what American literature needed—in the twentieth century as well as Poe's own time. "Either the New World must be mine as I will have it, or it is a worthless bog. There can be no concession. His attack was *from the center out.* Either I exist or I do not exist and no amount of pap which I happen to be lapping can dull me to the loss. It was a doctrine, anti-American. Here everything was makeshift, everything was colossal, in profusion. . . . It left, in 1840, the same mood as ever dominant among us. Take what you can get. What you lack, copy" (*IAG,* 219).

For it is only through this ruthless perfectionism and isolation that the American artist can slough off the makeshift culture stuccoed upon American reality. The genius of America, Williams warned, "is shy and wild and frail, the loveliest, to be cherished only by the most keen, courageous and sensitive. It may die" (*IAG*, 214). Or it may live and speak through the voices of its idealists and lovers like Columbus and Poe who—having lost all hope of realizing the genius of America in fact—allow its presence to fill their minds. It is after he has lost all hope of "the illusive bright future of a great empire" that Columbus remembers and writes of the first great moment of discovery that led to his glory and despair. It is after Poe's wife has died and he has become totally isolated that the essence of American reality lives in his writing. There it achieves realization.

Now, defenseless, the place itself attacked him. Now the thinness of his coat, the terror of his isolation took hold.

His imagery is of the desperate situation of his mind, thin as a flame to mount unsupported, successful for a moment in the love of—not so much his wife—but in the escape she filled for him with her frail person, herself afflicted as by "ghouls."

Disarmed, in his poetry the place itself comes through. This is the New World.

Poe stayed against the thin edge, driven to be heard by the battering racket about him to a distant screaming—the pure essence of his locality (*IAG*, 232-233).

Thus, throughout *In the American Grain*, Williams sees his subjects as being essentially "alive," his contemporaries, because their modes of response to America—both good and bad—were still available to modern Americans. For example, he believed that Cotton Mather's books did not "live" themselves, "but what is in them lives and there hides, as in a lair from whence it sallies now and then to strike terror through the land" (*IAG*, 115). Or he could write about Samuel de Champlain as "this man. This—me; this American; a sort of radio distributor sending out sparks to us all" (*IAG*, 70).

But this approach did much more than make Williams' subjects in *In the American Grain* relevant to his problems and values as a modern American; it also allowed him and his contemporaries to participate in American history. By writing *In the American Grain*, Williams could, in effect, influence American history by contributing to what he believed to be its valuable traditions. The defeat of Puritanism, the discovery of New Worlds, the achievement of American ideals—all of these issues ceased to be "closed" or "past" to Williams after he wrote *In the American Grain*. Now American history was, in part, his responsibility, and Williams accepted it as such. For the rest of his life he struggled to aid or attack the traditions he discovered in the subjects of *In the American Grain*.

His indictment of the Puritans as the destroyers and/or ignorers of the new was renewed in his attacks upon Hamilton and the universities as "usurers" in *Paterson I* and *II*, and his advice in *Paterson V:*

> no woman is virtuous
> who does not give herself to her lover
> —forthwith
>
> (V, iii, 266)

Moreover, much of Williams' attitude toward himself and his fellow American poets is prefigured by his conception of the American idealists and "wanderers" in *In the American Grain*. There he admired men like De Soto and Poe because they were not "content with little things," because they demanded the beauty of a "city greater than Cuzco" or a successful national literature. And throughout *Paterson II*, Williams berates his persona Mr. Paterson, and himself, because he cannot find beauty and "invent" a local literature:

> That the poem,
> the most perfect rock and temple, the highest
> falls, in clouds of gauzy spray, should be
> so rivaled   that the poet,
> in disgrace, should borrow from erudition (to
> unslave the mind): railing at the vocabulary
> (borrowing from those he hates, to his own
> disfranchisement)
>
> (II, iii, 99)

Above all Williams was an indefatigable searcher for New Worlds, like his heroes Columbus, Boone, Rasles, and Burr. In *In the American Grain* itself he portrays himself as responding to his Negro patients—a "new" race—in much the same way that Rasles responded to his "new" race, the American Indians.

For example, Williams notes that in his journals Rasles "speaks of his struggles with their [the Indians'] language, its peculiar beauties . . . he cited its tempo, the form of its genius with gusto, with admiration, with generosity" (*IAG*, 121). And in his chapter on the Negroes, Williams shows the same appreciation of a patient's speech: "Language grows in the original from his laughing lips. . . . It is water from a spring to talk with him—it is a quality. I wish I might write a book of his improvisations in slang. I wish I might write a play in collaboration with him" (*IAG*, 210-211).

Williams attempted to define what he considered the proper meaning of American liberty and freedom in his 1939 essay "Against the Weather." "When America became the escape for the restless and confined of Europe," he wrote,

the significance, as a historic moment, was not guessed. It has never been clarified. The commonly accepted symbol for it . . . was "freedom," in which the sense of an escape from a tyrannical restriction was emphasized. This was inevitable and in the first flush of release seemed thoroughly justified, but it left a great deal to be desired.

Liberty is the better word. It was liberty they needed, not so much liberty for freedom's sake but liberty to partake of, to be included in and to conserve (*SE*, 208).

In the special sense in which he uses the word, Williams' prose and poetry do "conserve" the reality which they possess. In his first "Paterson" poem, published in 1927, Williams vividly depicted his power to possess his spatial environment. The whole city is articulated so distinctly within the "ideas" of his persona Mr. Paterson that he senses its "facts" as his flesh.

> But who! who are these people? It is
> his flesh making the traffic, cranking the car
> buying the meat—
>
> . . . .
>
> They are the divisions and imbalances
> of his whole concept, made small by pity
> and desire, they are—no ideas beside the facts—
> (*CEP*, 234-235)

These "facts" include the tawdriest, most ephemeral parts of Williams' environment, but by possessing them in the "ideas" of his poetry Williams rescued them from the garbage dumps of New Jersey. They are reborn and preserved in the world Wil-

liams described in *Paterson V:* "the world / of the imagination
[which] most endures" (V, i, 248). Similarly, Williams' possession of his heroes' loves, hatreds, and ambitions in *In the American Grain* renewed these men and gave them new life and
relevance in the twentieth-century American imagination.[35]

[35]Even though it sold poorly, *In the American Grain* aroused the imaginations of contemporary artists more than any of Williams' other works. It
was praised by D. H. Lawrence and Kenneth Burke in their reviews. Hart
Crane was "very enthusiastic" about the book and called it "an achievement
that I'd be proud of" (Slate, "William Carlos Williams, Hart Crane and 'The
Virtue of History,' " 490). Charles Sheeler praised Williams as "the man I've
been looking for all my life" after reading portions of it in *Broom* (Constance Rourke, *Charles Sheeler,* New York, 1938, p. 49). Alfred Stieglitz took
the name of his gallery, An American Place, from the book, and Martha
Graham wrote to Williams that "she could not have gone on with her
choreographic projects without it" (*Autobiography,* pp. 236-237).

CHAPTER | FOUR

Williams' poetry during the 1930's is best understood as a continuation of his work of the 1920's with important modifications that were related to his development as an "objectivist"—the name which he, Louis Zukofsky, and a number of other poets used for their poetic movement during the late 1920's and early 1930's.[1]

Though he remained true to the basic tenets of Imagism throughout his career, Williams grew dissatisfied with the limitations of the movement early in the 1920's. "The insignificant 'image' may be 'evoked' never [ever?] so ably," he complained in *Spring and All*, "and still mean nothing" (*SAA*, 20). Because of his desire to enliven local materials and add significance to them, his poetry of the 1920's rapidly progressed beyond the bare, "pure" Imagism of a poem like "The Red Wheelbarrow." It was not until about 1930, however, that he adopted a new poetic theory to rationalize his new poetic practices.

[1] The chief poets associated with the Objectivist movement were Zukofsky, Williams, Basil Bunting, George Oppen, Carl Rakosi, and Charles Reznikoff. Ezra Pound had a peripheral connection with the group. Williams' comments on Objectivism are contained in *IWW*, pp. 51-52; *Autobiography*, pp. 264-265; "Objectivism" in the *Encyclopedia of Poetry and Poetics*, ed. Alex Preminger (Princeton, 1965), p. 582; also "A Note on Poetry" in the *Oxford Anthology of American Literature*, eds. W. R. Benet and N. H. Pearson (New York, 1938), pp. 1313-14; "The New Poetical Economy," *Poetry*, XLIV (July, 1934), 220-225; and the reviews cited in notes 12 and 15 below. See also Carl Rakosi, "William Carlos Williams," *The Symposium*, IV, 4 (Oct., 1933), pp. 439-447; Louis Zukofsky, "American Poetry 1920-1930," *The Symposium*, II, 1 (Jan., 1931), pp. 60-84; Louis Zukofsky, ed., " 'Objectivists' 1931," *Poetry*, XXXVII (Feb., 1931), 237-296; and note 5 below.

Williams was not influenced by the poetic principles of Objectivism in the same way that he was influenced by those of Imagism. Almost all of the differences between the poems in *The Tempers* (1912) and *Al Que Quiere* (1917) and *Sour Grapes* (1921) can be ascribed to Williams' acceptance of the doctrines which Pound began to expound in the March, 1913 issue of *Poetry*. On the other hand, Zukofsky based the theoretical principles of Objectivism upon poems already written by his contemporaries, among them Williams. In his preface to *An "Objectivists" Anthology* Zukofsky specifically cites Williams' "To Elsie," "The Botticellean Trees," "It Is a Living Coral," and "Full Moon" as being among the poems which exemplify his theoretical principles.

Thus Williams cannot have been guided by the Objectivists' theories because they were influenced by his own, earlier poetry. Nevertheless, these Objectivist principles are still useful for understanding his development.

Williams wrote many of his poems spontaneously, but he also liked to "work to" a theory. He believed that the artist should have aesthetic principles so that he could "recognize what is good and *why* it's good—and how to organize it into a satisfactory poem."[2] But he was not always able to formulate his "theories" to his own satisfaction.[3] At such times, particularly during the early part of his career, Williams was receptive to the theories of others if they fitted his own interests closely enough. "My mind was tough and not easily carried away by the opin-

[2]"Symposium on Writing," *The Golden Goose*, Series 3, No. 2 (Autumn, 1951), p. 94.

[3]Even though Williams believed that he should be guided personally as an artist by theories, he did not have a very high regard for his own powers as a literary critic or theorist. See *SL*, p. 94. The unevenness of Williams' literary criticism was caused by several factors. He was not an intellectual, and he had little respect for orderly, consistent thought as an end in itself. Unlike Eliot and Pound, for example, he had little or no desire to influence a general audience or propagandize his poetic theories. Much of his best criticism seems to have been written chiefly out of a sense of obligation to his readers and fellow poets who were interested but confused by what he was doing (*SL*, p. 294). Most important of all, he had too little spare time to devote it to criticism. In a letter to Louis Zukofsky he described the conditions under which he wrote his 1931 essay (*SE*, pp. 105-112) on Pound's *Cantos:* "The goddamn thing almost tore my heart out—first reading the text and then scribbling what I had to say on street corners—the backs of letters—prescription blanks—and transcribing at 1 AM [*sic*] holding my eyes open (one at a time) with my right hand while I typed with my left." Feb. 23, 1931. Yale Collection.

ions of others," he recalled; "I was a good listener but enjoyed most to take home what I had heard to chew it over and to accept it only when I had made up my mind" (*SE,* xii). Once "moved" by others Williams was sometimes able to build his own, original theories upon them. For example, he seems to have derived his concept of the need for American self-expression—stated in the "Prologue" to *Kora* and *The Great American Novel*—from ideas which were commonplaces in *The Dial, The Seven Arts,* and *The Little Review.* However, as his prose style advanced from that of *Kora* to the incisive eloquence and editing of *In the American Grain,* Williams' concept of Americanism evolved correspondingly. It rapidly grew from his simple theory of national self-expression to the passionate, sophisticated, and original theories about American experience which inform *In the American Grain,* "An Occasion for Music," and "The American Background."

Williams' poetic techniques definitely evolved during the late 1920's and the early 1930's, but he did not on his own achieve a corresponding evolution of his poetic theories. Instead, he seems to have adopted Zukofsky's Objectivist theories as an explanation of his changing poetic practices.

Two tenets of Objectivism[4] which are relevant to Williams' development are stated in the preface to the movement's anthology:

> An objective—rays of the object brought to a focus,
> An objective—nature as a creator—desire for what is
> objectively perfect. . . .[5]

Zukofsky's first tenet can be understood by comprehending how the "objective" of a lens system works. It forms an image of the object being photographed by bringing its rays to a focus. In this process the depth of field—the area within which all objects

---

[4]*Funk and Wagnalls Dictionary* is also helpful:
"**Objective** . . . 1. Free from or independent of personal feelings, opinions, prejudice, etc.; detached; unbiased. 2. Pertaining to what is external to or independent of the mind; real: opposed to *subjective.* 3. Treating, stressing, or dealing with external or actual phenomena, as distinct from inner or imaginary feelings and thoughts. . . . *Optics* A lens or combination of lenses . . . that is nearest to the object being viewed. . . . 4. In a camera or projector, the lens that makes the image of the object.
"**Objectivism** . . . *Philos.* a The doctrine that reality is objective or external to the mind." (1963 ed.)
[5]Louis Zukofsky, "Preface—'Recencies' in Poetry," *An "Objectivists" Anthology* (Var, France and New York, 1932), p. 10.

in a picture are clearly visible—is narrowed, but made more intense. Thus, less of the picture as a whole is in clear focus, but a part of the picture ("the object") is seen in very intense, clear focus. To objectify an image means both to intensify its qualities and to blur or eliminate the features of its surroundings. In the same way, a person who is "objective" eliminates all irrelevant or accidental responses in order to "focus" his mind more entirely on the subject of his experience. The operation of the objective of a lens is therefore analogous to the conventional meaning of objective as "free from or independent of personal feelings, opinions . . . detached; unbiased."

Williams described this type of objectivism in his own writing in "A Note on Poetry" (1937). "In my own work," he wrote, "it has always sufficed that the object of my attention be presented without further comment. This in general might be termed the objective method. But all art is sensual and poetry particularly so. It is directly, that is, of the senses, and since the senses do not exist without an object for their employment all art is necessarily objective. It doesn't declaim or explain; it presents."[6]

As an Objectivist, Williams carried the earlier impersonality of his Imagist poetry to its logical extreme. Imagism stressed the "direct treatment of the thing," but it still allowed some subjectivity as long as the approach was sufficiently direct. Objectivism, however, was more actively anti-subjective.

During the 1920's, in accordance with the Imagist principle of "direct treatment," Williams began to avoid similes and openly assertive statements. He carried this tendency much farther in the 1930's and in many of his poems almost entirely eliminated his "presence" as a poet. The differences between "An Early Martyr" and "The Yachts" are a good illustration of his increasing stylistic objectivity.

"An Early Martyr" was written about 1920 even though it was not published until 1936.[7] The subject of the poem is John Coffey, a young man who stole from expensive stores as a protest

---

[6]"A Note on Poetry," p. 1313.

[7]It was published as the title poem of *An Early Martyr*, but "Mrs. Williams recalled that *The Freeman* bought the poem, paid for it, but lost their nerve and didn't publish it." *IWW*, p. 56. Since *The Freeman* ceased publication in 1924, the poem must have been written in the early 1920's—probably at the same time that Williams wrote a letter to the editors about Coffey (see note 8 below). See also Williams' *Autobiography*, p. 299, where Coffey is referred to as "Coffee."

against capitalist society "to make out a case against the law itself."[8] However, Williams devotes only half of the poem to a sketchy, rather general summary of Coffey's "crimes" and trial. He devotes the rest of the poem to a highly emotional statement of his own feelings about Coffey's actions and their moral significance (*CEP*, 85-86).

On the other hand, in most of his poetry written during the 1930's Williams strenuously avoids a personal tone. Instead he strives to express his emotions and judgments through the presentation of specific, concrete details. His poem "The Yachts," for example, possesses just as definite a message as "An Early Martyr." It strongly condemns men's interests in objects like yachts—"all that in the mind is fleckless, free and / naturally to be desired"—when much of "beaten, desolate" mankind is drowning "in agony, in despair." However, Williams presents both the appealing perfections of the yachts and the agonies of mankind in a deliberately impersonal manner with as little explanation as possible.

> . . . the signal is set and they
> are off. Now the waves strike at them but they are too
> well made, they slip through, though they take in canvas.
>
> Arms with hands grasping seek to clutch at the prows.
> Bodies thrown recklessly in the way are cut aside.
>   (*CEP,* 106-107)

Similarly in his poem "To Elsie" which appeared in *Spring and All* (1923), Williams openly avowed his sympathy with the "pure products of America" (*CEP*, 270-272). But in "View of a Lake" which appeared in *An Early Martyr*, Williams describes the condition of the rural poor strictly in terms of the concrete details of their lives:

> Where a
> waste of cinders
> slopes down to
>
> the railroad and
> the lake
> stand three children
>
> beside the weed-grown
> chassis
> of a wrecked car
>   (*CEP,* 96)

[8]"A Man Versus the Law," *The Freeman,* I, 15 (June 23, 1920), 348.

Even in a highly emotional poem like "Death," which was
first published in 1930,[9] Williams struggles to eliminate or restrict a declamatory tone as much as possible. The rough drafts
of "Death" are filled with violent statements like: "He's
dead / the old fool / the goddamned dirty / old fool." In other
versions the corpse is referred to as a "stinking old bastard" and
a "hunk of crap." But as he edited "Death," Williams deleted
most of these phrases so that the final version of the poem is
much less declamatory, though it is still violently emotional in
tone. Even when he wrote about subjects as personal as his own
parents in "Adam" and "Eve," he tried (as he later recalled) to
construct the poems out of the "factual material" of their lives
(*IWW*, 57).

Besides becoming more "objective" Williams' poetry also became more austere during the 1930's. He had begun to take a
more serious view of poetry and to eliminate whatever seemed
easy or clever to him. He dismissed cleverness for its own sake as
playing "tiddlywinks with the syllables" and a waste of time
(*SE*, 103). Poetry, he wrote in 1929, "is a forceful, intensely
serious occupation," and therefore it should not be easy for
either the poet or the reader.[10] Only because of its seriousness,
he wrote in 1932, did poetry stand "equal to any endeavor. The
fact that it takes us, turns over the mind, because the required
form is not easy to come at, discloses its pertinence to the time
and the intelligence" (*SL*, 133).

The revisions in the poem "St. Francis Einstein of the Daffodils" are a comprehensive example of the changes Williams and
his poetry underwent during his development from an Imagist
to an Objectivist. He published the first version in *Contact* in
1921. In this version, he celebrates the arrival of spring as the
perception of April's new, vitalizing life and then elucidates its
relationship to March, the season of partial spring. Stanzas 1
and 5 of this version read:

> In March's black boat
> Einstein and April
> have come at the time in fashion
> up out of the sea

[9]*Blues*, I, 9 (Fall, 1930), 22-23. The present version of the poem is in *CEP*,
pp. 78-79. Its rough drafts are in the Buffalo Collection, tape 25.
[10]"For a New Magazine," *Blues*, I, 2 (March, 1929), 31.

through the rippling daffodils
in the foreyard of
the dead Statue of Liberty
whose stonearms
are powerless against them
the venusremembering wavelets
breaking into laughter—

. . . .

April Einstein
through the blossomy waters
rebellious, laughing
under liberty's dead arm
has come among the daffodils
shouting
that flowers and men
were created relatively equal.
Oldfashioned knowledge is
dead under the blossoming peachtrees.

This part of the poem celebrates Einstein's victory. He is regarded as St. Francis because his theory of relativity allows men
and nature to contact and unite with one another without
changing their essential natures—just as St. Francis' preaching
united birds, animals, and men without changing them. Because
of Einstein's theory, the daffodils enjoy a double spring. Not
only do they flower in the natural season of spring, they also
exist in the springtime of their new identity of relative equality
with man. Einstein has released them from their old inequality
and thus "freed" them.

In the second part of the poem an "old negro / with white
hair" tends his orchard and garden. The Negro is the local
manifestation of Einstein because his care for the plants and
trees causes them to blossom and bear fruit.

Connecting Einstein and the old Negro are an elaborate series
of political and natural analogies. The basic one equates political democracy with March. Democracy, symbolized by the Statue
of Liberty and "Thomas March Jefferson," signifies the "Oldfashioned knowledge" of the equality of men which preceded
the new, total equality of men and flowers—just as March pre-
cedes the total spring of April. In an obliquely analogous way,
the old Negro buries "a black cat in the freshturned / garden"
to enable his spring flowers and fruit to grow. His perception of
the spring cycle of life and growth out of death and decay

corresponds to the force of Einstein's perception in the intellectual world.

When Williams rewrote the poem before its 1936 appearance in *Adam and Eve and the City* he removed the political analogies which had connected Einstein with the Negro and his garden in a complex but coherent way. The second half of the poem dealing with the old Negro and the dead cat began on line 65 of the 1921 version; it begins on line 15 of the 1936 version. As a result, the poem is much more cryptic. Williams' editing, however, can be explained in terms of the Objectivist principles already discussed. Strictly speaking, the recognition of the similarity between Einstein and the old Negro is the object of the poem. Both, because of their perception, are a force for spring; they are both *loci* of the force. The political allusions to Jefferson and the Statue of Liberty really do not contribute to the *presence* of this comparison in the poem. They merely elucidate it. If, as Williams claimed in 1937, poetry "doesn't declaim or explain; it presents" the object,[11] then the political and natural metaphors could be eliminated because they were not structurally necessary for the object's presentation. Thus in the 1936 version the reader is left, as he was not in the 1921 version, to decipher the relationships between the particulars of the poem.

A considerable number of other lines in "St. Francis Einstein of the Daffodils" were probably deleted before 1936 not so much because they were contrary to Objectivist standards, but because they were not in keeping with Williams' more serious and austere conception of poetry. In the 1921 version of the poem there are many declamations, lyric outbursts that are charming, facile, and repetitious or tangential. Williams' systematic removal of them causes the poem to be far more austere. As a result, the following criteria which Williams applied to the Objectivists' poetry in their 1932 anthology can be applied to the 1936 version of "St. Francis Einstein":

There is nothing here that seductively leads the sense to acceptance by sensuous intrigue. Nor can it be called parody since there is no exaggeration or warping for false emphasis. Nor is reason used to cudgel the mind into unwilling submission. The attack is by simple presentation, perhaps confrontation would be the better term.

Each part is similar to, if not identical with the moments of the classics by having been scrubbed . . . clean of everything adventitious

---

[11]"A Note on Poetry," p. 1313.

which would make poetry a running amusement rather than a constantly renewed consistency of contemplation. . . .[12]

Williams' poetry of the 1930's does not violate any of his basic Imagist tenets. He still presents concrete imagery, keeps the poet's "role" to a minimum, uses colloquial language, and avoids all poetic diction or traditional meters. However, the elements of lighthearted humor and satire which had frequently made his work similar to Charles Demuth's paintings virtually disappear. He does not return to the type of relatively casual and entertaining poetry that often characterized his early work until the 1950's, in some of the poems of *Pictures from Brueghel*. Because of Objectivism and his increasingly serious attitude toward poetry, Williams' writing in the 1930's became more like the painting of his friend Sheeler. It grew more serious, austere, and obscure. By the late 1930's he was so indifferent to his earlier goal of enlivening his environment that he was willing to accept dullness if a poem was serious enough. "This book," he wrote in a review, "is all to the good. . . . There are moments . . . that are pretty dull, but that's bound to be the character of all good things if they are serious enough: when a devoted and determined person sets out to do a thing he isn't thinking first of being brilliant, he wants to get there even if he has to crawl. . . ."[13]

Williams discussed the principles of Objectivism on a few occasions. In these remarks he usually mentioned that Objectivism was formally superior to Imagism. Imagism, he wrote, "had been useful in ridding the field of verbiage," but it had "no formal necessity implicit in it" (*Autobiography*, 264). In a 1941 lecture he made the same observation, that Imagism "completely lacked structural necessity," and then went on to say that the Objectivist "attempted to remedy this fault by fusing with each image a form in its own right."[14] The changes discussed previously, in poems like "St. Francis Einstein," eliminate a great deal of "verbiage," but they are not in themselves a formal advance upon Imagism.

Williams' new Objectivist "formalism" was, in part, simply a

[12]"A New Collection of Modern Poetry," Yale Collection, ZA 15. This essay was published, in somewhat different form, as "An Objectivists' Anthology," *The Symposium*, IV, 1 (Jan., 1933), 114-117.

[13]"Muriel Rukeyser's 'US 1,' " *New Republic*, XCIV (March 9, 1938), 141.

[14]"The Basis of Poetic Form," lecture given at Harvard University, Feb. 14, 1941. Buffalo Collection.

desire for greater neatness. During the 1930's and late 1920's he began to try to tighten his poems by arranging the lines in neater stanzas (*IWW,* 65-66). But on a deeper formal level, Williams sought and achieved a stronger organic unity in his poems, one based on a more dramatic subject-object relationship than had existed in his previous poems. In a review of Norman Macleod's poems Williams praised Macleod's "welding" of the subjective elements of his poetry ("phrase," "thought," "passion") to the poems' "objects." "The phrase is compact," Williams wrote,

meaningful—and if not always, at least often enough to be important, bent upon the thing spoken of. This gives it pregnant sound instead of mere noise. The constraint, in that all poetry is constraint, lies in a fidelity to the object, the thought about it and their passionate welding. It is the movement of this constrained passion, limiting itself to the objective of its immediate purpose, which creates the meter as the obstructions in a river create the pattern of its flow.[15]

Williams' desire for "fidelity to the object" may be related to the second tenet of Zukofsky's Objectivist credo, the reference to "nature as a creator—[the] desire for what is objectively perfect." This tenet seems to be an application, to aesthetics, of the philosophic doctrine of Objectivism, "the doctrine that reality is objective or external to the mind." Philosophic Objectivism assumes that subjective knowledge needs continually to be corrected by objective realities. Similarly, the Objectivist poets assume that the subjective elements of a poem achieve excellence or perfection to the extent that they are "created" by natural, that is, by objective realities.

"The Source," first published in the November, 1928 *Dial* is one of the first examples of the poetic form Williams achieved by welding "phrase" to "object," and by letting nature act as a "creator."

The poem begins with a rather stiff and static series of images in which the poet self-consciously composes a scene: "a pasture which begins / where silhouettes of scrub / and balsams stand uncertainly / On whose green three maples / are distinctly pressed / beside a red barn" (*CEP,* 346). But these images of a static nature are "all cancelled" by an image of organic growth —lichen, twigs, and leaves growing from "a triple elm's inverted

15"Notes on Norman Macleod," *Mosaic,* I, 1 (Nov.-Dec., 1934), 28.

. . . triple thighs." This highly sexual and vital image of natural creativity ends part I of the poem (lines 1-23).

In part II of "The Source" (lines 24-53), the poet enters the woods beyond the pasture described in part I. Here he discovers images of a growing, changing, organically living nature: "pungent mould / globular fungi." But though this scene is disordered in human terms ("uneven aisles of / the trees / rock strewn"), it contains the more profound order of organic growth which radiates outward from the source of the wood's fertility and the scene's activity.

> A spring in whose depth
> white sand bubbles
> overflows
>
> clear under late raspberries
> and delicate-stemmed touch-me-nots
> . . . .
> the water is cast upon
>
> a stair of uneven stones
> with a rustling sound
>
> (*CEP*, 347)

The images in parts I and II of "The Source" present quite objectively—without explication or declamation—a contrast between human and natural order. The delicacy and fluency of natural growth around the spring are implicitly contrasted with the Cezanne-like composition of part I in which objects are "pressed" upon one another. At the end of part II the poet resolves the tension between the two orders. He implicitly chooses the natural order when he describes himself as a "profuse body" which "advances / over the stones unchanged"—in contrast to the water described earlier which

> . . . is cast upon
>
> a stair of uneven stones
> with a rustling sound
>
> An edge of bubbles stirs
> swiftness is moulded
> speed grows
>
> (*CEP*, 347-348)

Approximately the same sort of structure exists in Williams' "The Sun," which begins with the poet's contemplation of a refuse-strewn beach. The first part of the poem (lines 1-27) ends

with a commonplace cliché about the tawdriness of the modern
age.

> The slovenly bearded
> rocks hiss—
>
> Obscene refuse
> charms
> this modern shore—
> Listen!
> *(CEP, 412)*

The poet "listens" in the second half of the poem (lines 28-52)
by letting the sun act upon him as it acts upon nature, as a
healer and purifier. He goes "down past knowledge" and his
vision is cured. His earlier "knowledge" of nature as merely
corrupted is replaced by a deeper understanding—that nature's
magnitude is beyond man's ability to harm it more than temporarily. The screaming children on the beach have only "logged"
their delight of the "penetrable / nothingness" of the air and
the sea "whose heavy body / opens / to their leaps / without a
wound—" *(CEP, 413)*.

In poems like "The Sun" and "The Source," Williams' Objectivism is more than a mere absence of "personal feelings,
opinions, prejudices." Instead he is practicing Objectivism in its
philosophic sense "that reality is objective or external to the
mind." The structure of these poems dramatizes Zukofsky's second, cryptic tenet of Objectivism, "An objective—nature as a
creator." By allowing nature to correct and create his thoughts
and emotions, Williams achieves definite, distinct formal structures which are much stronger and more dramatic than those in
his previous poems. A poem like "The Source" has a distinct
beginning, middle, and end as it presents the action of its poet's
progress from a false vision of reality to his confrontation with
the "thing itself," and his final, emotional reconciliation of his
vision with the truth.

Paradoxically, this type of objective structure makes subjectivity an integral part of the poem. However, the presence of the
subjective mind in a poem like "The Source" or "The Sun" can
be explained in terms of Williams' desire for a more total objectivity. The human mind is an extremely sensitive medium for
communicating the most subtle qualities of objects. It may function like the photographic plate in a cloud chamber or the lens

of an optical instrument. The changes which events make upon its sensitivity may primarily reveal their identities rather than the mind's own qualities.

Moreover, among an object's qualities are its affective ones, those which can affect a man and have meaning to him. A poem which seeks to deal with the total qualities of an object must therefore present certain subjective responses as evidences of the object's nature.[16] Williams himself stated approximately this conception in his late poems "The Pink Locust" and "To Daphne and Virginia." When the poet faces his world, he wrote, "it will not do to say, / as he is inclined to say: / Not much. The poem / would be in *that* betrayed." Therefore, "The poet / cannot slight himself / without slighting / his poem—" (*Pictures,* 141). The mind, Williams admitted, can trick or agonize us, "But for resources / what can equal it? / There is nothing [else]. We / should be lost / without its wings to / fly off upon" (*Pictures,* 75).

The aesthetic principles underlying Williams' Objectivist works can be related fairly clearly to those which motivated his earlier poetry of the 1920's. In many of his early poems—those which resemble Demuth's paintings in spirit—Williams had demonstrated what he could do to his materials, how he could enliven and animate by putting them into a hard, lively, imaginative world. This process is reversed in his Objectivist works. In them his interest is in what "things" do to him, how they may change him. Or Williams' Objectivism can be seen as a coherent extension of the "classical" approach which he and Charles Sheeler used to add significance to their local images. In the poems in "The Descent of Winter," for example, Williams emphasizes the analogous, formal relationships which are possible between the human and the natural. After relating man and nature so intimately on a metaphorical level, it was a natural step for Williams to present the dramatic, active relationships which existed between the mind and the natural world it confronts.

[16]"One lack with imagism . . . is that it is not definite enough. It is true enough . . . to the immediate object it represents but what is that related to the poet's personal and emotional and intellectual meanings? No hint is given. . . ." "Zukofsky," closing note to Louis Zukofsky's *"A" 1-12* (Ashland, Mass., 1959), p. 291.

Williams' development as an Objectivist is further revealed by his major prose work of the late 1920's and the 1930's, his novel *White Mule* and its continuation, *In the Money*. The two novels deal with a few years in the lives of an immigrant family, the Joe Stechers, after the birth of their second daughter Flossie in 1893. The Stechers, who are fictionalized counterparts of Williams' wife and her family (*IWW*, 60, 67), are completely unexceptional people by most of the standards of fiction. Joe Stecher is a German-American printer, a dedicated craftsman. At the beginning of the novel he is the manager of a printing plant. Gradually he starts his own printing business and makes enough money to move with his family to the suburbs. His wife, Gurlie, is a paradoxically shy yet aggressive Norwegian woman, tremendously self-centered, who triumphs in assorted domestic and social campaigns to become something of a social lioness. The baby Flossie survives various childhood ailments, Gurlie's indifference, and her nurses' incompetence; by the end of *White Mule* she can talk and has managed to become part of the family's awareness. The major events of the novel are not much more exceptional than its characters. Joe wins a strike for his employers, Gurlie takes the children to Vermont for a summer, and the baby survives her illnesses.

Williams made it clear in his comments on *White Mule* that the principles of its composition were the same as those which underlay his poetry. Poetry, he wrote in a 1937 article, was hard to write, "hard to get published and hard to evaluate when bought," and therefore he had turned to prose for "relief." But this change in genre, Williams insisted, did not "imply . . . a relinquishment of the disciplines which poetry imposes. To turn to the writing of 'White Mule' from my usual interests in poetry meant no more to me than the carrying over of the same concerns for language into new conditions."[17]

An important similarity between *White Mule* and Williams' Objectivist poetry is that the novel is radically less subjective than almost all of his earlier prose. *Kora in Hell* and *The Great American Novel* are both chaotic works in which Williams aggressively asserts his passing moods, fantasies, and thoughts. Williams himself is the protagonist of *A Voyage to Pagany*. The

[17]" 'White Mule' Versus Poetry," *The Writer*, L (Aug., 1937), 243.

novel's events are based on his European experiences, and its women are Williams' conceptions of his wife Flossie (*IWW*, 45).

Late in 1927 Williams began a novel whose central event was the birth of a baby girl. The first versions of this novel, contained in "Notes in Diary Form" and *A Novelette and Other Prose*, are written in the same excited, stream-of-consciousness style which Williams had used in *Kora* and *The Great American Novel*. Then—in a work-note dated December 13, 1927—Williams complained that his first attempts at his new novel "were soft, romantic and tentative." "What I have written first," he wrote, "has been without the firmness of the imagination—or only vaguely guessed ([like] my earlier, luckier work) and wobbly between sentiment and guesses and excited realization."[18] Williams preceded these self-criticisms with a statement that describes his stylistic intentions for *White Mule*.

> In writing a new novel—a clear style—the dangers are on one side my formerly important irritibility, diffuseness—and on the other the "plain" novel style or stylelessness. . . . I must be assured that I am speaking true [*sic*]. That is the style, true to the sharpest, firmest present vision of which I am capable. . . . The first few lines of Djuna Barnes['] new chapter in *transition* are upon the track, later the English—provincial archaic language does not suit me. I want an actual language.
>
> But the "plain" novel style—Anderson, Hechst [*sic*], Bodenheim—is even worse. It is that they are unobservant and thoughtless of the things (too intent on the people and places and close stench) unbased on any solid conception. . . . They are false, false as newspapers which lose everything among the news.[19]

Williams' reference to his "formerly important irritibility" and "diffuseness" as dangers expresses his rejection of the chaotic, highly personal, and "romantic" style of so much of his earlier prose. In *White Mule*, like his Objectivist poetry, he always avoids an openly assertive tone. Except for an excitable New York pediatrician who appears in one chapter, none of *White Mule*'s characters sound remotely like the Williams of *Kora*, *The Great American Novel*, or the prose passages of *Spring and All*. None of the novel's characters is endowed with any "poetic," expressive insights or speech which would communicate his experiences eloquently but which would be inappropri-

---

[18]Rough draft of "Notes in Diary Form" in the Buffalo Collection.
[19]*Ibid.*

ate to his rather limited and prosaic personality. When they are calm, the tone of the Stechers' thoughts and speech is muted and understated. When they become excited, angry, or afraid, they are either laconic or vague and inarticulate. "They held me up," Joe tells Gurlie after being threatened by strikers.

He was extremely serious and low-voiced. Are you hurt? [asks Gurlie] No. Where were the police? Oh, they laid for me, at the entrance to the Chambers St. elevated station.
  What did they do?
  Stopped me. Put a pistol in my face.
  Joe! What did you do?
  Well, I'm here, ain't I?

                                                                    (*WM*, 113)

In order to be sure that he was using "actual language," Williams based much of the novel's dialogue on conversations "put down verbatim" from things his patients said. "I tried in every way not to distort anything of this" [the patients' speech], he explained, "never to mold it to my purposes." Instead he tried to write throughout the novel in such a style that anything he heard in common speech "would be naturally a part of it."[20] Later Williams was very pleased by Alfred Kazin's insight that he had avoided the common fault of poets who write novels and foist their "poetic insights" onto their prosaic characters to produce "the lyric novel, wherein farmers talk like angels and machinists sing too, too prettily at work."[21]

Williams' criticism of the " 'plain' novel style" indicates the extremely careful selectivity which he exercised in his choice of the commonplace details which make up *White Mule,* his determination to use only those facts, incidents, and conversations that were related to a "solid conception" and not mere "news." This intention corresponds very closely to Williams' Objectivist credo that poems should contain absolutely no mere "noise" or "padding."[22]

The "conception" which underlies *White Mule* is never stated explicitly in the novel—just as the themes or meanings of his Objectivist poems are never overt. "Plot," Williams wrote in

[20]" 'White Mule' Versus Poetry," 245.
[21]Alfred Kazin, "White Mule," *New York Times Book Review* (June 20, 1937), p. 7. Williams' favorable comment appeared in " 'White Mule' Versus Poetry," 244.
[22]"Notes on Norman Macleod," 28.

1934, "is like God: the less we formulate it the closer we are to the truth" (*SL,* 146). However, in a 1937 article on *White Mule* he asserted that the novel dealt with the same themes that had concerned him in *In the American Grain.* He had spoken in *White Mule,* he wrote, "for the idealism of America, for the great themes of American life and aspiration in the past, in my 'In the American Grain,' in the foreword to my libretto to 'The First President,' in the appreciation of Alfred Stieglitz published in 1936—so, as a writer, it became my duty to include the whole of that in my style."[23]

Naturalization is the theme most common to all these works. Himself a second-generation American, Williams was fascinated by the process through which men and women became natives of America, discovered the New World, and then more or less successfully possessed it for their own uses. "I felt from earliest childhood that America was the only home I could ever possibly call my own," he wrote in 1939 about *In the American Grain;* "I felt that it was expressly founded for me, personally, and that it must be my first business in life to possess it" (*SL,* 185). In *In the American Grain* he had assessed the abilities of Americans to possess their land through intensive analyses, comparisons, and contrasts of men like Columbus, Boone, and Mather—who were "representative men," exceptional, notable examples of good or bad forms of American experience.

When Williams began *White Mule* in 1927 he had collected materials for a projected second volume of *In the American Grain.* He intended to begin this volume with Jefferson and come "with a big jump" up to Grover Cleveland and Pancho Villa (*Autobiography,* 237). His subject would presumably have been the American scene and the varieties of American possession which were characteristic of the late nineteenth and early twentieth century. But Williams was unable to find a publisher for this book, and he apparently channeled its theme into *White Mule,* where it appears in a domesticated, radically concentrated form.

This domestication of the "great themes of American life and aspiration" presented Williams with a difficult stylistic problem. How could he deal with a subject as extraordinary and complex

---

[23] " 'White Mule' Versus Poetry," 244.

as the "idealism of America," and yet restrict himself to such seemingly simple and ordinary materials as the Stechers' lives? It had been relatively simple for him to present the subjects of *In the American Grain* with little or no explanation, since they all possessed some eloquence of word or action that enabled the significance of their experiences to be revealed clearly and dramatically. This is most obviously true in the cases of Columbus, Franklin, Mather, and John Paul Jones, whose words were quoted verbatim or edited by Williams. But even Boone and Houston, who left no reliable accounts of themselves that Williams could use, had nevertheless acted in ways that were obviously significant and eloquently expressive of American experience. Joe and Gurlie Stecher, on the other hand, possess virtually no such obviously eloquent "language" of either words or actions to convey the significance of their experiences. And, as an Objectivist, Williams could not resort to the overt explanations or declamations that he often uses in *In the American Grain* to communicate the truth of his characters' lives.

One key to Williams' technique in *White Mule* lies in a rather casual remark which he made in his 1937 introduction for Sidney Salt's *Christopher Columbus and Other Poems*. "For myself," he wrote, "I never tire of the Columbus story. . . . In the Columbus legend lies the one opportunity all Americans can have to feel together as brothers. We together are the New World and there can never be another."[24] In other words, the essential experience which can be common to all Americans is the "Columbus legend." When *White Mule* and *In the Money* are analyzed in terms of Williams' Columbus legend—as presented in *In the American Grain*—a subtle pattern emerges. Each chapter of the novels is a "voyage" of discovery for the Stechers. In most chapters one of them visits a new place, a personal New World. Or, if the Stechers stay at home, then some sort of change occurs in the chapter which makes the home itself significantly different, potentially a New World to them; in other words, the new comes to them.

Thus instead of the heroic voyages of conquest and discovery which occur in *In the American Grain, White Mule* has the Stechers' trips to parks, business offices, and new apartments or

[24]"Introduction" to Sidney Salt's *Christopher Columbus and Other Poems* (Boston, 1937), p. 8.

houses in the suburbs. Yet the "aspiration" which animates the journeys in both books is the same; all are expressions of the desire to have one's own "land of heart's desire" in the New World. "A small place in the suburbs," Joe muses, "not too far from the city—with a green, well-kept lawn. Flowers, a few trees about it. *Ein Obstgarten.*"[25]

This theme is developed through a structural pattern which is essentially similar to that of Objectivist poems like "The Source." Williams himself cryptically summed up this structural formula when he remarked in the middle of a chapter: "First the situation then the reaction" (*Money,* 301).

The "situation" in each chapter is based upon one of the Stechers' confrontations with something new. Williams then has the chapter's main character or characters react to this new situation. He never bluntly names the nature of this reaction, as he frequently did in *In the American Grain.* Instead he usually provides each chapter with a cast of characters whose reactions to the situations differ subtly but significantly from the main character's. By letting him make his own comparisons and contrasts, Williams allows the reader to draw his own conclusions about the qualities of the characters' reactions and the nature of their personalities.

The essentially dramatic nature of this structural pattern—in both Williams' prose and poetry of the 1930's—is simplified in this diagram:

	Rising Action	Climax	Falling Action
WM	arrival or	confrontation	character resolves
Money	departure	with new	his relation to the new

	"SITUATION"		"REACTION"
Objectivist poem, e.g., "The Source"	movement by poet to nature	poet confronts nature truly	poet resolves a new relation to the natural

In a poem like "The Source" this action occurs in the realm of personal, mental experience: vision, perception, and emotion. In

---

[25]*WM,* p. 279. Williams hints at the theme of all voyages being microcosms or macrocosms of one another in his poem "Voyages" where a mirror, a painting of "Ulysses / at Sea," and a "girl of nine" facing the sea are all implicity equated (*CLP,* p. 84).

his prose, particularly *White Mule,* the action occurs on the social plane: the individual, the family, and American society—business, manners, economics, politics.

Williams develops the naturalization theme of *White Mule* and *In the Money* through a beautifully unified but dualistic plot structure. First, the entire world is entirely new to the new-born Flossie. In fact, a baby's memory is so brief, Williams believed, that the world seems new to them each time they awaken. "Each time they wake from sleep it is as if they were just born," one of the Stechers' relatives says about Flossie.[26] At the same time America, as well as Flossie, is new to Joe and Gurlie Stecher, who are recent immigrants.

The presence of the new in the lives of the old is an implicit challenge to them. To satisfy the unexpected demands of the new being, new responses and responsibilities are demanded of them. The old, in effect, must become new themselves if the new being is to grow and realize itself. Previously latent powers and sensibilities will thus be realized; and the old, by contact with the new, will attain a greater self-realization. But all this is possible only if the old have some capacity for growth.

The old often seek self-realization by appropriation, not growth. Resisting change, they realize themselves by appropriating others' lives, by making others extensions of their limited selves. For this reason, they see the new being only as an opportunity to realize themselves, not itself. If the new disappoints their expectations, they react to it with anger or indifference. This is Gurlie's reaction to Flossie. Unable to discover any feminine means of expressing her aggressiveness and daring, Gurlie's great wish is to be a man. She desires sons so that she may appropriate their lives. "If it had only been a boy," she thinks after Flossie's birth, and Williams comments: "There had not been a horse on the farm she had not dared to ride, even as a child. Once . . . she had climbed the mast of a schooner. . . . She had wanted boys, six boys" (*WM,* 25). When Flossie disappoints Gurlie's expectation, her reaction is brutal. "Another girl," she says to the midwife, Mrs. D.

[26]*WM,* p. 171. This same idea is stated in *Kora,* p. 69.

Agh, I don't want girls. Take it away and let me rest. God pardon you
for saying that. Where is it? Let me see it, said the mother. . . .
   She took the little thing and turned it around to look at it. Where is
its face? Take off that cap. What are these shoes on for? She took them
off with a jerk. You miserable scrawny little brat, she thought, and
disgust and anger fought inside her chest, she was not one to cry—
except in a fury (*WM*, 7).

   Once the first rage of Gurlie's disappointment is over, she
reacts to Flossie as the old more commonly react to the new,
with indifference and ignorance. She wished to appear a compe-
tent mother because of her immense egotism, and she attends to
Flossie's material needs adequately—particularly when there is
someone present to be impressed by her brash competence. But
though she does not assault Flossie openly—as the older
daughter Lottie does—she practices the more subtle aggression
of indifference. Once when the baby cries "Gurlie's look came
back from the street to stare at the struggling infant—not be-
wilderedly but absently with some amazement but no recognition in it. Then she stood up, comforted the baby gently for a
moment against her breast and—though it was still crying—
placed it in its crib and walked away. She closed the door behind her, walked to the other end of the house and sat at the
back window, there to continue looking out" (*WM*, 57). There
is nothing to be seen from the back window of the apartment
but drying clothes; Gurlie prefers taking an interest in nothing
at all rather than in Flossie. So she leaves the infant to the
mercies of her illnesses and fifteen-year-old nursemaids who can
be hired for two dollars a day. Fortunately, the illnesses aren't
fatal, the nursemaids care for the child as best they can, and
Flossie survives.

   But Gurlie's indifference has its effect upon Flossie. The baby
quickly learns that adults, particularly her mother, usually must
be coerced to satisfy her needs, and she rapidly develops the
persistence needed to gain their attention. This stubbornness
becomes one of the chief traits of Flossie's personality. Because
of her "spirit"—and her paleness—she receives the nickname
"White Mule" which Williams uses as his title.[27]

[27]Flossie does not get the nickname until the first chapter of *In the
Money*.

In contrast to his wife, Joe Stecher has some capacity for growth. He sympathizes instinctively with Flossie's struggle to grow and reacts to her with tenderness and pity. "Somehow," Williams wrote of Joe's first look at Flossie, "this bit of moving, unwelcome life had won him to itself forever. It was so ugly and so lost" (*WM*, 5). Desiring his children's growth and health, Joe is rewarded by the growth of his own powers of generosity and affection. Once when bathing his daughters, Joe sees them naked and is startled by the realization that he has created these beings so different from himself, yet so alive and interesting.

Joe had never really looked at his children like this before, never realized that he, Joe Stecher, possessed—if you call it that—two such amusing sprouts of feminine exuberance.
. . . He was tasting a world with which he was not familiar even among his own family (*Money*, 107).

Equally important, Joe's love for his children and his desire for their healthy growth causes his vision of himself and the purpose for his work to "grow"; when Flossie is born he achieves an understanding of the purpose of his energies which is far healthier than that possessed by the money-grubbing society around him. "Today he could see light, it had to do with all that is awake early and moves and grows stronger. It [life] is a nice thing to keep, if you can keep it well and happy. A man must keep on, he must keep on working and then, finally, he will see the light. He will come out of poverty and be able to keep everyone happy. What is lovelier than a place in the country with small children playing in the grass, or picking flowers" (*WM*, 46).

Unfortunately, the contribution Joe makes toward his children's growth is too often limited because he accepts the conventional role of father. "She ought to be out in the park these days," he thinks of Flossie, "But I won't push the carriage. That's a woman's job. I'll work, I'll provide, I'll be responsible for everything you want of me—but I'll be damned if I'll push a baby carriage. That's the place for a baby—out in the country" (*WM*, 47). As a result, Joe's generous impulses toward the children are often stifled by Gurlie on the grounds that he, a mere male, can scarcely know what they need or should have. Nevertheless, he is enough in contact with Flossie for her to develop a genuine charm, signified by her tiny "crooked grin," as she responds to his warmth and love with a love and warmth of her own.

Though Flossie's development is shaped by contact with the older persons around her, the motive force for her self-realization is very much her own. Throughout the novel she exhibits an unceasing, instinctive determination to grow through contact with the world. Only the world and the people and things in it can provide her with food for her body, excitement and interest for her mind. But to enjoy the world's benefits, Flossie must be able to communicate her needs and desires and Williams records her growth and self-realization essentially in terms of her achievement of a language.

It is Flossie's lack of any means of communication that most threatens her when she is born. When her ear becomes abscessed she can only cry and strike at her head. She is entirely dependent upon the ability and willingness of Joe, Gurlie, and the midwife to understand what is wrong with her, and they are too indifferent or inexperienced to do so. Luckily the abscess breaks by itself and she recovers. Gradually, chiefly by crying, she becomes more able to communicate her physical needs and her existence becomes more secure.

But the true measure of the baby's development lies not so much in her ability to have her physical needs satisfied, as in her growing capacity to comprehend new experiences and situations and manage to relate them to her own interests.

At first she is able to respond to a new thing or person only by a fascinated attention. When her nursemaid takes her to the park, Flossie "looked wide eyed at the stranger, lost in wrapt attention" (WM, 117). Then, when she is a year old and visits a doctor, the baby is able to understand his intentions and cooperate in a rudimentary way (WM, 192). Near the end of White Mule Flossie is able to respond to new people and situations with some imagination. When old Mrs. Payson, whom the baby has just met, tries to take off a tight dress, she tells Flossie to put up her hands. Flossie does this, but she also "put her hands up to push as she could" (WM, 255).

At the end of White Mule Flossie is surrounded by new people, the neighboring Ferry children, and given a new food, a berry to eat. "Flossie got one and sucked it seriously, smacking her lips and blinking her eyes. More! she said presently" (*WM*, 289).

Scarcely more than a year before, when she was born, "nothing lasted for long—since she had no strength to bear it" (*WM*, 30). But now Flossie can meet the new children, decide that they are friendly, eat the new food, decide that it is good and ask for more. She has finally "arrived." Now she is truly a part of the world around her, a native of it, because she has a language. Now she is an integral, vital part of the cycle of life around her. Williams states this subtly and symbolically at the end of *White Mule*: "The children were standing back in a fascinated circle, the baby's face smeared with berry juice, her hands sooty, quite part of it all" (*WM*, 291). Life and death, the earth and its fruits, "all" are around Flossie, and she has grown to be part of them. Now she is one of the children, not isolated as "the baby." She stands in the "circle" of life around her, unified with it, part of it.

The corresponding theme of Joe and Gurlie's naturalization to America is implicitly contrasted with Flossie's growth throughout *White Mule* and *In the Money*. Just as the baby "arrives" in the world she is new to and achieves a place in it, so Joe and Gurlie establish themselves in American society; and the respective qualities of the baby's and her parents' developing contacts with their environment subtly define one another.

Compared to her parents' contact with the world, Flossie's is virtually omnivorous. She ignores nothing. She is interested in anything that will interest her, and she responds warmly to anyone who will be interested in her. In contrast, Joe and Gurlie's contact is partial, for they ignore many of the vital and interesting qualities of America in their drive for wealth. The unity of the novels is enhanced by the fact that Joe and Gurlie ignore America in much the same way that they ignore the baby; their responses to the American scene are prefigured by their responses to Flossie in the early chapters of *White Mule*.

Just as she almost totally ignored Flossie because the child did not satisfy her desire for a son, so Gurlie ignores everything in America which does not promise immediately to fulfill her expectations. These expectations are immense but crude. "Money is everything in this country," Gurlie cries, when her sister advises her to let Joe and herself relax and enjoy life.

"What do I want to be rich for! What do you want to live for? Of course I'm not satisfied with what I've got. I want to go places. . . . I want to see everything there is to see that I'm interested in. He doesn't want anything," she jerked her head at her husband, "that's why he needs *me*. He'd be satisfied to walk around in the woods. . . . I'm different. . . . I want to go to the theatre and sit in the best seats— where I have never sat more than once or twice. I want to go to a good restaurant afterward—if I want to—everything!" (*Money*, 195).

The pathetic irony of Gurlie's life is that she really does so little. Because she is obsessed with making money and dominating others—activities she confuses with genuine wealth and social status—Gurlie ignores virtually all of the potential richness of the life around her. Without knowing why, she remains violently dissatisfied. She refuses to join in the rich neighborhood social life of clubs, picnics, and excursions which surrounds the family when they live in New York City in the 1890's because it does not satisfy her vague but vigorous social pretensions.

The Stechers had gone to the fishing club once, on Decoration Day, to a jamboree, a big kettle, set into the broad brick fireplace, steaming with clam chowder—the children spreading tomato catsup on Pilot biscuits till it ran down the front of their dresses. An apron and necktie party—No, they were too nervous, too shy—too prone to find fault.

Gurlie would roar afterward. "Huh! When I think of the kitchen at Sonderheim and those beautiful things *hundreds* of years old, the silver and the copper kettles, the chairs and the tables cut from the finest wood! What do they think they know in this country?" (*Money*, 100).

When she first arrives at the Payson farm in Vermont with the children, Gurlie responds to the freedom and beauty of the mountains with instinctive pleasure.

She took deep, repeated breaths of the sweet air and went off for a few rods walking on the soft grass. . . . There after a moment she sat down facing again the magnificent view, northward. . . .
She laid her bare hands on the grass, then she lay back in it stretching out her arms, resting her head on the soft turf (*WM*, 232-233).

She proclaims her love of nature, but she spends the summer rushing about the countryside "organizing" the farm and dominating the Paysons—activities which feed her egotism and sense of self-importance as loving nature does not.

Ultimately Gurlie is interested in America only as a place whose material opportunities will give her the quick wealth she needs to dominate others and purchase the social status she desires. "Oh, how I should like to be rich! That's why we came here," she tells the Paysons.

> We are all the same, we that come from the other side. We didn't come here for love of the country, but to better ourselves. How can we love this country? We are from Europe. That's our country. That old love of home sticks to the second and third generation. That's why America is all for greed. . . .
>   . . . Here, we don't care. Nobody cares. If you go to jail and you make money anyhow, who cares? (WM, 238).

The consequences of Gurlie's attitudes are plainly implied by Williams. Because she and persons like her—De Leon and the Norsemen in *In the American Grain,* Joe's competitors in *In the Money*—arrive in the New World determined that it shall satisfy their material expectations, they ignore America and refuse to love it. Because of this limited vision, they cut themselves off from those aspects of America which could genuinely satisfy them. Dissatisfied, they exploit America even more vigorously, cut themselves off even more from its vitalizing qualities, and create the worst American conditions: opportunism, ruthlessness, and corruption.

Joe's relationship with Flossie is much better than Gurlie's. He loves her and is interested in her, yet he limits the good he might do for her because he remains committed to his conception of the father as provider and little else.

In the same way Joe remains so deeply committed to his early ideals of workmanship and orderliness that he ignores many of the vitalizing and exciting aspects of the American environment. He remains aloof from his workmen in the same way that Gurlie ignores her neighbors. He is just to them in a paternalistic way, but refuses to befriend them because they are greedy and do not live up to his ideals of disinterested, devoted craftsmanship. Similarly he remains almost entirely aloof from America's urban and natural environment because it does not correspond to his ideal of a perfectly orderly, Edenic natural beauty. He dreams of his childhood in Germany where his father was an *oberförster,* and ignores the world around him most of the time. He "sleepwalks" through New York, repelled by the dirt and disorder, ignoring the excitement and interest. Only during a snowstorm is he able to accept the city because then "everything was muffled, giving the illusion of peace . . . an unreality—a softness" which contents him. To his friends and business associates he presents a cryptic mask of good-humored efficiency, but "very deep inside him moved another man—under water, under earth—among the worms and fishes, among the plant roots—an impalpable atmosphere through which he strode freely without necessity for food or drink, without breathing and with unthrobbing heart" (*WM,* 45).

When Joe sets out to realize his dream of orderliness and cleanliness in America, he knows it will be difficult, but he is determined that he shall have his *Obstgarten* in the suburbs with a lawn, flowers, and trees. Therefore after Flossie is born he deliberately throws himself into the maelstrom of founding his own business so that he can earn the money to "leave the city—go out to the suburbs, take a house, have a garden—and begin to live" (*WM,* 16).

But though he does not realize it at the time, Joe sacrifices himself when he makes this decision. Earlier his family had wished to send him to the university because of his sensitivity and intelligence; but, after his father's death, Joe had emigrated to America so he could support and educate his mother, brother, and sisters. Joe's success should have given him a second chance for a full life, but the brutal pressures and anxieties of the business world rapidly destroy his capacity for leisure. Gradually he becomes less and less able to enjoy the rich, orderly, relaxed life which his work and success were supposed to earn for him. At the beginning of *White Mule* the other, "underground," Joe Stecher is very close to the surface of his life. He loves to hike and fish, read Goethe, and play the violin. By the end of *In the Money* when his friends ask him what he is going to do with his life now that he is rich, Joe can only reply with the single word, "Work" (*Money,* 269, 288, 295). He declares that he only feels happy when he is working, and, Lemon, his business friend, sadly realizes that he and Joe have become addicted to their work as some men are to whiskey or women because they wished to be drugged, to be unable to think (*Money,* 295).

Joe has his family, which he loves, and his business, which he does not love. His life is not, Williams implies, a bad one but it could have been a great deal more. Practically all the benefits of his potentially great sensitivity and intelligence are denied him, and there is the further tragedy that these qualities are also denied to the American environment that needs them so badly. Lemon, who greatly admires Joe's integrity and courage, tries to persuade him to go into politics or law, or to become a business or labor leader. "You'd have made a great lawyer," Lemon tells him. "You've got the eye for it, and the character for it too. And how badly *that* is needed in our courts today. But business needs it quite as much. Really, sometimes I wonder why you abandoned labor. . . . It was a great pity, for them (*Money*, 291).

In this way, Williams implies, as the honest and sensitive Joe Stechers withdraw into their jobs and families, every element of American society grows more corrupt, ruthless, shoddy, and inhumane. In this respect Joe is similar to men like De Soto, Poe, and Raleigh in *In the American Grain*—talented, idealistic men whose idealism prevents them from accepting American reality as it is. Even worse, their idealism so estranges them from their societies that they cannot make the contributions to American life which are so desperately needed. Despite Lemon's pleas, Joe adamantly refuses to extend his responsibilities beyond his immediate family and business. He will not "play ball" with either capital, big business, or labor; nor will he commit himself to any innovation, such as profit-sharing, which might resolve the conflicts which so disturb his society. "You'll be picked off," Lemon warns him. "Is that what you want? . . . Are you not just inviting your own destruction sooner or later if you don't join one or the other group? Many men do that. . . . It's very common and you're too good for it" (*Money*, 294-295). "They were not peasants," Williams wrote about such men a few years before he started *White Mule*, ". . . they were tragic men who wasted their wits on the ground—but made a hard history for me—not for me only, I think" (*FD*, 219).

There is a definite similarity between the dramatis personae of *In the American Grain* and *White Mule* and *In the Money*. Gurlie and Joe's business competitors correspond approximately to the ignorant exploiters and destroyers of the New World. Joe can be identified with the dissatisfied American idealists who never fully enjoy the "land of heart's desire" which they seek. Flossie can be identified with America itself. "She is," Williams wrote, "in many ways . . . really the only authentic 'Miss America.' That's what I wanted her to be."[28]

Finally there are the lovers and discoverers of America whom Williams celebrated and praised in *In the American Grain*. Who in *White Mule* corresponds to Columbus, Boone, Rasles, and Lincoln? The answer, simply, is Williams himself—but as the author of the novel rather than one of its characters. For the ethical and emotional ideal which he advocated in *In the American Grain* is realized in part in the aesthetic principles of Objectivism which underlay the style of *White Mule* and *In the Money*.

Philip Rahv, in his review of *White Mule*, noted that Williams was not content merely "with the perception of facts and the feeling of them." Instead, Williams' description and selection of details was "instinct with natural piety and pure in its virile tenderness, so alive with sensory detail recreated in language that is swift, bare, tonic, and elated by its closeness to the object." This very "closeness" to his material affected Williams' style, because it released "in him a sensibility of springtime that in itself becomes the source of a new poetics."[29]

This receptivity to the new is exactly the quality of mind which Williams so appreciated in men like Boone, Rasles, and Burr: "men intact—with all their senses waking" who were therefore able to appreciate the wilderness, the Indian, the Negro, the "common people," and give themselves to the realization of these new beings (*IAG*, 206). It is this loving appreciation of the strange, the new, and the different that is truly *"moral:* to be *positive,* to be peculiar, to be sure, generous, brave—TO MARRY, to *touch*—to *give* because one HAS . . . to create, to hybridize, to crosspollenize,—not to sterilize, to draw back, to fear, to dry up, to rot. . . . In Rasles one feels THE INDIAN emerging from within the pod of his isolation from eastern understanding, he is released AN INDIAN. He exists, he is—it is an AFFIRMATION, it is alive" (*IAG*, 121). The characters in *White Mule* and *In the Money*, even Joe who

[28]"'White Mule' Versus Poetry," 244.
[29]"Torrents of Spring," *The Nation*, CXLIV (June 26, 1937), 733.

is the best of them, continually draw back in fear from Flossie or the American life around them. They refuse to give themselves wholly because they are committed more to order than they are committed to life itself. They have ordered their lives in terms of ease, greed, ambition, and ideals. But life itself is a very disorderly activity, and *new* life is particularly disturbing because it is only interested in living—not in "living up to" other people's ideas about what is good, clean, and useful or comfortable. "Babies," wrote Williams, "don't give a damn what goes on and they let go with everything they have and sometimes it's not too attractive" (*IWW*, 61).

At the beginning of *White Mule,* for example, the midwife is angered because Flossie defecates in her clean diaper. Gurlie is enraged because the baby disappoints her desire for a boy. Even Joe, dreaming about his *Obstgarten,* is worried that his children may not pick the right flowers, "wild flowers and peonies. . . . They have to be taught not to take the things that are planted in the gardens—they are children. They want to take things that don't belong to them. That's the Unions. Revolutionists" (*WM,* 46-47).

Williams, on the other hand, is not so fastidious. "That which is possible is inevitable," he wrote at the beginning of a story; "I defend the normality of every distortion to which the flesh is susceptible, every disease, every amputation. I challenge anyone . . . to prove that health alone is inevitable" (*FD,* 208). In other words, whatever is, exists—no matter how disorderly or "unhealthy" it may be, no matter how it disturbs our conception of what is proper and practical. Therefore he is able to recognize and describe these things as themselves, in terms of their living, and not condemn or ignore them as disorderly.

Yet Williams never violates the "objectivity" of his presentation by openly explaining what he describes. "The baby's awakening consciousness," wrote Willard Maas, "is made known to the reader not through direct narration, but by implication, through the introduction of events circumventing her. Details are furnished with the tenderness of the common and real that makes Williams's characters and their action self-revealing without comment or explanation. . . ."[30] As a pediatrician, Williams was thoroughly experienced in communicating with pa-

[30]"A Novel in the American Grain," *Books* (July 11, 1937), p. 4.

tients through his powers of observation rather than their limited powers of expression. He was able in this way to create a
language to communicate Flossie's experiences which is a synthesis of her actions and his description of these actions.

Williams is particularly skillful in presenting the exact
sensory detail which will, by implication, convey the baby's experience. For example, shortly after Flossie's birth, Gurlie and
the midwife attempt to make her nurse:

> Mrs. D [the midwife] came. She insisted it should nurse. They tried.
> The baby waked with a start, gagging on the huge nipple. It pushed
> with its tongue. Mrs. D had it by the back of the neck pushing. She
> flattened out the nipple and pushed it in the mouth. Milk ran down
> the little throat, a watery kind of milk. The baby gagged purple and
> vomited (WM, 8).

Instead of being fed, the baby is being attacked. This is communicated by the detail of the "little throat" and the "huge
nipple" which must be flattened and pushed into the infant's
mouth. The baby could not, naturally, *say* that this first feeding
was a horrible experience; she can only gag and vomit. The
nature of her experience is conveyed by Williams' description of
Gurlie's and Mrs. D's actions.

But more than acute sensory observation was needed for the
reader to understand Flossie. Many of the facts of the newborn
child's life would be repugnant to the reader if presented with
strict sensory neutrality. One common unattractive fact of new-
born life is presented at the end of Chapter One. The midwife
has just changed the baby's diaper, and

> feeling the nice fresh diaper, cool and enticing, now the baby grew red
> all over. Its face swelled, suffused with color. Gripping its tiny strength
> together, it tightened its belly band even more.
>
> And with this final effort, the blessed little thing freed itself as best
> it could—and it did very well—of a quarter pound of tarrish, prenatal
> slime—some of which ran down one leg and got upon its stocking
> (WM, 9-10).

By the emotional tone of approval in the last sentence and the
detail of the baby's use of its "tiny strength" Williams induces
the reader to understand and approve of the defecation in its
true nature as a great accomplishment for the child. The "language" of the baby is implicitly increased because the reader's
fastidiousness, which might be a barrier to his understanding of

the true nature of this activity, has been overcome, and Flossie can be better understood as herself.

Williams also uses his knowledge as a pediatrician throughout *White Mule* to make the significance of the baby's behavior intelligible to the reader. In the passage quoted above, for example, it is his knowledge of the baby's weakness, communicated to the reader, that makes the baby's action seem such a worthy accomplishment.

In effect, Williams directs his sensory, emotional, and intellectual powers to the presentation of his subjects' experiences in *White Mule*. They are used, not to express Williams' identity, but to give the baby and the Stechers a "language" by which their identities and situation can be realized in the reader's mind. In the same way, the heroes of *In the American Grain* give their whole souls "with greatest devotion . . . to the New World" which they love and have discovered (*IAG,* 139). Thus, as Williams suggested, "the great themes of American life and aspiration" are included in the very style of *White Mule* and *In the Money.*[31]

In a sense, there is something more feminine than masculine in this ethical-aesthetic ideal of an art which "gives life" to its material. Williams himself described the maternal element in the art of *White Mule* and related it to his profession. "I take care of babies and try to make them grow," he wrote. ". . . Nothing is more appropriate to a man than an interest in babies. He should today substitute his interest for that of the obsolete mother. Women today merely have babies. It takes a man to bring them up. And it had better be a man with an interest in good style in order that we don't load up the little composition with 'lies.' "[32] Similarly, he compares Lincoln to an orchestra conductor and a woman in *In the American Grain* as he describes his act of bringing the American people to their identity and thus "giving birth" to them.

Mengelberg, a great broad hipped one, conducts an orchestra in the same vein. It is a woman. He babies them. He leans over and floods them with his insistences. It is a woman drawing to herself with insatiable passion the myriad points of sound, conferring upon each the dignity of a successful approach. . . .

[31]See note 23 above.
[32]" 'White Mule' Versus Poetry," 244.

It is Lincoln pardoning the fellow who slept on sentry duty. It is the grace of the Bixby letter. The least private would find a woman to caress him, a woman in an old shawl—with a great bearded face and a towering black hat above it, to give unearthly reality.

Failing of relief or expression, the place tormented itself into a convulsion of bewilderment and pain—with a woman, born somehow, aching over it, holding all fearfully together (*IAG*, 234-235).

It is this "maternal" commitment to his materials that distinguishes Williams' Objectivism from the art of the many other modern artists who have similarly acclaimed the ideal of "the thing itself," of bringing their subjects to self-expression by purely objective means. His art is radically different from the more conventional "ironic" objectivity, described by Northrop Frye, in which the artist "makes the minimum claim for his personality and the maximum for his art."[33]

Objectivism, as practiced by Williams, makes maximum demands upon both the artist's art and his personality. In his mature works, starting with those of the 1930's, Williams raises all aspects of his subject to objective self-expression. Even those elements of his theme in *White Mule* which are most blurred and debased contribute to the novel's most pure and tender moments, and they are realized with the same objective skill no matter how repugnant they must have seemed to Williams. Gurlie's vanity and indifference to her children, the ruthless brutality of Joe's employers—these qualities are just as potent enemies of new life and growth as the Puritans in *In the American Grain* ever were, and Williams must have hated them accordingly. Yet his treatment of these things is always clear, objective, and accurate; it never descends to caricature or condemnation. These things, sordid as they are, effect what is good and new in the novel, the lives of the Stecher children. They are part of Flossie's, the Stechers', and Williams' America; and therefore they must be described as truly, generously, and fearlessly as Boone and Rasles faced the dangers, treacheries, and sordidnesses of the New World which they possessed: "to create, to hybridize, to crosspollenize,—not to sterilize, to draw back, to fear, to dry up, to rot. It is the sun" (*IAG*, 121).

[33]Northrop Frye, *Anatomy of Criticism* (Princeton, 1957), p. 61.

CHAPTER | FIVE

During the 1930's Williams was an exception to the general trend in American writing toward greater political and ideological commitment. His political activities were limited to his chairmanship of a local committee to send medical aid to Loyalist Spain. In his writings he expressed a definite but limited amount of social consciousness which did not greatly increase during the depression.[1]

The major development in Williams' theory and practice of writing was his growing concern with what Wallace Stevens called the "anti-poetic." Williams had assumed, ever since "The Wanderer," that poets had complete freedom in their choice of subjects and that all subjects were potentially valid for poetry. American verse, he wrote in 1917, "must be free in that it is free to include all temperaments, all phases of our environment, physical as well as spiritual, mental and moral. It must be truly

[1]It is difficult to judge the precise nature of Williams' political commitments because he made few extended or significant ideological statements. There are a few relevant sources however. In a letter to the *Partisan Review* he rejected Marxism as opposed to the American tradition (*SL*, pp. 157-158). He showed an interest in Major Douglas' Social Credit theories and contributed articles to *New Democracy*, the movement's American publication (see *New Democracy*, V, 4 [Oct. 15, 1935], 61-62; V, 5 [Nov. 1, 1935], 81-83; and VI, 2 [April, 1936], 26-27). However, Williams shared none of Pound's fascination with fascism. He seems to have regarded Social Credit as a local, "democratic" form of economic development—sort of a Greenback, populist position. In this respect, Williams' Social Credit theories are simply an economic application of his theory of the local culture which he developed in the 1920's. See Chapter Two above and *SE*, pp. 134-161.

democratic. . . ."[2] And in *Kora in Hell* he explained a chaotic improvisation by arguing: *"A poem can be made of anything. This is a portrait of a disreputable farm hand made out of the stuff of his environment"* (*Kora*, 65).

During the late 1920's this premise gradually became stronger and more explicit. In both his prose and his poetry Williams used less and less "eloquent" or "poetic" subjects. This tendency was accelerated and clarified by Wallace Stevens' claim—in his preface to the 1934 edition of Williams' *Collected Poems*—that much of the material of Williams' poems was "anti-poetic." Stevens argued that Williams—because he was a romantic poet —was balanced between the sentimental and the anti-poetic, and that Williams' poetry was the product of the "fecundating" interaction of these two opposites. The sentimental attitude was produced by the romantic poet's "strong spirit" as it rejected "the accepted sense of things." This tendency could produce only fantasy if unopposed. Williams and other romantics therefore needed "the anti-poetic . . . that truth, that reality to which all of us are forever fleeing."[3]

Stevens almost certainly meant this criticism to be praise of Williams as a man whose "imagination remains pure" because he neither stifles nor senselessly indulges it.[4] However Williams interpreted Stevens' comments as an insult to his subject matter. It is possible that he did not understand Stevens' criticism fully, for the "very phrase anti-poetic apparently enraged him" (*IWW*, 52). Williams recalled later that he had been "nettled" by Stevens' claim that he was "interested in the anti-poetic." Poetry, he protested, is "all one to me—the anti-poetic is not something to enhance the poetic—it's [poetry is] all one piece. I didn't agree with Stevens that it was a conscious means I was using. I have never been satisfied that the [term] anti-poetic had any validity or even existed."[5] In other words, Williams seems to

[2]"America, Whitman, and the Art of Poetry," *The Poetry Journal*, VIII (Nov., 1917), 29.

[3]Wallace Stevens, "Williams," preface to Williams' *Collected Poems 1921-1931* (New York, 1934), pp. 1, 2.

[4]Daniel Fuchs, *The Comic Spirit of Wallace Stevens* (Durham, N.C., 1963), p. 117.

[5]*IWW*, p. 52. Williams seems to have understood Stevens' term as meaning that his subjects were too vulgar or "low" to be poetic. I believe, however, that Stevens meant the term "anti-poetic" to mean simply that Williams' subjects were against *conventional* (i.e., "sentimental") poetic prac-

have believed that Stevens praised him for consciously, almost cynically, using anti-poetic realities to enhance poetic ones. Such praise would have been libel to Williams, for one of his basic tenets was that life was a single thing, not divided, and there-fore the materials of art should never be put into such categories as high or low, proper or improper, poetic or anti-poetic. The true significance of Shakespeare's fools, he wrote in a 1929 de-fense of Joyce's *Ulysses*, "is to consolidate life, to insist on its lowness, to knit it up, to correct a certain fatuousness in the round-table circle. Life is not to run off into dream but to remain one, from low to high" (*SE*, 88). And in a poem dated 1928 in the Buffalo Collection, he wrote that "a green truck / dragging a concrete mixer" through the street had "the clatter and true sound / of verse—" (*CEP*, 59).

Coincidentally, Williams seems to reply to Stevens' preface in his 1932 editorials in *Contact*. He wrote in the May issue that "if we cannot find virtue in the object of our lives, then for us there is none anywhere." He admitted in October that there was an idea "that poetry increases in virtue as it is removed from contact with a vulgar world," but that this was heresy since "nothing is beyond poetry. It is the one solid element on which our lives can rely, the 'word' of so many disguises, including as it does man's full consciousness, high and low, in living objec-tivity."

Williams seems to have become more conscious of his own, contrary attitude toward his subjects after he read Stevens' pref-ace. He wrote to Marianne Moore in 1935 that poetry is "limit-less in its application to life" and that if a poet is unsuccessful with his subjects, "he fails through the lack of power [and] not through the material he employs." "There is a good deal of rebellion still in what I write," Williams commented, "rebellion against stereotyped poetic process—the too meticulous choice among other things. In too much refinement there lurks a steril-ity that wishes to pass too often for purity when it is anything but that. Coarseness for its own sake is inexcusable, but a Rabe-lasian sanity requires that the rare and the fine be exhibited as coming like everything else from the dirt. There is no incompatibility between them" (*SL*, 155-156). Williams explained

---

tice. In this sense, "anti-poetic" is a valid generalization, and I have used it to describe Williams' work despite his disapproval of the term.

himself further in an imaginary conversation that he included
in his introduction to Sidney Salt's *Christopher Columbus,* which
was published in 1937. Williams' reader-critic complains in the
dialogue that he cannot enjoy modern poetry. Just when the poet
is writing "so beautifully," he is apt to commit some "eccentricity"
or refuse to "adopt more accepted modes of expression." "That
you may not enjoy as you would like to," Williams argues.

"What do you think beauty is, since you speak so glibly of the beautiful?
You think it's a partial thing, something here against something 'ugly'
there. Impossible. It's the whole thing at once. Or nothing."
   "So you refuse to write what we like, for us?"
   "Yes, we refuse. Because what you think is lovely is in reality hor-
rible. . . ."
   "I am not perfect, I know that. Make me nearer to perfection, then.
It is the ideal which you should hold before us. Everything in the arts
should be beautiful—as we wish to be."
   "Horrible, horrible, horrible—as you are! But art is beautiful, except
not—as you wish [it] to be. . . ."
   ". . . I am a chemist and I tell you your life is your soup. . . . Your
life is made of vegetables, of meats, of water and of salt..."
   "Is that a joke?"
   "It belongs to the soup. Your life is one thing all together. It is a
whole. And what you see in a work of art is like that. It is a whole. . . .
Do you think there is something poetry cannot touch? Yes, you do
think so. Because they are not 'lovely' things. There's your old lie again.
Nothing is lovely but the whole. You want the world to be flat, you do
not want to see that it is round—you do not want to see back of the
picture. . . ."

Williams' poem "To All Gentleness" is his most thorough
poetic defense of his materials.[6] In it he develops the idea that
there are no incompatibilities or dichotomies in reality. Everything is part of the world's beauty and "gentleness." Both "a
cylindrical tank fresh silvered" and a "profusion / of pink roses"
speak to him "of all gentleness and its / enduring" (*CLP,* 24).
   He then assails persons who would deny the "tank fresh silvered" its poetic identity because it is anti-poetic: "And they
speak, / euphemistically, of the anti-poetic! / Garbage. Half the
world ignored... / Is this praise of gentleness?" In the rest of
the poem Williams gives concrete examples of the half of the
world ignored as anti-poetic.

   [6]*CLP,* pp. 24-29. The source of the title is presumably *Love's Labour's Lost,*
V, ii, in which Holofernes rebukes his mockers with the words: "This is not
generous, not gentle, not humble."

The flower is our sign.

Milkweed, a single stalk on the bare
embankment (and where
does the imagination begin?

                Violence and
gentleness, which is the core? Is
gentleness the core?)

                Slender green
reaching up from the sand and rubble (the
anti-poetic they say ignorantly, a
disassociation)

            premising the flower,
without which, no flower.

                      (CLP, 28)

In relation to the rose, the milkweed may seem anti-poetic. But as
a flower it premises all flowers, including the rose, to the imagination which properly associates things. Therefore it is an ignorant disassociation to dismiss it—or the sand and rubble it grows
in—as anti-poetic.

"The poetic and the anti-poetic are a dichotomy / to the split
mind,"[7] argued Williams. For in reality, he believed, "the
phase, is supreme!" and all seeming dichotomies are seasons of
it. Ugliness and beauty, the high and low, violence and gentleness, the poetic and anti-poetic, all are part of the "longer arc,
upgrade or downgrade."

Williams was equally explicit in his 1938 credo "A Note on
Poetry" that nothing could be excluded from the realm of the
poetic. "By listening to the language of his locality," he wrote,
"the poet begins to learn his craft. It is his function to lift, by
use of his imagination and the language he hears, the material
conditions and appearances of his environment to the sphere of
the intelligence where they will have new currency. Thus anything that the poet can effectively lift from its dull bed by force
of the imagination becomes his material. Anything. The commonplace, the tawdry, the sordid all have their poetic uses if the
imagination can lighten them."[8] This statement sums up Williams' poetic practice during the 1930's so well that almost any
poem in *An Early Martyr* or *Adam and Eve and the City* will

[7]These lines are on a rough draft of the poem. Buffalo Collection, tape 26.
[8]"A Note on Poetry," in *The Oxford Anthology of American Literature*,
eds. W. R. Benet and N. H. Pearson (New York, 1938), p. 1313.

exemplify its principles. The very titles of poems like "Lovely
Ad" and "Picture of a Nude in a Machine Shop" proclaim their
subject matter's tawdriness and commonness.

The subjects of Williams' "anti-poetic" poems of the 1930's
are not markedly different from those he wrote about during the
late teens and the 1920's, but his approach to them is different
in one key respect. In a poem like "January Morning"—published in *Al Que Quiere*—Williams' mood and the poem's emotional tone dominate the poem's materials.

> The young doctor is dancing with happiness
> in the sparkling wind, alone
> at the prow of the ferry! He notices
> the curdy barnacles and broken ice crusts
> left at the slip's base by the low tide
> and thinks of summer and green
> shell-crusted ledges among
> > the emerald eel-grass!
> > > *(CEP,* 164)

The imagery of the poem is made up of what the young doctor
notices, and he notices exactly those lively things in the landscape which will sustain his happiness. He practices the selectivity of Laforgue which Williams recommended in his 1922
Contact editorial: "a building upon the basis of what is observed, what is proved, what is of value to the man in the welter
as he found it, and a rigid exclusion of everything else" *(SE,* 36).

The landscape of "Morning" is virtually the same as that of
"January Morning." But in this poem—dated "Jan 18/38" in
the Buffalo Collection—the "young doctor" is twenty years
older, and, equally important, he is an Objectivist rather than
an Imagist poet. "Morning" is a quieter, far more intense poem
than "January Morning." The poet's mood is a response to the
poem's materials, the product of his involvement with them. He
accepts all of his environment for what it is, including its most
sordid, futile, and ugly parts. He struggles to *discover* what is
"of value to the man in the welter," and he discovers far more
than the "young doctor" noticed.

The same picturesque humor of "January Morning" is present in "a church spire sketched on the sky, / of sheet-metal and
open beams, to resemble / a church spire—." But "Morning"
contains much that the earlier poem does not. It has the pathos,
futility, and tragedy of Williams' environment: a woman kneel-

ing daily, praying for her dead husband, "alone on the cold / floor beside the candled altar, stifled / weeping—and moans for his lost / departed soul" (*CEP,* 396). It has the terrible poverty of a world where nothing can be lost; everything no matter how grimy or worthless must be "Covered, swaddled, pinched and saved / shrivelled, broken—to be rewetted and / used again." Yet equally important, "Morning" also has the vitality of Williams' environment, a vitality which is powerful even though it is not picturesque or pretty: "Kid Hot / Jock, in red paint, smeared along / the fence" (*CEP,* 395). And from this vitality there often comes a sober, intense relish and keen enjoyment of even the poorest details of Williams' environment, no matter how seemingly insignificant or sordid they may be.

Because he often enjoys his environment—poor as it is—and because he presented it so objectively, Williams' poems of the 1930's never seem proletarian—even when they are constructed of classically proletarian materials. His poems have none of the dutiful dreariness or preachy indignation characteristic of so much proletarian writing. They celebrate a world which may be completely wrong economically and socially but which is still, Williams insists, fit for poetry; for it is part of reality and therefore deserving of poems.

Williams did not omit social comment from his poems because he lacked social theories or opinions. Like Pound he was a believer in Major Douglas' Social Credit theories and a contributor to *New Democracy.* He expounded his detailed, personal theories of American culture in articles and prefaces like "The American Background" and "An Occasion for Music." However, he felt poetry had a more important task than proselytizing or propagandizing. "The poem alone focuses the world," he wrote in 1941.

It is practical and comprehensive and cannot be the accompaniment of other than an unfettered imagination. . . . To limit it is to kill it.

We seek as far as we are American to take in the difficult . . . the GOLD of it no matter how the ornament is shaped or what may be the purpose to which it seems to be put. To reject the spurious. . . . To reveal the rare and the curious relationships which are the mind's true business (*SE,* 242-243, 244).

The process is alchemical, to transmute facts so their "rare and curious" qualities may be discovered. Therefore the poet must not be "seduced by political urgencies" which would limit his imagination and debase his materials to stereotypes. "I hope," he wrote about a young poetess in 1938,

Miss Rukeyser does not lose herself in her injudicious haste for a "cause," accepting, uncritically, what she does as satisfactory, her intentions being of the best. I hope she will stick it out the hardest way, a tough road, and invent! make the form that will embody her rare gifts of intelligence and passion for a social rebirth the chief object of her labors. Her passion will not be sacrificed, on the contrary it will be emphasized, by the success of such attention to technical detail. So will the [social] revolution.[9]

On the other hand, Williams shows a distinct consciousness of society's workings and great sympathy for the poor in his short stories. "I was . . . obsessed by the plight of the poor," he later said of his stories. "I was impressed by the picture of the times, depression years, the plight of the poor. I felt it very vividly. I felt furious at the country for its lack of progressive ideas. I felt as if I were a radical without being a radical. The plight of the poor in a rich country, I wrote it down as I saw it" (*IWW*, 63, 49).

In Williams' mind the poor were the human equivalent of the anti-poetic. "As in the poem," he wrote in 1950, "it must be stressed, that the short story uses the same materials as newsprint, the same dregs" (*SE*, 295). Like the anti-poetic the poor were ignored because of the prejudices and stereotypes of society, i.e., literate society. "I saw," Williams wrote,

how they [the poor] were maligned by their institutions of church and state—and "betters." I saw how all that was acceptable to the ear about them maligned them. I saw how stereotype[s] falsified them.

Nobody was writing about them, anywhere, as they ought to be written about. There was no chance of writing anything acceptable, certainly not salable, about them.

It was my duty to raise the level of consciousness, not to say discussion, of them to a higher level, a higher plane. Really to tell.[10]

Williams' duty was motivated by more than pity for the poor.

[9]"Muriel Rukeyser's 'US 1,'" *New Republic*, XCIV (March 9, 1938), 142.
[10]*SE*, p. 300. Ironically, the officially "proletarian" magazines would not buy Williams' stories either, because they too had their stereotypes of the poor. According to Fred B. Miller, the editor of *Blast*, to whom Williams donated several stories, leftist magazines alternated between hackneyed leftist writing and a "bourgeois respectability" which was worse than the *Atlantic Monthly*'s. "They're off the hackneyed formula stuff (the strike, the worker bunged by a cop . . .) for good. Good! (But are they any closer to an appreciation of William Carlos Williams' stories? Like fun they are.)" Fred

He considered them important because he felt their struggles to live and realize themselves against odds really constituted the human condition. As the depression worsened, he began to despise any poetic vision of life which emphasized the beautiful, pastoral side of reality. Williams had depicted himself in "The Wanderer" as flying from the ugliness of the city into the New Jersey countryside where he would be "safe" (*CEP*, 8). But in a later poem, he grimly acknowledged: "do not believe that we can live / today in the country / for the country will bring us / no peace" (*CLP*, 52). Lyric, pastoral poetry was only possible "long ago! when country people / would plow and sow with / flowering minds and pockets / at ease— / if ever this were true" (*CLP*, 52).

Now the true circumstances of human life could be seen, Williams wrote about his short stories, in the figure of an old woman "passing my own house, unnamed . . . with heavy poorly fitting glasses, bare headed in the September heat, limping from her arthritis but dragging some sort of vehicle behind her." He was touched by this sight because in the woman he recognized "the situation into which we are all plunged up to our necks and over them."[11] Similarly, he warned the readers of his short story "Life Along the Passaic River" that they could not "do anything" with a drunk wandering the streets of Paterson "except not miss him. . . . He's up against it; he's got to be what he is" (*FD*, 112).

Just as the ugly is the obverse of the beautiful, the poor are the "other side" of the reality of society. They are "up against it." They have to live life as it is—not as it is dreamed to be. Therefore, Williams believed, their attitudes and experiences are likely to be particularly authentic. "I knew it was an elementary world that I was facing," Williams wrote, "but I have always been amazed at the authenticity with which the simple-minded often face that world when compared with the tawdriness of the public viewpoint" (*Autobiography*, 357). More important, Williams believed that the poor had achieved virtues that the rest of society had not been forced to acquire. "The times [the depression]—that was the knife that was killing

B. Miller, "*The New Masses* and Who Else?" *The Blue Pencil*, II, 2 (Feb., 1935), 5.

[11]Williams, "The Short Stories of William Carlos Williams," unpublished introduction for an anthology. Yale Collection, ZA 223, p. 10.

them," he said of the poor, "I was deeply sympathetic and filled with admiration. How amusing they were in spite of their suffering, how gaily they could react to their surroundings" (*IWW*, 49-50). In an even more detailed and moving tribute to the poor of the depression years, he wrote:

Let us dare to vaunt our claims to fame alongside that of those defeated and puzzled but valorous lives of these men, women and even children of the South during the depression years. It is a spiritual courage which . . . carried them transfigured in spite of all barrier[s] which were enough to wipe out a race, on to survival. They showed a tenacity of initiative that be [*sic*] an inspiration to the entire nation. But the spirit of their lives, the humerous [*sic*] patience of the colored, the high belief in their own importance of the poor whites and their women living as they could. . . .[12]

Courage, humor, tenacity, the ability to endure tragedy—certainly such virtues were of great potential value to society; but society, Williams was convinced, knew the poor only through its stereotypes, which "falsified" and "maligned" them.

Like his Objectivist poems, the structure of Williams' best stories is based on the theme of discovery. The world of these stories, the world of those who are "up against it," is a Dance of Life—very much like that of his poem "Perpetuum Mobile: The City."

In Holbein's *Dance of Death*, Death intervenes everywhere. No one can escape him; no institution can exclude him. In Williams' poems and short stories it is life which intervenes with the same persistence. Everywhere men and women seek to live. Always they are driven by love and desire. Whether they are driven ignorantly, brutally, gently, beautifully, creatively, or destructively is less important to Williams than the life which drives them. That they follow dreams which are "more / than a little / false"—this too is less relevant than the fact that they can dream.

> There is no end
> to desire—
>
> Let us break
> through
> and go there—
> (*CEP,* 386)

---

[12]"The Most Overlooked Book of the Past Quarter Century," unpublished review of James Agee and Walker Evans' *Let Us Now Praise Famous Men.* Yale Collection.

He began *In the American Grain* with the assertion that he had sought in the American past "to draw from every source one thing, the strange phosphorus of the life, nameless under an old misappelation." He performs the same task for the American present in his short stories. His technique is simple. First he begins with a concern or involvement, a vision of his subjects' "essential qualities (not stereotype), the courage, the humor (an accident), the deformity, the basic tragedy of their lives—and the *importance* of it" (*SE*, 300). This concern then becomes focused upon a hero or heroine, "a standout personality round which to build, whose history gradually becomes known as the story progresses."[13]

Then, Williams believed, the writer must simultaneously free his subjects from society's stereotyped "misappelation" and gradually reveal their intrinsic, unique merits. All short stories, he claimed, deal with

a trait of some person raised from the groveling, debasing . . . fixed by rule and precedent, of reportage—to the exquisite distinction of that particular man, woman, horse or child that is depicted. The finest short stories are those that raise, in short, one particular man or woman, from that Gehenna, the newspapers, where at last all men are equal, to the distinction of being an individual. To be responsive not to the ordinances of the herd (Russia-like) but to the extraordinary responsibility of being a person (*SE*, 297).

Assessing a subject's response to "the extraordinary responsibility of being a person" implies a process of implicit evaluation which Williams described as a diagnosis. ". . . my business [as a writer-physician], aside from the mere physical diagnosis, is to make a different sort of diagnosis concerning them [his patients] as individuals, quite apart from anything for which they seek my advice. . . . From the very beginning that fascinated me. . . . For no matter where I might find myself, every sort of individual that it is possible to imagine in some phase of his development, from the highest to the lowest, at some time exhibited himself to me" (*Autobiography*, 358).

Williams' short story techniques may be summarized in two related processes. He tries to individualize subjects who are stereotyped in the "public view" by emphasizing their unique qualities. Second, he tries to assess them as persons by diagnos-

---

[13]"The Short Stories of William Carlos Williams," p. 2.

ing their achievements and virtues. This process of "personal" diagnosis sometimes involves an implicit social diagnosis or criticism, since he has to describe the obstacles to his subjects' development if he is to evaluate their achievements.

The process by which Williams progressed from the stereotyped to the unique can be examined in the rough drafts of "The Farmers' Daughters." For example, he wanted to emphasize at the beginning of the story that Helen and Margaret came from the poor-white South and had had good reason to escape north to New Jersey. In the first draft of the story, Williams alludes to a stereotype to make this point: "She came from Georgia, the back country celebrated by Erskine Caldwell."[14]

Williams dilutes the cliché by making it vaguer in his second and third drafts of the story.

Helen was from Georgia, the back country made notorious by recent fiction—the picture is familiar and often sentimentalized. . . . [Second draft.]

There were two women, two young women, who before landing in the suburb where I practiced medicine as a young man lived south of the Mason and Dixon line. [Third draft.]

In the back of the folder which contains these rough drafts, however, there are prescription blanks upon which Williams scrawled: "Chick Peas & Fatback." There is also a brief character sketch of Margaret, entitled "Dick Street" and "The Doctor's Story," which begins:

> What did you eat as a kid?
> Chick peas and fat back
> That ought to have put more meat on your bones.
> I hated 'em, used to throw 'em under my chair.

Williams used this version, with minor changes, to begin the fourth and final drafts of the story (FD, 345).

Williams' "chick peas and fat back" detail gives all the information that the Caldwell or Mason and Dixon allusions do, and it gives the information more concretely, vividly, and immediately. Most important, it lifts Margaret from the stereotype of the poor-white slut by establishing the unique, violent spirit of dissatisfaction which characterizes her. In this way, the "chick peas and fat back" detail helps to express Williams' diagnosis of

---

[14]"The Farmers' Daughters," rough draft in Yale Collection.

how well Margaret has raised herself from the "ordinances of the herd" and responded to the "extraordinary responsibility of being a person" (*SE*, 297).

This process can also be seen in the plot development of stories like "Pink and Blue," "The Use of Force," and "A Face of Stone." Williams first depicts his subjects in these stories as stereotypes and gradually discloses their unique qualities until they are individualized at the end.[15] Williams even calls his subjects "types" at the beginning of "A Face of Stone."

He was one of these fresh Jewish types you want to kill at sight, the presuming poor whose looks change the minute cash is mentioned. . . .

People like that belong in clinics, I thought to myself. I wasn't putting myself out for them, not that day anyhow. Just dumb oxen. Why the hell do they let them into the country. Half idiots at best. Look at them (*FD*, 167).

But by the end of the story, Williams has discovered that the woman nearly starved to death in World War I in Poland. Her protectiveness toward her child and her worries about its health are caused by her memories of her own childhood, not by idiocy. Nor is her husband merely a "fresh Jewish type" and chiseler. He both deeply loves and is ashamed of his wife; it is an act of heroism for him to expose her and himself to the certain rudeness of strangers.

Williams first presents Belle, the heroine of "Pink and Blue," as "a face—like the countryside, a country woman dressed up to be photographed; that vague, placeless look of our rural anonymities (*FD*, 69-70). Any sort of self-development by a rural woman in such an environment would seem impossible, but Belle achieves it, particularly in her costumes: "a plump attractive thing dressed all in pink from head to foot, hat, dress, stockings, shoes, even her complexion touched up to match. She

---

[15]In this respect the effect of Williams' stories is the same as that of his early poems. In both, the local, anonymous object or person is discovered to possess qualities potentially universal in their validity, through Williams' presentation of their concrete "facts." In his early poems, however, Williams seems to have begun with a vision of the object as unique, fresh, and immediately significant—see *Pagany*, p. 13. He then sought a correspondingly fresh and immediate language to induce this vision in his readers' minds. In contrast, he often begins his stories with clichés and only gradually discovers or arrives at a vision and expression of his subjects' uniqueness. See Chapter Seven below.

was really a picture—a veritable azalea bush in blossom" (*FD*, 70).

Williams seems interested chiefly in diagnosing the personalities and recognizing the individuality of his subjects in these stories. He is most concerned with breaking through stereotypes to discover their unique qualities no matter how absurd or deeply hidden they may be. In other stories, however, Williams seems equally interested in social diagnosis—in discovering the social conditions that warped or obscured his subjects' development.

Williams almost perfectly balances these two concerns in "Jean Beicke." He considered this story his best,[16] and I agree with him. It contains some of his most incisive and unflinching diagnoses of his society and its limitations. It is also probably the best example of his ability to articulate the uniqueness of the most seemingly worthless and anonymous human material.

Jean Beicke was a sick, grotesquely deformed infant who was abandoned at Passaic General Hospital and eventually died. In the story she is at first only one more unwanted child suffering from malnutrition and disease. She is merely one more of the "poor kids" who made Williams "wonder sometimes if medicine isn't all wrong to try to do anything for them at all" (*FD*, 160). But gradually Jean's will to live and thrive, against all odds, makes Williams and her nurses recognize and love her as an individual. "Boy! how that kid could eat!" Williams wrote. "As sick as she was she took her grub right on time every three hours, a big eight ounce bottle of whole milk and digested it perfectly. In this depression you got to be such a hungry baby, I heard the nurse say to her once. It's a sign of intelligence, I told her. But anyway, we all got to be crazy about Jean" (*FD*, 162).

As he is increasing the reader's concern for Jean, Williams is also subtly presenting a social diagnosis of the causes of her death. Most obviously guilty is Jean's father, who callously abandoned her mother, returned to conceive Jean, and then abandoned his family again. Next there is the depression, which prevented the mother from adequately feeding or caring for Jean. Finally, there are the hospital's doctors and nurses, who should have known how to save Jean but did not. "We went over her

---

[16]"Technically and from the depth and breadth of it's [*sic*] humanity I never did better. The sharpness of its detail, not over crowded, nothing overlapping." "The Short Stories of William Carlos Williams," p. 33.

six or eight times," Williams wrote, "three or four of us, one after the other, and nobody thought to take an X-ray of the mastoid regions. It was dumb, if you want to say it, but there wasn't a sign of anything but the history of the case to point to it" (FD, 163). The story ends with an explicit medical autopsy and an implicit social autopsy. Nothing and no one responsible for Jean's death are excused.

Then the diagnosis all cleared up quickly. The left lateral sinus was completely thrombosed and on going into the left temporal bone from the inside the mastoid process was all broken down.

I called up the ear man and he came down at once. A clear miss, he said. I think if we'd gone in there earlier, we'd have saved her.

For what? said I. Vote the straight Communist ticket.

Would it make us any dumber? said the ear man (FD, 165-166).

In stories in which Williams' subjects are eccentric, perverted, or grotesque, there is usually a good deal of this type of social diagnosis though it is never propagandistic or even very explicit. Williams can take his subjects' uniqueness more for granted in these stories and concentrate his attention upon the social conditions which limited or warped their developments.

Most of Williams' grotesque subjects appear in *The Knife of The Times,* his first collection of stories. They are adults who had scarcely more opportunities than a Jean Beicke to realize themselves, who are as warped from emotional or spiritual unsatisfaction as she was malformed by physical starvation. Their individuality is often limited to a sort of flawed or unsatisfactory perfection which they achieve despite the limitations of their environment.

Williams blamed the inadequacies of American culture for both the emotional and economic plight of many of his subjects. During the 1930's, he later wrote, artists were deeply affected by the poverty and inequalities visible everywhere. He believed that persons denied normal or constructive satisfactions often turned to revolutionary, self-destructive, or perverted means to fulfill themselves. "It was the indifference to sex driven to fury by sheer hunger, physical hunger (along with the rest of the appetites) which filled our stories. . . . I saw the regressions and deprivations, the bread lines—that filled me to [sic] anger. . . ."[17]

---

[17]*Ibid.,* pp. 12, 14.

However, Williams also believed that some of these persons might have "perfect" responses to their flawed desires. That is, though their desires may be warped, they still act upon them shrewdly, passionately, and courageously. Dago Schultz, Doc Rivers, the "Colored Girls of Passenack," the boy Stewie in "A Descendant of Kings"—all are persons who possess the audacity to achieve some distinction or "perfection" in their very regressions. "They had no knowledge and no skill at all," Williams wrote about such persons.

They flunked out, got jailed, got "Mamie" with child, and fell away, if they survived, from their perfections.
    There again, a word: their perfections. They were perfect, they seemed to have been born perfect. . . .
    . . . they were there full of a perfection of the longest leap, the most unmitigated daring, the longest chances (*Autobiography*, 288).

Writing about Belle of "Pink and Blue," Williams warned: "When for any reason our cultral [*sic*] roots have been allowed to waste away there may occur a situation as occured [*sic*] in the story *Pink and Blue*. Resourceful people will cast themselves about at randon [*sic*] and take hold where they are able."[18] but he also stressed that she had shown a certain "genius" which should not be ignored. "A man has to be on the alert" among the illiterates, he commented, "a genius, such a man as Mark Twain, is likely to put in an appearance at any moment. Sparks of his genius may appear in some such innundated [*sic*] character as . . . Belle."[19]

"Old Doc Rivers" is Williams' most comprehensive and sensitive diagnosis of the poverty of his environment and the flawed perfections which were endemic to it. Potentially Rivers was a man and physician of great virtues. "He was far and away by natural endowment the ablest individual of our environment . . . a man trying to fill his place among those lacking the power to grasp his innate capabilities" (*FD*, 89-90). Yet most of Rivers' good qualities were wasted or perverted because of his environment; "the provincial bottom of New Jersey" lacked the culture needed for him to realize them constructively.

There were a few healthy releases for Rivers' temperament:

[18]*Ibid.*, p. 23.
[19]*Ibid.*, p. 25.

visits with a rich French family possessing "a continental culture," hunting trips in the Maine woods where he could "plunge into something bigger than himself." However, there were many more unhealthy releases in his environment. Rivers was chiefly a drug addict who used "all the ordinary hypnotics—morphine, heroin, and cocaine also." But there was also alcohol and plenty of backwoods women. "His sensitiveness, his refinement, his delicacy—found perhaps a release in this backhanded fashion" (*FD*, 99). There was overwork when "the heart beats faster, the blood is driven to the extremities of the nerves, floods the centers of action and a man feels in a flame. That's what Rivers wanted, must have wanted . . ." (*FD*, 102). And finally there was the excitement of irresponsibility which also became a habit and indulgence.

He began to slip badly in the latter years, made pitiful blunders. But this final phase was marked by that curious idolatry that sometimes attracts people to a man by the very danger of his name. . . .

They seemed to recreate him in their minds, the beloved scapegoat of their own aberrant desires—and believed that he alone could cure them.

He became a legend and indulged himself the more (*FD*, 100).

This fearful devotion to Rivers, even in his worst days, was no accident. Because of their environment's lack of an adequate culture, Rivers' townspeople were unable to comprehend his capabilities. So they turned his skills into something they could understand and respond to: magic.

It is a little inherent in medicine itself—mystery, necromancy, cures—charms of all sorts, and he knew and practiced this black art. . . .

But most feared him—in short, dared not attack him even when they knew he had really killed someone.

In reality, it was a population in despair, out of hand, out of discipline, driven about by each other blindly, believing in the miraculous, the drunken, as it may be. Here was, to many, though they are diminishing fast, something before which they could worship, a local shrine, all there was left, a measure of the poverty which surrounded them. They believed in him: Rivers, drunk or sober. It is a plaintive, failing story (*FD*, 101, 102, 104).

Here Williams' social diagnosis is, though half implied, as precise as any medical one. Rivers' environment lacked the culture which would have enabled him to realize his full and satisfactory excellence as a physician. Therefore, he achieved a perverse, regressive "perfection" in the more primitive role of sachem.[20]

In his later stories, most of those in "Life along the Passaic River" and "Beer and Cold Cuts," Williams wrote about poor people who possessed qualities which were less colorful but more constructive than those of a Belle or Doc Rivers. It was about such persons that Williams wrote in his *Autobiography:* "Let the successful carry off their blue ribbons; I have known the unsuccessful, far better persons than their more lucky brothers" (358). Williams' social diagnosis in these stories is generally limited to a noncommittal presentation of his environment's poverty. His emphasis is upon the virtues of the poor, the courage and good humor, which constitute their unrecognized triumphs.

The pattern of these stories is simple. A destructive element of the environment strikes. Death in some form—poverty, illness, violence—threatens to end human fulfillment. But somehow Williams' subjects have the courage to go on living without retreating from their environment. Sometimes stoically, sometimes comically, they reassemble the meagre materials available to them so that a livable world is once again constructed.

"The Accident," for example, begins with life seemingly completely defeated.

After twelve days struggling with a girl to keep life in her, losing, winning, it is not easy to give her up. One has studied her inch by inch, one has grown used to the life in her. It is natural.

She lies gasping her last: eyes rolled up till only the whites show, lids half open, mouth agape, skin a cold bluish white, pasty, hard to the touch—as the body temperature drops the tissues congeal. One is definitely beaten (*FD,* 221).

Seeking relief from his defeat and despair, the narrator-physician of the story rushes out into the spring fields with his little son. Very little happens. They see people, goats, and the child has an "accident." He falls but does not hurt himself, and then a far greater "accident" occurs. Miraculously life and growth return to the world.

[20]The term "sachem" indicates Rivers' nature and his relationship with his society fairly precisely. See Joseph Campbell's discussion of Shamanism in *The Masks of God* (New York, 1959). Vivienne Koch's reading of "Old Doc

In the windows of the Franco-American Chemical Co. across the way
six women have appeared in two windows, four in one and two in the
other. They watch the baby, wondering if he is hurt. They linger to
look out. They open the windows. Their faces are bathed with sun-
light. They continue to strain out at the window. They laugh and
wave their hands.
Over against them in an open field a man and a boy on their hands
and knees are planting out slender green slips in the fresh dirt, row
after row (*FD*, 224).

Williams uses a recognizable technique in many of his stories
to invite the reader's recognition of the humble virtues of the
poor. He presents the indefatigable facts of death and poverty.
With them he intertwines the equally significant facts of speech
and behavior which convey the limited but real triumphs of the
poor over death and poverty. An excerpt picked almost at random illustrates this.

I'm sorry we ain't got no light in there. The electricity is turned off.
Do you think you can see with a candle?
Sure. Why not? But it was very dark in the room where the woman
lay on a low double bed. A three-year-old boy was asleep on the sheet
beside her. . . . Everything was clean and in order (*FD*, 138).

In such passages in which the forces of life are so intermingled
with the forces of death and poverty, the reader is invited to
recognize that the forces of life are derived from the individual
human's qualities of courage or integrity. He is thus exposed to
"the exquisite distinction of that particular man, woman, horse
or child that is depicted" and is himself made more "responsive
to the extraordinary responsibility of being a person" (*SE*, 297).

Sometimes Williams' characters possess the eloquence to assert
their own virtues—the charity and dignity of the mother's
speech at the end of "Danse Pseudomacabre"—for example. But
in most of his stories Williams aids the reader's comprehension
of the distinctions of his short story subjects by a simple device.
He intersperses the implicitly admirable facts of his subjects'
lives with his own explicitly admiring comments. For example,
in the middle of "Comedy Entombed: 1930" Williams suddenly
shifts from notation to admiring evaluation.

I have seldom seen such disorder and brokenness—such a mass of
unrelated parts of things lying about. That's it! I concluded to myself.

Rivers" is quite similar to mine. See her *William Carlos Williams* (Norfolk,
Conn., 1950), p. 217.

An unrecognizable order! Actually—the new! And so good-natured and calm. So definitely the thing! And so compact. Excellent. And with such patina of use. Everything definitely "painty." Even the table, that way, pushed off from the center of the room (*FD*, 327).

These comments do not explicate or create the significance of the facts of the lives of the poor; they simply recognize that significance. In the process they articulate the significances of the lives of the poor in ways that the poor themselves cannot.

Williams' short story techniques premise a definite relationship between the articulate writer-narrator and his ineloquent, "anti-poetic" subjects. As in *White Mule* and his objectivist poetry, Williams "lends" his powers of selection, organization, and appreciation to his subjects so that they may realize themselves in a world which would otherwise ignore them.

Such a relationship between an articulate, relatively eloquent individual and his inarticulate fellow citizens is an ideal one— even for the artist, as Williams himself confessed. He admitted in his *Autobiography* that "we see through the welter of evasive or interested patter . . . penetrate to some moving detail of a life" only occasionally and by chance. "The difficulty is to catch the evasive life of the thing, to phrase the words in such a way that [a] stereotype will yield a moment of insight. That is where the difficulty lies. We are lucky when that underground current can be tapped and the secret spring of all our lives will send up its pure water. It seldom happens. A thousand trivialities push themselves to the front, our lying habits of everyday speech and thought are foremost . . ." (359).

In his play *Many Loves,* written during the late 1930's, Williams dramatized a more pessimistic relationship between articulate and inarticulate persons which prefigured his treatment of this theme in *Paterson.*

Williams started with three playlets dealing with inarticulate, provincial subjects—factory workers, farmers, a suburban housewife. "The theme of each 'playlet,' " Williams wrote in a Synopsis,

and of the counter-play, is love—of a sort.

In the first sequence, a young man loves an older, married woman. In the second, a young man and young woman of high school age . . . are assailed by the girl's father. In the third of these prose playlets, an older man and a younger woman engage in a mild intrigue (*ML*, 3).

In all three playlets, love is defeated and the woman is denied fulfillment because of some sort of male failure or betrayal. The dance of life becomes a dance of death. Genuine marriage, the meaningful relation of male and female, is not achieved.

Serafina, the title character of the first playlet, is a factory worker's wife. Her husband's interest in his marriage is confined to whether "That goddamned woman" is going to be home to fix his supper. Serafina's boyfriend is no more satisfactory. He has gotten her pregnant and is leaving to join the army. Laddie, a poor student, seems to love Serafina with some sensitivity but because of his timidity he confesses his love too late to help her.

Ann, the young girl of the second playlet, is denied fulfillment by her father Pete, who hates and envies her. He discourages her desires for an education or career and scares away any young men who might court her. The only boy with the nerve to risk Pete's rage by dating Ann is Horace, who is as reckless and insensitive as the rest of her environment. Trapped between her father's brutality and Horace's crassness, Ann innocently steps into the arms of a chic lesbian who seems the epitome of female freedom and self-development.

In the third playlet a suburban doctor, obviously intended to represent Williams, flirts with Clara, a frustrated housewife. Clara is aroused, but the Doctor is interested in her only as an audience for his monologues and has no serious interest in her. When she embraces him, he overcomes his indifference to her enough to respond sluggishly, but they are interrupted when Clara's sick child awakens.

In all the playlets the characters are not articulate enough to understand their situations with the clarity needed to resolve them. None of the unsatisfied women, for example, can recognize the type of male inadequacy which betrays her fulfillment. Nor can they recognize that their supposed escapes from their dilemmas lead only to different forms of betrayal.

The form of the three playlets closely corresponds to their subjects. In conventional dramatic terms they are "anti-dramatic" —just as Williams' poems and short stories are "anti-poetic"— because of their fidelity to characters who are intractable to ordinary dramatic development. The characters are unable clearly to articulate their basic concerns or situations, and the dialogue of the playlets is correspondingly groping and half-relevant.

Nothing in the characters' lives is genuinely resolved or fulfilled, so the playlets end abruptly and arbitrarily. Peter, the play's backer who expected a conventionally well-made drama, cries: "Can't you see it? It's [the third playlet's] unresolved, / floating, too silly. The old goat / gets nowhere" (*ML*, 87-88). But that is exactly the point of the playlet. Clara and the Doctor are floating and getting nowhere and their relationship will not be resolved.

But if the playlets are thus flawed—in conventional terms—to imitate their subjects' flaws, they are also strengthened by their subjects' strengths. They are forceful, candid, and emotionally moving, for Williams' characters express themselves bluntly and vividly. They have few delusions about themselves and little desire to create them in others. "I'm not shy and I'm not timid," says Clara in "Talk," "I'm no blushing violet. I tell you just as I'd tell anybody else—I'm trying to do my job as a sweet mother and it's killing me. I'm telling you—killing me. If I quit the whole mess of this having children and sent it to hell and gone out of my sight, I'd be a better woman—" (*ML*, 76-77). Finally, Williams' characters, particularly the women, intensely desire love and fulfillment. Their clumsy gropings for these things are the most moving parts of the play. "I haven't felt so relaxed in months," Clara tells the Doctor. "It's marvelous to find someone you can say anything to—anything at all, and he'll understand it. I can't open my mouth except to a couple of girls—and I can't tell them everything. I can't tell my mother, I can't tell my husband . . ." (*ML*, 86).

Williams did not articulate the theme of love in his playlets by grafting an alien glibness onto their characters' speech. Instead he revealed their basic situation by repeating it in an articulate context: the sophisticated minds and language of the playlets' "author," his leading actress, and his backer. For the counter-play, like the playlets, also deals with "love—of a sort," as Williams pointed out in his Synopsis.

In the counter-play, the love is between two men, an elder and another, younger one. Here the dramatic action hinges on the necessity for the younger, who is the author of the three short pieces, to get the older man . . . to finance the production of his play—but without concessions. For the poet-playwright is in love with and about to marry his leading lady . . . (*ML*, 3).

Two of Williams' comments on Shakespeare may be applied to the relationship between Hubert, the playwright, and his playlets. "By writing," Williams claimed, Shakespeare

escaped from the world into the natural world of his mind. The unemployable world of his fine head was unnaturally useless in the gross exterior of his day—or any day. By writing he made this active. He melted himself into that grossness, and colored it with his powers. . . .

Therefore his seriousness and his accuracies, because it was not his play but the drama of his life. . . .

When he speaks of fools he is one; when of kings he is one, doubly so in misfortune.

He is a woman, a pimp, a Prince Hal—(*SE*, 69-70).

Writing about a speech by John of Gaunt in *Richard II*, Williams argued that its words should be "related not to their sense as objects . . . but as a dance over the body of his condition accurately accompanying it" (*SAA*, 91).

In the same way Hubert's playlets, though they have their own autonomous identities, can be considered an expression of his condition, a dance accompanying and articulating his own dilemmas in love. Like the males in his playlets, Hubert is tempted to use and betray the female opportunistically. He can use Alise's talents to make his play a success and then betray her by returning to Peter. Also, just as poor marriages limit the fulfillments of the women in his playlets, Hubert's dependence on Peter limits his fulfillment as a man and an artist.

Despite these similarities in theme, the counter-play and playlets have far different forms of dramatic development. The counter-play has all the conventional devices of the drama—which the playlets lack—to move its characters' situation to a resolution. There is rising action, Peter's pursuit of the truth. There is suspense: will Hubert be forced to choose between play and fiancée? There is a catastrophe, Peter's discovery that he has lost Hubert to Alise. Finally there is the climax as Peter plays *deus ex machina* and lets Hubert have his marriage.

However, Peter's and Hubert's lives have the limitations as well as the advantages of a well-made play. Their passions are satisfied in art and talk, not life. Because of this the counter-play is rarely forceful and moving. Alise is its only passionate character, and her passion is lost in the mixture of Peter's fatuous witticisms and Hubert's evasions which make up the dialogue.

Peter and Hubert do not authentically or directly confront their situation, because they are able to "clothe" it in their fictions of manners, evasions, and innuendoes. The inarticulate characters of the playlets are like the poor in Williams' stories. They are "up against it" and cannot escape what they are and the condition of their lives. But Peter and Hubert can escape. Peter, for example, rarely expresses the possessiveness of his emotional relationship with Hubert. He conceals it in his economic control over him. Similarly, Hubert's desire to free himself is never openly stated. It is implied in the rebellion and frustration of his characters. Peter sums up their situation in an insult which can be applied to himself as well as Hubert: "you seem to have a knack / to avoid coming face to face, / whether with yourself—or me. . . . You're slick as a dance floor, my friend" (*ML*, 90).

The relationship between the articulate and the inarticulate in *Many Loves* significantly resembles that in *Paterson*. The force, rough intensity, and unresolved structures of the prose playlets counterpoint the smoother, more articulate and finished form of the counter-play which is written in verse. Also, the counter-play forms a frame which articulates the significance of the playlets by clarifying their common theme of love in a more sensitive medium, the speech of Hubert, Peter, and Alise. In the same way Dr. Paterson's poetic monologues in *Paterson* contrast the form of the poem's prose passages and articulate their significances.

Equally important is the contrast between the ways the articulate and inarticulate experience life in both works. In *Paterson*, as in the playlets, the inarticulate experience authentically but have no language.

> They do not know the words
> or have not
> the courage to use them
> —girls from
> families that have decayed and
> taken to the hills: no words.
> They may look at the torrent in
> their minds
> and it is foreign to them
> . . . .

> —the language
> is divorced from their minds,
> the language   .   .   the language!
> (I, i, 20-21)

Unable to comprehend their own experiences, the inarticulate cannot resolve them, and they therefore perish, unsatisfied and unfulfilled. In contrast, the articulate, poetic Dr. Paterson—like Hubert, Alise, and Peter—has a language and comprehension but fails to experience life directly and authentically. "You've never had to live, Dr. P.," a disappointed poetess accuses Dr. Paterson,

> —not in any of the by-ways and dark underground passages where life so often has to be tested. The very circumstances of your birth and social background provided you with an escape from life in the raw; and you confuse that protection from life with an *inability* to live. . . .
> But living (unsafe living, I mean) isn't something one just sits back and decides about. It happens to one. . . . Or else it doesn't happen. And when it does, then one must bring, as I must, one's life to literature; and when it doesn't then one brings to life (as you do) purely literary sympathies and understandings, the insights and humanity of words on paper *only* . . . (II, iii, 111).

Divorced from life, the articulate are no more capable than the inarticulate of evading destruction and achieving fulfillment. The only solution to the dilemma is for some fertile connection to occur between the poetic and prosaic, the articulate and inarticulate, so that both may survive and have fulfillment.

This connection is a simple one in *Many Loves*. When the articulate characters of the counter-play recognize their situation in the coarsely authentic medium of the prose playlets, they can respond to it and resolve it. The purpose of the play, Williams wrote, was to make the audience look within themselves,

> . . . for what I shall discover.
> Yourselves! Within yourselves. Tell
> me if you do not see there, alive!
> a creature unlike the others, something
> extraordinary in its vulgarity,
>
> . . . .
>
>   . . . something
> which in the mind you are and would
> be yet have always been, unrecognized,
> tragic and foolish, without a tongue.
> (*CLP*, 13)

In the counter-play of *Many Loves* Peter achieves this act of
recognition which leads to resolution. Peter's involvement in the
playlets increases as he realizes their relevance to his and Hubert's situation. His indignant asides and protests not only
interrupt the action of the playlets; they also reveal Peter's
change from a detached spectator to an unwilling participant in
Hubert's little dramas. When Ann, the heroine of the second
playlet, expresses her desire to escape her home and family,
Peter recognizes Hubert's desire to free himself (*ML,* 51). Then
Peter fully recognizes his own situation and the possibility that
he may be exploited and humiliated by his affection for Hubert
when he sees Horace badger Lil, a fat, unwanted girl, for the
money to elope with Ann. Having seen the unvarnished realities
and possible consequences of his loss of influence over Hubert,
Peter is able to respond to his situation and resolve it to his best
advantage. He compromises his control over the play and accepts Hubert's marriage to Alise, thus salvaging something of his
affection.

But first Peter had to descend to the vulgar, authentic, prosaic
realities of his relationship with Hubert. In the process he reluc-
tantly discovers the relevance of the "anti-poetic" world of the
playlets which he had formerly despised and ignored as alien to
himself. Similarly, in Williams' anti-poetic poetry the reader is
invited to descend and discover the potential benefits of the
ignored "half the world." In his short stories there is also the
invitation to descend and discover the lives, integrity, and virtues of the poor, the human equivalent of the anti-poetic. In all
these works of the 1930's Williams emphasized the need for the
articulate to descend and recognize their community of condition with the inarticulate, frustrated, unfulfilled objects and
persons which fill the American environment.

CHAPTER | SIX

By the late 1930's Williams had accomplished what he conceived to be the artist's task in the world: "to quicken and elucidate, to fortify and enlarge the life about him and make it eloquent."[1] In his poems, short stories, novels, and plays he had articulated many of the elements of his environment—even the most inarticulate and intractable or "anti-poetic" ones. But he still wished to write *the* poem, the single work which would gather together and articulate all the elements of his world. "The poem," he wrote in a 1950 letter, "embraces everything we are." It should be an attempt to lift "an environment to expression," to communicate a "total culture." "The poem," he concluded, ". . . is the assertion that we are alive as ourselves—as much of the environment as it [the poem] can grasp" (*SL*, 286).

Williams intended *Paterson* to be this poem which would articulate his entire environment. When he began the poem, it was his conscious intention to find "an image large enough to embody the whole knowable world about me. The longer I lived in my place, among the details of my life, I realized that these isolated observations and experiences needed pulling together to gain 'profundity' " (*Autobiography*, 391). He sought to make the poem inclusive of both the local realities of his environment and of their universal implications. He felt that his task as a poet was

[1]"Sermon with a Camera," *New Republic*, XCVI (Oct. 12, 1938), 283.

to write particularly, as a physician works, upon a patient, upon the thing before him, in the particular to discover the universal. . . .

I took the city as my "case" to work up, really to work it up. . . . Paterson as Paterson would be discovered, perfect, perfect in the special sense of the poem, to have it—if it rose to flutter into life awhile—it would be as itself, locally, and so like every other place in the world (*Autobiography*, 391, 392).

Williams' desire to make *Paterson* inclusive of all elements of his environment created a formal problem. How were the aspects of his environment which he had written about in *In the American Grain*, *White Mule*, and his short stories to be included in a poem? He had written about these subjects in prose because they were not "poetic." Sometime during the late 1930's he decided that this problem could not be solved by eliminating such subjects, nor by changing them into poetry. In "Against the Weather," a long essay on poetic form written in 1939 when he was beginning *Paterson*, he reasoned that compactness and coherence, rather than uniformity, of parts constituted poetic excellence.

Another characteristic of all art is its compactness. It is not, at its best, the mirror. . . . It is the life—but transmuted to another tighter form.

The compactness implies restriction but does not mean loss of parts; it means compact, restricted to essentials. Neither does it mean the extraction of a philosophic essence. The essence remains in the parts proper to life, in all their sensual reality (*SE*, 198).

Instead of destroying one another, all the elements of the world coexist in the work of art because it possesses "that which must draw them together—without destruction of their particular characteristics; the thing that will draw them together because in their disparateness it discovers an identity" (*SE*, 199). "Ugolini and Ariel," wrote Williams on a rough draft of *Paterson*, "both dwell in the poem and by that get their reason [for existing?], point blank. Without the grill work of the poem to contain them, make a cage of words[,] a barrier between them and authority, which would destroy them, they could not exist for us."[2]

Thus Williams seems to have conceived of the poem as a sort of Prospero's island upon which all varieties of being coexist and thereby define and influence one another—each in the "sen-

---

[2]Yale Collection, ZA 188. See Dante, *Inferno*, XXXIII.

sual reality" of its own language whether prose or poetry. He strove to make *Paterson* inclusive of his world in the same way that Shakespeare made *The Tempest* inclusive of his—by mixing prose and different types of poetry.

This technique was not new to Williams. In *In the American Grain* he mingled objective, prose accounts by other authors with his own varied, more poetic reactions. As early as 1927 he attempted to apply this technique to his local environment. In a rough draft of the "Dolores Marie Pischak" section of "Notes in Diary Form" he wrote:

JEWELS ana [*sic*] PASTE
Fill in the rest of the story afterward, cold *
The city of Gaefield [*sic*] was settled (copy from the Hist [*sic*] of Bergen Co.) etc. Thus t[o] make it consecutive, the Saddle River, the Strike the dye stuff—etc. etc.[3]

Despite the interval between "Notes in Diary Form" and *Paterson,* the poem's mixed style is a development of the techniques used in the earlier work. The significance this technique had for Williams can be further understood by studying his rationale for it.

The simplest theory Williams used to justify his mixing of prose and poetry was derived from Ford Madox Ford's essay on Swinburne (1937). According to Ford, the modern reader had good reason for being bored by long, conventional poems. "Man," Ford argued, ". . . has as definite a need of the patterns of rhythm in his life as he has of salt in his diet. To get it he must dance ceremonial dances, chant in numbers, listen to rhymes. But when his normal life of the street, public conveyance, and suburb is perpetually interspersed with mechanical rhythm he will have little use for the long onrolling of classical metres evolving slow and not unusual thought."[4] Williams agreed with Ford and quoted him on a rough draft of a preface to *Paterson:* "   .   the enfeebled mind, weary of travelling the rivulet of print between top to bottom of page,   . But you would think that, with effort, one ought to be able to keep one's mind down on pages and pages of verse   .   .   Who in fact does want to read poetry   .   .   ?   F.M.F."[5]

[3]Buffalo Collection, tape 25.
[4]*Portraits from Life* (Chicago, 1960), pp. 266-267.
[5]Buffalo Collection, tape 53. This passage is quoted in *ND 17* (p. 307) with slightly different punctuation. It is derived from pp. 257, 263 of Ford's

Williams hoped to avoid this monotony by using different types of poetry and by adding passages of documentary prose. He conceived of the poem as a representation of a mind and a river, full of swift currents and sudden eddies.[6] He intended the prose to be like the river's obstacles. They would "break up the poetry" and "help shape the form of the poem." Also, if carefully chosen they could increase the reader's interest. "I wanted," Williams recalled, "to make the thing topical, interesting to the reader. I knew the reader, any reader, would be interested in scandal so scandal went in. The documentary notations were carefully chosen for their live interest, their verisimilitude" (*IWW*, 73).

Williams' conception of propriety in language was another reason for his mixing of prose and poetry.

In his dialogue "The Basis of Faith in Art," he asserted that the poet "lives in a world of the imagination where there is nothing but truth and beauty." There are no frustrations in this "Olympus." "All our destinies are solved" there, for "in that country nothing detracts a man from following his bent, honestly" (*SE*, 189). Williams expanded this conception significantly in a 1948 lecture. He began by accepting Freud's theory that the "poem is a dream, a daydream of wish fulfillment" and that the "*subject matter* of the poem is always phantasy." "We may mention," he continued, "Poe's dreams in a pioneer society, his dreams of gentleness and bliss. . . . Yeats's subject matter of faery. Shakespeare—the butcher's son dreaming of Caesar and Wolsey. No need to go on through Keats, Shelley to Tennyson. It is all, the subject matter, a wish for aristocratic attainment—a 'spiritual' bureaucracy of the 'soul' or what you will" (*SE*, 281-282). Naturally such a "subject matter" could only be expressed in the most "poetic," the most idealized language possible: "the 'beautiful' or pious (and so beautiful) wish expressed in beautiful language" (*SE*, 282).

But, argued Williams, the world and its values changed:

with the industrial revolution, and steadily since then, a new spirit—a new *Zeitgeist* has possessed the world, and as a consequence new values have replaced the old, aristocratic concepts. . . . A new subject matter

---

Portraits from Life which Williams specifically praised in " 'White Mule' Versus Poetry," *The Writer*, L (Aug., 1937), 244.

[6]See *Paterson*, I, i, 16.

began to be manifest. It began to be noticed that there could be a new subject matter and that that was not in fact the poem at all. Briefly then, money talks, and the poet, the modern poet has admitted new subject matter to his dreams—that is, the serious poet has admitted the whole armamentarium of the industrial age to his poems—(*SE,* 282).

In other words, before the industrial revolution poets could believe that their "phantasy" was essentially synonymous with reality. Therefore they could express all of life in the aristocratic, "beautiful language" of poetry. But after the industrial revolution, men could not ignore the existence of a "new subject matter," "money," the economic condition of man. This subject could not be expressed in beautiful language; it could not be fitted into the poem, because it had not and could not achieve the "aristocratic attainment" which poetry expresses. "Money," commerce, the marketplace, cannot be reconciled with "dreams of gentleness and bliss." They are too crude and too prosaic, yet they are now so essential to human life that they cannot be omitted from any work of art, including a poem, which wishes to deal with the totality of life.

In his poem "Raleigh Was Right," Williams agrees with Raleigh's condemnation of Marlowe's "The Passionate Shepherd to His Love," but he condemns Marlowe's idyllic pastoral for a different reason. Raleigh accuses the pastoral idealist of ignoring "Time [which] drives the flocks from field to fold," fades beauty, and betrays lovers' promises. Williams blames modern poets for ignoring poverty. Once poets had been able to sing of the loveliness of rural life, but that was "long ago! when country people / would plow and sow with / flowering minds and pockets / at ease— / if ever this were true" (*CLP,* 52). Now "empty pockets make empty heads," and it is the poet's duty to "cure" poverty if he can. In another poem, "The Mind's Games," Williams attacks the whole artistic tradition which ignores "money" as the antithesis of the aesthetic life. Wordsworth wrote,

> The world is too much with us; late and soon,
> Getting and spending, we lay waste our powers:
> Little we see in Nature that is ours;
> We have given our hearts away, a sordid boon!

and many later poets have agreed with him. In "The Mind's Games" Williams admits that a man can find wholly aesthetic, beautiful things in the world, "one / small fly still among the petals." To such a man, the world is radiant "and even the fact / of poverty is wholly without despair." But all such beauty was rendered irrelevant by the sufferings of the "systematically / starved."

> What good then the
> light winged fly, the flower or
> the river—too foul to drink of or
> even to bathe in? The 90 storey building
> beyond the ocean that a rocket
> will span for destruction in a matter
> of minutes but will not
> bring him, in a century, food or
> relief of any sort from his suffering.
>
> The world too much with us? Rot!
> the world is not half enough with us—
> *(CLP,* 109)

Beauty becomes a "fly-blown putrescence / and ourselves decay," he wrote, if all men cannot enjoy the earth's richness. Therefore such prosaic subjects as economics belong with the beautiful and the poetic in the poem. But they belong there as prose, not as poetry. In a review of Muriel Rukeyser's *US 1,* he noted that

her material, *not* her subject matter but her poetic material, is in part the notes of a congressional investigation, an x-ray report and the testimony of a physician under cross-examination. These she uses with something of the skill employed by Pound in the material of his "Cantos." She knows how to use the *language* of an x-ray report. . . . She knows, in other words, how to select and exhibit her material. She understands what words are for and how important it is not to twist them in order to make "poetry" of them.[7]

Another reason Williams gave for mixing prose and poetry in *Paterson* was that—despite their differences in quality—there was no essential dichotomy between poetic and prosaic experiences. "Life," he once remarked, ". . . isn't any more poetry than [it is] prose" *(IWW,* 64). Prose and poetry were not exclusive of one another; life was inclusive of both. The identities which existed between prose and poetry were more important than the differences.[8]

Since the poem has to include all of life, Williams reasoned

[7]"Muriel Rukeyser's 'US 1,'" *New Republic,* XCVI (March 9, 1938), 141.

[8]"All the prose . . . has primarily the purpose of giving a metrical meaning to or of emphasizing a metrical continuity between all word use. It is *not* an antipoetic device. . . . It *is* that prose and verse are both *writing.* . . .

that it had to include prose as well as poetry: ". . . verse (as in Chaucer's tales) belongs *with* prose, as the poet belongs with 'Mine host,' who says in so many words to Chaucer, 'Namoor, all that rhyming is not worth a toord.' Poetry does not *have* to be kept away from prose . . . it goes *along with* prose . . . it is the same: the poem" (*SL,* 263).

During the composition of *Paterson,* Williams had definite ideas about how prose and poetry were connected in life and how they should be connected in the poem.

In a work-note for *Paterson* he wrote of prose as being—in relation to poetry—unfinished or formally unsatisfactory language. Throughout the poem, he decided,

there are to be completely worked up parts in *each* section—as completely formal as possible: in each part well displayed.

BUT—juxtaposed to them are unfinished pieces—put in without fuss— for their very immediacy of expression—as they have been written under stress, under LACK of a satisfactory form—or for their need to be just there, the information.

Grades of verse in different sizes of type—
  14 point *the* main thesis
  12 pt[.]—the lesser verse & the prose

P. [Pound] You're [*sic*] interest is in the bloody loam but what I'm looking for is the finished product I. [Williams] When you reject the earth, you reject that which sprang from it and leaves there, also, its seed.[9]

Here the poem's resemblance to *Many Loves* is illuminating. Like that drama, *Paterson* can be considered "two races in a counterpoint / of feeling."[10] The "completely worked up" or formal parts of *Paterson* are the poem's poetry which occur in the stream-of-consciousness of Dr. Paterson, Williams' *persona.* Like Hubert, Alise, and Peter in the counter-play, he belongs to the "race" of articulate, imaginative persons who are capable of expressing themselves poetically. His poetic reveries in the poem correspond to their poetic dialogue.

Poetry does not *have* to be kept away from prose . . . it goes *along with* prose . . . without aid or excuse or need for separation or bolstering, shows itself by *itself.*" "The truth is that there's an *identity* between prose and verse, not an antithesis. It all rests on the same time base, the same measure." *SL,* pp. 263, 265. All italics are Williams'.

  [9]Yale Collection, ZA 188.

  [10]Rough draft of "Author's Prologue to a Play in Verse," Buffalo Collection, tape 26. See Chapter Five above.

On the other hand, the prose passages in *Paterson* express the being of the "race" of unpoetic, inarticulate persons who are the poet's townspeople. Like the playlets of *Many Loves*, the prose passages of *Paterson* are deliberately presented in forms that are unsatisfactory from a literary standpoint. Because they were produced under "stress, under LACK of satisfactory form" they are highly appropriate to a region like Paterson where both the population and the environment lack "articulation" or realization because of the absence of a satisfactory local culture—where everything and everyone suffer from the stresses of ignorance and poverty.

In another work-note for *Paterson,* Williams hints that prose and poetry are not confined to their finished or unfinished states. One can turn into the other or be a different form of the same thing. "Poetry," he wrote, "demands a different material than prose. It uses another facet of the same fact. . . . Facts, but just before and just after the incident which prose (journalism) would select and, by that, miss the significance poetry catches aslant."[11] In *Paterson* there are two images, water and radium, which are useful for understanding how poetry and prose can be different facets of the same facts.

Hubert uses the image of water in *Many Loves* to explain how prose can be turned into poetry by a dramatist:

> simple, simple as water flowing...
> that was ice, and made it flow, so
> that it appears an easy matter: to
> give the word a metaphorical twist by
> the position it assumes, the elevation
> it induces—without pictorial effects—
>
>   (ML, 9)

In *Paterson* this connection is implied by Williams' use of the Paterson Falls as an image of reality and language—"the roar, / the roar of the present, a speech" (III, iii, 172). In winter the waters of the Falls exist in all three of the medium's states—mist, liquid, and ice. Similarly in *Paterson* the medium of language exists in many possible forms.[12] Within a few pages in Book I, for example, the following styles occur:

[11]Buffalo Collection, tape 25. Quoted in *ND 17,* p. 305.
[12]An excellent study of the varieties of verse in *Paterson* is contained in Chapter 4 of Linda W. Wagner's *The Poems of William Carlos Williams* (Middletown, Conn., 1964).

How strange you are, you idiot!
So you think because the rose
is red that you shall have the mastery?
(I, iii, 41)

Who restricts knowledge? Some say
it is the decay of the middle class
(I, iii, 46)

Cornelius Doremus, who was baptized at Acquackonock in 1714, and died near Montville in 1803, was possessed of goods and chattels appraised at $419.58½ (I, iii, 45)

Radium is a second image in *Paterson* that helps explain the relation in the poem of prose to poetry. In Book III Williams refers to his chief prose source, Nelson's *History of Paterson,* as "the Book of Lead," and he speaks of the book's flood of prosaic facts as "leaden." On the other hand, he identifies poetry with radium at various places in the poem. The poet is identified with Madame Curie in Books III and IV. She works "with coarsened hands / by the hour, the day, the week / to get" the "LUMINOUS" stain of pitchblende (IV, ii, 209). The poet in Book III questions whether he will be able to "separate that stain / of sense from the inert mass" of his prosaic environment (III, i, 132).

"A work of art," Williams claimed, "is important only as evidence . . . of a new world which it has been created to affirm" (*SE,* 196). And art alchemically transmutes material reality into a new world in the same way that radium transmutes matter into new elements. The historical archetype of radium, for Williams, was Columbus' discovery of the New World. In Book IV of *Paterson* he equates Columbus' discovery with Madame Curie's, and he claims that the social equivalent of radium and poetry are love and "credit" which create new private and public worlds.[13]

Thus the prose in *Paterson* may be considered the "leaden" communication of the world's material. The poem's poetry, on the other hand, is the "radiant gist" in the pitchblende; it will become lead eventually, but in the interval of its decay it will make the elements of the world luminous and enrich, cure, and transmute them so they are made new.

[13]Compare this conception with Williams' equation of the poetic process with alchemy in *SE,* p. 244.

The metamorphic nature of these images for language in *Paterson* verifies the criticisms that the poem's images and symbols are "metamorphic" and "loose and protean."[14] However, there is a difference between the metamorphoses of water and those of radium.

Water, particularly at a falls, is suddenly and unpredictably variable. In the same way Williams' language in the poem often varies swiftly from prose to poetry to correspond to the sudden changes of the mind and of the environment. In this respect, *Paterson* fulfills Williams' prescription for an inclusive, living language

which will not be at least a deformation of speech as we know it—but will embody all the advantageous jumps, swiftnesses, colors, movements of the day—

—that will, at least, not exclude language as spoken—all language (present) as spoken (*SE*, 109).

The image of radium as poetry implies a metamorphic process that is less immediate and unpredictable. It encompasses all the slow, gradual factors—which Williams analyzed in "The American Background" and *In the American Grain*—which had caused American experience and American reality to decay from the intrinsic poetry of Columbus' New World, to the utilitarian prose of Hamilton's colonial Paterson, to the present, leadenly prosaic level of "the vilest swillhole in christendom" (*IAG*, 195). Yet since radium can cure even though it decays, this image also incorporates Williams' hopes for a "redeeming language," a poetry which might slowly transmute American reality so it becomes more beautiful or "poetic."[15]

When he began *Paterson* in the early 1940's Williams was determined that the poem should do more than merely include all the poetic and prosaic facts of his environment. He also believed that it should "raise" these facts to universal significance in accordance with the theory of the local that he had derived from Dewey and Keyserling: "not to talk in vague cate-

[14]See Sister Mary Bernetta Quinn, *The Metamorphic Tradition in Modern Poetry* (New York, 1966), pp. 90 ff.

[15]"We, let us say, are the Sermons of Launcelot Andrewes from which (in time) some selector will pick *one* phrase. Or say, the *Upanishad* that will contribute a single word!" *SE*, p. 285.

gories but . . . to discover the universal: in the particular (*Autobiography,* 391).

The universal can be discovered in the particular, Williams believed, because the way in which any man interacted with his particular locale is potentially analogous to the ways all men interact with their environments. "Being an artist," Williams wrote in 1939, "I can produce, if I am able, universals of general applicability. If I succeed in keeping myself objective enough, sensual enough, I can produce the factors, the concretions of materials by which others shall understand and so be led to use—that they may the better see, touch, taste, enjoy—their own world *differing as it may* from mine. By mine, they, different, can be discovered to be the same as I, and, thrown into contrast, will see the implications of a general enjoyment through me."[16] In *Paterson* he attempts to present exactly how man in Passaic County had used or "enjoyed" his world in a way that would be relevant to all men's relationships with their environment. In his "Author's Note" to the poem, he claimed that "a man in himself is a city, beginning, seeking, achieving and concluding his life in ways which the various aspects of a city may embody —if imaginatively conceived—any city . . . all that any one man may achieve in a lifetime."[17] Thus the city and the individual men of the poem represent this "one man" of the region: "Williams, anyone living in Paterson, the American, the masculine principle—a sort of Everyman."[18] The chief manifestation of this American Everyman in the poem is the person of Dr. or Mr. Paterson, the "sleeping giant" of Book I. The action of the poem occurs within his mind as a dream and interior monologue. Sometimes he is the expositor and sometimes he is a specimen of the region's male virtues and vices. He is more or less Williams himself, the author of *Paterson,* and therefore he is referred to in both the first and third persons during the poem.

Mr. Paterson's historical analogue is Sam Patch, a nineteenth-century folk-hero who jumped into the Falls. Lesser, local manifestations are the men whose actions are described in specific

[16]*SE,* pp. 197-198. See also, "The Fatal Blunder," *Quarterly Review of Literature,* II, 2 (1945), 125.

[17]According to Williams, this "idea" was his basic "metaphysical conception" of the poem. *IWW,* p. 72. Also see Chapter Two above.

[18]Robert Lowell, "Paterson II," *The Nation,* CLXVI (June 19, 1948), 692.

sections of the poem or its documentary prose passages: David
Hower, Klaus Ehrens the evangelist, Alexander Hamilton, Allen
Ginsberg, and others. There are also natural images of the male
which symbolize particular aspects of Paterson's condition: the
river and city, "a bud forever green, / tight-curled, upon the
pavement," and the "indifferent gale: male" of the Falls. Finally
there are a few outsiders, men from other regions or cultures
who are compared to Paterson, e.g., Ezra Pound and Columbus
in Book III.

All of these men are essentially the same man, Paterson, meta-
morphosed as he appears in various historic and contemporary
identities. He is the local representative of the universally
relevant, perpetually contemporary "artist" whom Williams
wrote about in "Against the Weather." The symbolic truth of
his works and his identity are "the expression of all truths,"
because of "the continual change without which no symbol remains permanent. It [the truth] must change, it must reappear
in another form, to remain permanent. It is the image of the
Phoenix" (SE, 208).

Contrasted to the universal male Paterson are the "innumerable women" Williams wrote of in Book I: "A man like a city
and a woman like a flower. . . . Innumerable women, each like
a flower." They are "Everywoman, any woman, the feminine
principle, America."[19] These women are the local, material soil
from which the male's or artist's universal activities grow—the
particular rock from which every Sam Patch–artist must leap to
realize his art. In Williams' criticism of the 1940's this feminine
principle is spoken of as the local, concrete "society" or "place"
where universally valid art had to begin. The artist, he wrote in
1946, "will continue to produce only if his attachments to society continue adequate. If a man in his fatuous dreams cuts
himself off from that supplying female, he dries up his sources
. . . heading straight for literary sterility."[20]

Like the male principle, the female in Paterson exists in a
number of identities. She first appears in the poem as a giantess,
asleep with the giant Paterson. In the course of the poem her
identity is dispersed among various women whom Paterson has

[19]Ibid., 693.
[20]"Letter to an Australian Editor," Briarcliff Quarterly, III, 11 (Oct.,
1946), 208.

known or has read about: "C" or "Cress" (Cressida); Mrs. Cumming, a minister's wife who fell into the Falls; a poetess who writes letters to Paterson; the "beautiful thing" of Book III; the young nurse in Book IV. She also exists in nature, chiefly as the park on Garrett Mountain and the rock at the base of the Falls.

> The scene's the Park
> upon the rock,
> female to the city

—upon whose body Paterson instructs his thoughts
(II, i, 57)

Finally there are a few outside women whose achievements are used to contrast the sorry condition of woman and nature in Paterson, e.g., Madam Curie and the Abbess Hildegarde in Book IV.

The catastrophic "divorce" which characterizes the relationship between the male and female principles in Paterson is intended to represent all "alienations" or "dissociations." The poem has "universal import," writes David Ignatow, because its theme is the causes of all upheaval in the world: "the failure of language, the failure of communication . . . the basic failure among men themselves in their attitude towards one another and towards life." The consequence of this failure to communicate is a separation or "divorce" of the male and female principles of life "from which springs those calamities that we now witness among men, women and nations."[21]

Williams stated his personal experience of the proper form of "marriage" or communication between the sexes in his Autobiography. "Men," he wrote, "have given the direction to my life and women have always supplied the energy."[22] From this experience Williams derived his conception of a good society or culture: a culture in which women supply emotional potency to life, and men—particularly artists and scientists—provide it with direction and purpose.

Williams' short story "A Night in June" is one of his most beautiful evocations of the best sort of marriage between a man and a woman. The faith-filled union between Williams the doc-

[21]David Ignatow, "Introduction," Williams Carlos Williams: A Memorial Chapbook, The Beloit Poetry Journal, XIV, 1 (Fall, 1963), 2.
[22]P. 55. See also ibid., xi-xii and "Faiths for a Complex World," American Scholar, XXVI (Fall, 1957), 453-457.

tor and his patient Angelina also implies the ideal union between "science and humanity" (*FD*, 141), the mind and the flesh, the cultured person and the primitive. Ironically, Williams and Angelina cannot speak the same spoken languages—she is Italian and speaks very broken English—but they possess a far more significant language of mutual emotional responsiveness. Each complements the other's limitations so perfectly that both are fulfilled. He arrives at three in the morning to deliver her ninth child, alert, concerned, and perfectly prepared: "everything [in his medical kit] was ample and in order. . . . Even the Argyrol was there, in tablet form, insuring the full potency of a fresh solution. Nothing so satisfying as a kit of any sort prepared and in order . . ." (*FD*, 138). The birth is difficult, and Williams grows tired, but his responses remain excellent. "Do you mind if I give you the needle? I asked her gently. We'd been through this many times before. She shrugged her shoulders as much as to say, It's up to you. So I gave her a few minims of pituitrin to intensify the strength of the pains. I was cautious . . ." (*FD*, 141). Then at the climax of the story it is the women, Angelina and her sister-in-law, who give Williams the strength to go on and deliver the baby successfully.

Her [the sister-in-law's] two hands grabbed me at first a little timidly about the right wrist and forearm. Go ahead, I said. Pull hard. I welcomed the feel of her hands and the strong pull. It quieted me in the way the whole house had quieted me all night.

This woman in her present condition would have seemed repulsive to me ten years ago—now, poor soul, I see her to be as clean as a cow that calves. The flesh of my arm lay against the flesh of her knee gratefully. It was I who was being comforted and soothed (*FD,* 142).

Because so much of his life and profession was dependent upon this "marriage" between the male and the female, the mental and the physical person, Williams terribly feared its breakdown. As early as the 1920's he described the grim social and psychological effects of such a "divorce" in his poem "To Elsie" and in the "Jacataqua" chapter of *In the American Grain.* In "Jacataqua," the female is spiritually barren, only a brood animal or shallow "pal" to men (*IAG*, 179). "Women—givers (but they have been, as reservoirs, empty). . . . They are our cattle, cattle of the spirit—not yet come in. None yet has raised benevolence to distinction. Not one to 'wield her beauty as a scepter' " (*IAG,* 180-181). Their sexuality lacks all joy, all

"aesthetic or emotional" affectiveness (*IAG*, 182), and therefore
like Elsie all they can do is fearfully give or withhold themselves
physically, "succumbing without / emotion / save numbed terror
/ under some hedge of choke-cherry / or viburnum—" (*CEP*, 270-
271).

Uninspired by the flesh, imaginative Americans lose all desire
for contact with the "soil" of reality. They refuse their responsibility of "husbandry," of improving their environment by giving
it purpose and direction. They become "New England eunuchs,
—'no more sex than a tapeworm' . . . Rider [Albert P. Ryder]:
no detail in his foregrounds just remote lusts, fiery but 'gone,'—
Poe: moonlight. It is the annunciation of the spiritual barrenness of the American woman" (*IAG*, 181). Consequently,
sophisticated Americans, particularly the men, treat "the earth
under our feet" as the "excrement of some sky / and we degraded prisoners / destined / to hunger until we eat filth"
(*CEP*, 271-272).

Williams believed that there is only one way out of this cycle
of squalor and estrangement. Men must devote their whole
powers to the creation of a "language," a valid culture which
will produce communication between the male and the female,
the mind and the flesh, the human and his environment. Only
through such a "language" will men be able to serve the female
"soil" of their lives and be nourished by it.[23]

Thus in *Paterson* the consequence of "divorce" is "premature
death": life without fertility or fruition, life in which fulfillment is "only / a dream or in a dream" (IV, iii, 224). Because
of separation, the failure to communicate, the male exists as "a
bud forever green, / tight-curled, upon the pavement, perfect / in
juice and substance but divorced, divorced / from its fellows, fallen low—" (I, ii, 28). And the women of the region "wilt and disappear" because "—the language / is divorced from their minds"
(I, i, 21).

The cause of separation in *Paterson* lies in the indifference of
power to life, "the indifference of certain death / or incident
upon certain death" (III, i, 129). Throughout his career Wil-

[23]Significantly, one of the only poems which Williams wrote for music and
public performance is his hymn "Rogation Sunday," *CLP*, p. 260. See also
"At Kenneth Burke's Place," *CLP*, pp. 256-257. For some other statements by
Williams of his conception of a proper culture see his *Autobiography*, pp.
332-334, 370, 374-376 and "The American Background," *SE*, pp. 134-161.

liams was concerned with power. He possessed power himself, the power to achieve a rich and full family life, deliver two thousand children, become head of pediatrics and then Chief of Staff at Passaic General Hospital, write *Paterson* and a dozen other books of poetry, three plays and a libretto, five novels, and four volumes of short stories, autobiography, letters, and essays. The reason for Williams' survival and success as a man and a poet, Kenneth Rexroth says, was that he possessed "the perfect security of that power" which underlies our civilization. "It is the illusion of power that has made so many of your contemporaries soft and silly. . . . They think they have power. Or one poor demented old man is crazy because he always wanted power and never got any. But you have never had any doubt about the nature of power—in life, in human affairs, in art."[24]

But though Williams may have never had any doubts about the presence of power, he had many doubts about its uses. In many of his works, particularly his prose, his subjects are powerful, forceful persons. Washington in *In the American Grain* is introduced as

ninety percent of the force which made of the American Revolution a successful issue. . . .

Here was a man of tremendous vitality buried in a massive frame and under a rather stolid and untractable exterior which the ladies somewhat feared, I fancy. He must have looked well to them, from a distance . . . but later it proved a little too powerful for comfort (*IAG*, 140).

Often, however, Williams portrayed his subjects as—unlike Washington—using their power in violent, amoral, destructive ways. The Norsemen and conquistadors in *In the American Grain,* Gurlie Stecher in *White Mule,* Dago Schultz in "An Old Time Raid," the Doctor in "The Use of Force"—all express their powers with brutal indifference to their own lives or the lives of others. Deeply disturbed by the poverty of the Depression and the destruction during World War II, Williams gradually formulated the idea that power should serve human life rather than its own aggrandizement. He best expressed this ethic in a 1944 letter to Robert McAlmon about Ezra Pound. Everyone, Williams wrote, is "born with a certain authority at his

[24]*Assays* (Norfolk, Conn., 1961), p. 203.

command which is innate," and some persons possess a great deal more of this authority than others do—"Something that is in the man himself, really great—and unaccountable" (*SL,* 220-221). But even though the sources of this authority may be inexplicable or "unaccountable," its uses are subject to moral judgment. "Some Negroes," Williams concluded the letter,

have that authority in the way they wear their clothes. I know a colored porter on the Erie like that. He's a better man than another just by the way he walks up the street. Some women have it. . . . What is it? Damned if I know. Even some little children have it, even infants when they are born. To me it is an immoral quality. I suppose Napolean and Alexander had it to perfection. It makes a man think he is better than anyone else. But unless he uses it for others, to make himself a servant in some sense for humanity, to man, to those about him who need him—he turns out to be a selfish bastard like Pound, like Napolean—like the Negro porter, like the infant as soon as he grows up (*SL,* 223).

This letter states in general terms the ethic which underlies *Paterson.* As Robert Lowell pointed out, the poem is about the myth of American power—a myth which is founded upon the brutal fact of American power. *Paterson,* wrote Lowell, "depends on the American myth, a myth that is seldom absent from our literature—part of our power, and part of our hubris and deformity. At its grossest the myth is propaganda, puffing and grimacing. . . . But the myth is a serious matter. It is assumed by Emerson, Whitman, and Hart Crane; by Henry Adams and Henry James. For good or for evil, America *is* something immense, crass, and Roman."[25] In *Paterson* this power is almost entirely evil, the destructive producer of an "America grown pathetic and tragic, brutalized by inequality, disorganized by industrial chaos, and faced with annihilation."[26]

The poem's universal symbol of power is the "ignorant sun" of the preface which is later described as blindly and terribly creating and destroying things, "winding the yellow bindweed about a / bush," without concern for their fulfillment (I, ii, 34). The great local symbol of power in the poem is the Passaic River and its Falls, "the great, roaring, dumb Passaic waterfalls pouring down from above the city its torrent of power without

[25]Robert Lowell, "Paterson II," 693.
[26]*Ibid.*

direction, except as dying in the sea, without purpose, without soul, which is to say without language."[27] "Sound / married to strength," the Falls in *Paterson* are the force that created the city, turns its mills, and animates its citizens. Its roar is a voice, a "language (misunderstood) pouring (misinterpreted)" which calls its citizens to its service and their destructions.

This is stated in Book I through the experiences of Sam Patch and Mrs. Cumming, the archetypal man and woman of the region.

The causes of Mrs. Cumming's death are presumably intended to represent the causes of all women's premature deaths, both physical and spiritual, in *Paterson*. A recently married minister's wife from Newark, she stood with her husband "for a considerable length of time" at the brink of the Falls, and then fell. Throughout the poem the female, the natural and the material, are drawn to the powerful and wonderful. They seek impregnation and fulfillment but receive destruction.

> All these
> and more—shining, struggling flies
> caught in the meshes of Her [the giantess'] hair, of whom
> there can be no complaint, fast in
> the invisible net—from the back country,
> half awakened—all desiring. Not one
> to escape, not one .   a fragrance
> of mown hay, facing the rapacious,
> the "great"
>
> (IV, iii, 225)

They are like the Indians of the Ponce de Leon chapter of *In the American Grain* "who ran to the shore . . . who cried, 'Heavenly Man!'" only to be murdered or enslaved. They are the women in Williams' plays who lack satisfactory marriages and turn confused to forceful but irresponsible men who betray them.

The danger to woman in *Paterson* is that she will be caught and lose herself in the "indifferent gale: male" of the Falls. The danger to the male in *Paterson* is that he is tempted to imitate the Falls, to realize his potency in the same "deaf," irresponsible way. He can exist, like Sam Patch and the Falls, as an image of "crude force."[28] Until he "makes himself new" in Books III and

---

[27]Ignatow, *William Carlos Williams,* 2.
[28]See *Pictures,* p. 171 and Chapter Eight below.

IV of the poem, the artist is the obverse of Williams' Washington, who disciplined his impulses the better to respond to the needs of his society. Instead he is "the selfish bastard like Pound, like Napolean" of Williams' letter to McAlmon. He is the artist whom Peter describes in *Many Loves*, an emotionless "machine grinding toward its end."

> There is
> something in this man—as in
> any man—not to be benefited by a marriage.
> . . . .
> . . . this man,
> as you are a woman, will remain...
> as cold as ice in his heart—toward you,
> as toward every other feeling
> thing about him, completely cold...
> . . . .
> He has
> only one ambition—to get out!
> Out from within himself, where he
> is freezing. There is only one door.
> Writing! Stop him and he'll destroy you
> —or himself, with as much indifference
> as he'd eat a potato.
> (*ML,* 101-102)

Hubert's spiritual condition is Patch's physical fate in *Paterson*. Both are indifferent and self-destructive because they are motivated only by a desperate emotional impetus that is too innocent—or ignorant—to accept limitation.[29] After his first leap into the Paterson Falls, Patch went on to become nationally famous as a daredevil jumper. After leaping into Niagara Falls and the Hudson, he was killed at the Genessee Falls on November 13, 1829. His corpse, frozen into an ice-cake, was found downstream the following spring.

Why did Patch leap? "He appeared and made a short speech. . . . A speech! What could he say," Williams wonders, "that he must leap so desperately to complete it?" (I, i, 27). The answer is found not in *Paterson,* but in one of the poem's sources. "Napolean was a great man," Patch boasted, "and a great gen-

---

[29]Though Williams despised such "ignorant" forcefulness in persons like himself and Pound, he approved of it in nature and among essentially primitive, natural persons. See *CLP,* p. 122; *FD,* p. 225; *Autobiography,* pp. 287-288; Chapter Five above.

eral. He conquered armies and he conquered nations. But he couldn't jump the Genessee Falls. Wellington was a great man and a great soldier. He conquered armies and he conquered nations, and he conquered Napolean, but he couldn't jump the Genessee Falls. That was left for me to do, and I can do it, and will!"[30] In other words, Patch desired to be great, wonderful, powerful, and potent—like the Falls. But his strength and daring were wasted just as the Falls' power is wasted. Like the Falls he had no language which would make his potency creative instead of destructive. "Speech had failed him. He was confused. The word had been drained of its meaning" (I, i, 27). Like Doc Rivers in Williams' short story, he destroyed himself because no satisfactory local culture (i.e., "language") was available for him to realize his talents constructively. Therefore, the male, like the female, is destroyed by the Falls. Both "leaped (or fell) without a / language, tongue-tied / the language worn out" (II, iii, 103).

This destruction, Williams explained, was the result "of a failure to untangle the language and make it our own as both man and woman are carried helplessly toward the sea (of blood) which, by their failure of speech, awaits them" (*ND 17*, 254). Because of his lack of language or comprehension, man in *Paterson* is divorced from the vital knowledge he needs in order to relate the forces of his world to life. "What passes for knowledge" is

> divorced from rhododendrons, from traprock.
> from the city hall and the court-house
> . . . .
> Divorce! Divorce! Knowledge is divorced
> from its source and men like laboratory animals
> with their spinal cords severed
> celebrate the new wra [*sic*]—or the new hospital[31]

Moreover, because of fear, ignorance, coldness, and indifference, men lack the potency of mind required to invent or create a language and achieve knowledge. "The city!" cried Williams,

> is a husband who has lost
> the desire of husbandry, rushes away
> away without finding

[30]Jenny Marsh Parker, *Rochester, a Story Historical* (Rochester, 1884), p. 188. Quoted in Quinn, *The Metamorphic Tradition*, p. 99.
[31]Rough draft of *Paterson* in Buffalo Collection, tape 53.

> It is the crime of husbands that have lost
> the desire of husbandry, that rush away
> and do not build, that cannot love. . . .[32]

Because they are unable to possess these forces, men will therefore remain their imitators and victims.

Paterson's universality lies in its questioning of the opportunities for redeeming power. Virtually every form of potency in the poem, both human and natural, is seen as somehow ignorant, brutal, or indifferent and therefore ultimately destructive of the self and the world. Patch's daring is suicidal; the poet Paterson's search for beauty is condemned as indifference to reality; Ezra Pound's erudition leads to madness and treason; science creates the bomb which will end everything. The poem is only too grimly relevant to a world and century in which millions of beings have been annihilated.

[32]*Ibid.*

CHAPTER | SEVEN

Despite its universal relevance, *Paterson* is rigorously local in its language and imagery. Except for a few of the letters to Mr. Paterson, everything in the poem happened or was spoken within a few miles of the Passaic River. One of the basic tenets of Williams' theory of the local is that though men's dilemmas are universal—"man has only one enemy: the weather"—the solutions they achieve have to be local to be valid (*SE*, 209). Americans, Williams wrote in 1938, "go about blind and deaf. We fight off convictions that we should welcome as water in the desert, could we possibly get ourselves into the right mind. The artist must save us. He's the only one who can. First we have to see, be taught to see. We have to be taught to see *here,* because here is everywhere, related to everywhere else."[1]

In *Paterson* Williams attempted to increase his readers' vision of their localities by presenting the local details of his environment in a deliberately fragmentary manner. As early as 1934 he dismissed the surface coherence of pictorial realism as too easy. " 'Simply physical or external realism,' " he maintained,

has an important place in America still. We know far less, racially, than we should about our localities and ourselves. But it is quite true that the photographic camera will not help us. We can though, if we are able to *see* general relationships in local setting, set them down verbatim with a view to penetration. And there is a cleanliness about this method which if it can be well handled makes a fascinating

[1]"Sermon with a Camera," *New Republic,* XCVI (Oct. 12, 1938), 282-283.

project in which every bit of subtlety and experience one is possessed of may be utilized.

Plot is like God: the less we formulate it the closer we are to the truth (*SL,* 146).

In a 1939 review of Williams' works, Vivienne Koch wrote that his poetry of the late 1930's retained the "earlier interaction with the reader as 'filler-in' of the incomplete image" but had become "more uncompromising and economical in what it supplies for this job."[2] Williams praised Koch's criticism as instinctively right about the "trend" of his development[3] and in a deleted preface to *Paterson* he referred to it as "A fragmentary sort of poem, in four parts, strung together with notes and comments for what may come of it; a design to off-set the shortsightedness and indifference of the present age—a near Paradise what with plenty staring us in the face on all sides—by defects of a different order."[4] If *Paterson* can teach the reader to see the "general relationships" in the fragmentary, local particulars of Williams' world, it will increase the "subtlety and experience" of his perception and "off-set the shortsightedness and indifference" of the age. The reader will thus be better equipped to see his own, local world, and the poem will have attained the universal relevance and significance Williams desired.

Williams achieved considerable inner coherence beneath the surface fragmentation of *Paterson* by choosing the Passaic River, the chief geographical feature of his locality, as his model for the poem's form. "I took," he said, "the river as it followed its course down to the sea; all I had to do was follow it and I had a poem. There were the poor who lived on the banks of the river, people I had written about in my stories. And there was the way I felt about life, like a river following a course."[5]

Each book of the poem represents a different season of life. Book I is "spring," II is "summer," and so forth.[6] The forms of

[2]"All the Differences," *Voices,* 96 (Winter, 1939), p. 48.
[3]Buffalo Collection, tape 25.
[4]Buffalo Collection, tape 53. Quoted by John C. Thirlwall in *ND 17,* pp. 305-306. Thirlwall's punctuation of this quote differs slightly from mine.
[5]*IWW,* p. 73. Williams'· choice of the river as the locus of the poem was also influenced by his short story "Life Along the Passaic River." In a work-note for the poem he wrote that James Laughlin had induced him to "find and to reread" the story, and that it was what Williams had been looking for. Buffalo Collection, tape 53.
[6]Buffalo Collection, tape 53. "Many years ago I was impressed with the four-sided parallelogram, in short, with the cube. Shifting at once, to save

local details in each book correspond to stages in the seasons' and river's passages. Thus the forms each detail assumes are roughly analogous to the forms taken by all life which exists within a cyclical or seasonal existence.

Paterson Book I is intended to represent the river's upstream sources. "A stream has to begin somewhere . . ." Williams wrote of this book. "The concept of the beginning of a river is of course a symbol of all beginnings" (*IWW*, 74). Since he considered Book I the equivalent of spring, this part of *Paterson* symbolizes the most potent and creative season of the year as well as the beginning of the river, the most creative, fertilizing force in the environment.

Because the river is also an image of the mind throughout *Paterson*, Book I also probably represents the mind at the beginning of the creative act, when it is least distracted by the mundane details of life and when the imagination is most potent. This is the state of the artist's mind which Williams described in *Pagany* and his poem "the Flower": "when I am fresh, in the morning, when / my mind is clear and burning—to write."[7]

At this stage of their beings, all of these creative forces—the river, the seasons, the mind—are characterized by great clarity. The river is near its sources, and its waters are clear and unpolluted. The world and its parts, both prosaic and poetic, have the wonderful newness and precision which they possess in spring. The poet is able to apprehend and communicate this new world because his mind is correspondingly fresh and clear.

According to Williams, he has just discovered his immediate locality, and his great desire is to express its reality clearly. "Only of late, late! begun to know, to / know clearly (as through clear ice) whence / I draw my breath or how to employ it / clearly—if not well" (I, ii, 31). In Book I all the major images of *Paterson*—Sam Patch, the poet Paterson, Mrs. Cumming, the divorced women, and the other "archaic persons of the drama"—are visualized with clarity and a certain monu-

time, the trinity always seemed unstable. It lacked a fourth member, the devil. I found myself always conceiving my abstract designs as possessing four sides. That was natural enough with spring, summer, autumn and winter always before me. To leave any one of them out [of *Paterson*] would have been unthinkable." *SL,* p. 333.

[7]*CEP*, p. 238; see *Pagany*, pp. 155-156.

mental simplicity. The passages of poetry in this book are fairly long, coherent, and precise in both thought and mood even though they convey a considerable variety of emotion and complexity of thought. The prose passages are equally coherent, largely because Williams quotes them in considerable length and organizes the poem so that their contents have clear relationships with the poetry.

This clarity is very similar to that which Williams found in the writings of his own family and the early explorers of America he read for *In the American Grain*. On a rough draft of *Paterson,* beneath a copy of an 1877 letter by his father, Williams wrote: "How to recover that clarity and directness, I do not know. an [*sic*] era in a few words, ended."[8] And in *In the American Grain* he praised Rasles' letters as "a river that brings sweet water . . . peculiarly sensitive and daring in its close embrace of native things. His sensitive mind . . . blossoming, thriving, opening, reviving—not shutting out—was tuned" (*IAG,* 121).

This clarity of vision, this "embrace" of American reality was natural for Rasles and Williams' father; they possessed an America almost untainted by brutality and exploitation. For the poet "Mr. Paterson" in Book I, however, this clarity is artificial. The facts of his environment exist in his mind, Williams stresses, not as reality but as a "complement exact . . . a mathematic calm, controlled" of his city's vulgar slum streets. The brutality of senseless rapes and the tawdriness of plaster saints and glass jewels all possess a "forthright beauty" within his mind. Because he ignores the human misery and economic deprivation which these images signify, Mr. Paterson is like the man Williams described in "The Mind's Games." "The world / to him is radiant and even the fact / of poverty is wholly without despair." The world is not too much with him. He does not waste his powers on "getting and spending," and there is nothing about money in his mind or this book of the poem.

Throughout Book I the poet's lack of passionate attachment to his world is stressed. Mr. Paterson's character is largely based upon the lines from Williams' 1927 poem "Paterson" that por-

[8]Yale Collection, ZA 188. Williams was also impressed by the presence of this purity in Greek and medieval art; see *Pagany,* pp. 138-140, 150 ff.

tray him as a fatuous pseudo-intellectual who must go away "to rest and write."

> Twice a month Paterson receives
> communications from the Pope and Jacques
> Barzun
> (Isocrates). His works
> have been done into French
> and Portuguese.

(I, i, 17-18)

Williams carefully omitted the lines, which were the climax of the 1927 poem, that asserted Mr. Paterson's discovery of community with his townspeople and their miserable world. "But who! who are these people? It is / his flesh making the traffic, cranking the car / buying the meat—."[9] Instead of using these lines, Williams inserted a letter at the end of Part 2 of Book I which accuses Paterson of coldness and of having made a "hoax cleavage" between his life as a man and his life as an artist.

Nevertheless, Mr. Paterson's intentions are good. In Part 2 he struggles to awake and know more of his world, and the poem becomes more specific. For example, the women "divorced" from language, who were spoken of quite abstractly in Part 1, become "Two halfgrown girls hailing hallowed Easter"; and the poet admits that their "unfledged desire, irresponsible, green" challenges *his* awakening to reality. Mr. Paterson also begins to mix poetic and prosaic experiences instead of keeping them separated but clearly connected as in Part 1. He contemplates Sam Patch and Mrs. Cumming and wonders what meaning their fates may have for him.

In Part 3 of Book I, the poet attempts to diagnose the causes of the region's poverty. He discovers plenitude everywhere. There is the aesthetic, contemplative richness of the mind whose thoughts can soar "to the magnificence of imagined delights," and there is the material richness of the land which can yield, "In time of general privation / a private herd, 20 quarts of milk / to the main house and 8 of cream, / all the fresh vegetables, sweet corn. . . ."[10] But he also discovers a blighting parsi-

[9]*CEP*, p. 234. This poem was first published in *The Dial*, LXXXII (Feb., 1927), 91-93.

[10]I, iii, 45. Similarly, Gurlie is shocked when she discovers that the Paysons give their neighbors their surplus milk. *WM*, pp. 250-251. See also *SL*, p. 259.

mony and greed which cause the inhabitants to waste their minds' and the environment's resources or cruelly withhold them from one another. The universities restrict knowledge; the "special interests / . . . perpetuate the stasis and make it / profitable" (I, iii, 46).

During Part 3 the distance between the poet and his world is decreased slightly because Mr. Paterson-Williams obliquely includes himself in the above indictment. A doctor hypocritically ignores his patients. "He was more concerned, much more concerned with detaching the label from a discarded mayonnaise jar . . . than to examine and treat the twenty and more infants taking their turn from the outer office, their mothers tormented and jabbering" (I, iii, 44). An unidentified man, perhaps the poet or doctor, refuses to impregnate a young Negro woman and "Refused / she shrank within herself. She too refused" (I, iii, 44-45).

Near the end of this part the poet confesses he is "moveless," part of the stasis of the region. He envies the men he knew who escaped and became expatriates in lands where they discovered a directness, clarity, loveliness, and authority in the world which he failed to find in his environment (I, iii, 48). Moreover, the poet fears that there is no alternative to his separation from the world around him. He believes that if he leaps into the maelstrom of its chaotic, tawdry life, he will suffer Patch's fate—or the fate of an unnamed man in a prose excerpt who was swept over the Falls and crushed in the machinery of the town water works in 1875 (I, ii, 48). He feels that he has no choice but to be, like everyone else, an escapist and drive "in his new car out to the suburbs, out / by the rhubarb farm—a simple thought— / where the convent of the Little Sisters of / St. Ann pretends a mystery" (I, iii, 50). He pleads that he must be repelled or alienated by the sordidness of his environment and the brutality of its people.

> What can he think else—along
> the gravel of the ravished park, torn by
> the wild workers' children tearing up the grass,
> kicking, screaming?
>
> (I, iii, 49)

Obsessed by these thoughts, the poet ends Book I with an image of ominous foreboding. Repelled by the "torrent" of life, the mind may withdraw entirely from reality; and, because men will then lose all communication with their world, the earth itself will be a meaningless mystery, a "chatterer."

> Thought clambers up,
> snail like, upon the wet rocks
> hidden from sun and sight—
>   hedged in by the pouring torrent—
> and has its birth and death there
> in that moist chamber, shut from
> the world—and unknown to the world,
> cloaks itself in mystery—
>
> . . . .
>
> And standing, shrouded there, in that din,
> Earth, the chatterer, father of all
> speech   .   .   .   .   .[11]

Paterson Book II represents summer. The period of beginnings is over; the state of being, of fruition, has begun. According to the "Author's Note" the time of the poem has similarly advanced from "the elemental character of the place" to the "modern replicas" of the immediate present.

The action of this book describes the poet's journey out of the clear aesthetic world of the beginning of the creative state and into the real material world where he must accomplish the poet's task he defined in Book I—the invention of a language for his locality. He has left the unspecified place where he read of and contemplated Patch and Mrs. Cumming. Now he visits Garrett Mountain Park in the center of Paterson on a late spring Sunday afternoon: the contemporary world of his townspeople where "the picnickers laugh on the rocks celebrating / the varied Sunday of their loves."

Appropriately, but self-consciously, the poet begins to think in terms of "risks and costs." He optimistically assumes, as he climbs the mountain, that he will be able to find beauty in this grossly materialistic world and be able to possess it aesthetically.

"Arrived breathless, after a hard climb he, / looks back (beautiful but expensive!) to / the pearl-grey towers! Returns / and starts, possessive, through the trees" (II, i, 58).

This ascent is Paterson's test of potency. He has come into "the rock, / female to the city / —upon whose body" he "instructs his thoughts." The key word in his mind is "invent."

---

[11]I, iii, 51-52. See "The Clouds," *CLP*, pp. 126-127.

> Without invention nothing is well spaced,
> unless the mind change, unless
> the stars are new measured, according
> to their relative positions, the
> line will not change, the necessity
> will not matriculate: unless there is
> a new mind there cannot be a new
> line, the old will go on
> repeating itself with recurring
> deadliness. . . .
>
> (II, i, 65)

Here Williams seems to use "invent" in all three of its meanings: the modern word meaning to construct newly, the archaic usage meaning to discover, and the Latin root *inventus* which means to "come upon" or "come into," i.e., impregnate.[12] Presumably Mr. Paterson, like Wordsworth upon Mount Snowdon or Hart Crane on Brooklyn Bridge, seeks to achieve the great, romantic "over view" of reality which will express his sense of loving unity with his world.

According to Williams' poetics, this invention was an absolute necessity for society. In 1947 he wrote that "until your artists have conceived you in your unique and supreme form you can never conceive yourselves, *and have not, in fact, existed.*"[13] "No world," he claimed in a 1946 review, "can exist for more than the consuming of a match or the eating of an apple without a poet to breathe into it an immortality."[14] However, as Mr. Paterson ascends Garrett Mountain, Williams portrays him as unqualified to achieve such an act of conception. As Book II proceeds, Williams dissects Paterson's impotence with the same pathological precision that he observed in the Viennese clinics and praised in Joyce's work.[15]

The chief causes of Paterson's failure are anger and fear

[12]A somewhat similar use of the term "invent" by an American artist occurs in Henry James's story "The Madonna of the Future": "Nothing is so idle as to talk about our want of a nursing air, of a kindly soil, of opportunity, of inspiration, of the things that help. The only thing that helps is to do something fine. There's no law in our glorious Constitution against that. Invent, create, achieve. . . . What else are you an artist for?" Williams quoted the phrase "Invent, create, achieve" in "Preface," *Quarterly Review of Literature*, II, 4 (1946), 346.

[13]"An Approach to the Poem," *English Institute Essays, 1947* (New York, 1948), p. 60.

[14]"Preface," 348.

[15]*Pagany*, pp. 205-210; *SE*, p. 78.

caused by disappointment. Paterson arrives at the park expecting to find beauty but does not. "These women are not / beautiful and reflect / no beauty but gross," he broods. Only the distant view, the sight of a budding tree, and a dog being groomed by its master satisfy him. Williams uses lines from "The Wanderer" to show Paterson's disgust at the animal vitality of his townspeople: ". . . the ugly legs of the young girls, / pistons too powerful for delicacy!   . / the men's arms, red, used to heat and cold, / to toss quartered beeves and. . . ."[16] But Paterson has no "old queen" to immerse him in the vulgar vitality of the world of the "filthy Passaic"; he is more like Cortez, De Soto, and Poe in *In the American Grain,* whose searches for beauty in the New World ended in destruction.

Paterson is disappointed by more than his failure to find beauty. He also suffers the disappointment of seeing the images, the "beginning words," which he imagined in Book I subtly diminished in significance and dignity in the real world of the park. They, like the summer river, have lost their "spring" freshness, purity, and power. In particular, the colossal images of the sleeping giant and giantess which were delineated in Book I are reduced to a pair of drunken, vulgar lovers who, asleep in the park, enact a parody of coition.

> She stirs, distraught,
> against him—wounded (drunk), moves
> against him (a lump) desiring,
> against him, bored   .
>
> flagrantly bored and sleeping, a
> beer bottle still grasped spear-like
> in his hand   .

(II, i, 75)

Similarly the daring performance of Patch's leap into the Falls is reduced to an evangelist's claim, in a sermon at the park, that he has dared give up his money to follow the Lord. Or, the almost monumental despoilations of the wilderness in Book I are reduced in Book II to an 1878 account of how two policemen chase a wild mink (I, i, 65).

[16]II, i, 58. Williams' quotation of these lines *(CEP,* p. 7) is significant because "The Wanderer" was his first "realistic" poem. They reflect his own early attitude toward the lower classes when, as he phrased it, "the aesthetic shock occasioned by the rise of the masses upon the artist receives top notice." *SL,* p. 259. See Chapter One above.

The consequence of disappointment, as Williams had written in *In the American Grain,* was anger: "the evil of the whole world; it was the perennial disappointment which follows, like smoke, the bursting of ideas. It was the spirit of malice which underlies men's lives and against which nothing offers resistance" (*IAG,* 27). Book II is filled with accounts of violence and parsimony of a particular sort: a panicky destructiveness caused by fear that some "order" will be violated by a new force. In 1880 on the same Garrett Mountain, a man named Dalzell murdered a member of a singing society on its way to the park. "Dalzell claimed that the visitors had in previous years walked over his garden and was determined that this year he would stop them from crossing any part of his grounds" (II, i, 60). An unsigned letter recounts the impregnation of a bitch named Musty who was entrusted to the letter-writer's care. *"Every few seconds I would run to the end of the line or peek under the sheets to see if Musty was alright. She was until I looked a minute too late. I took sticks and stones after the dog but he wouldn't beat it. . . . You won't think so highly of me now and feel like protecting me. Instead I'll bet you could kill..."* (II, i, 69-70). Finally, Hamilton devised America's elaborate system of banking ("usury" to Williams and Pound) to keep its population from possessing their country and ruining his plans. "Hamilton saw more clearly than anyone else with what urgency the new government must assume authority over the States if it was to survive. He never trusted the people, 'a great beast,' as he saw them . . ." (II, ii, 84).

The poet Paterson's disappointment and fear of his world take an extremely subtle form in Book II. He denies the potentiality of his environment and instead discovers only images of decay. In effect, Williams accuses his protagonist of abusing contemporary reality in the same way that he believed Eliot and Pound did: by using the past "to howl down the present."[17] Throughout Book II the poet sees the men and women of his environment not so much as themselves but as parodies of some other, better expression of human nature. For example, he sees some people enjoying a traditional peasant picnic. One old woman is dancing, but instead of being impressed by her spirit, Paterson uses her to emphasize the lack of true, pagan exuber-

[17]"In Praise of Marriage," *Quarterly Review of Literature,* II, 2 (1945), 148. See also *SE,* pp. 210 ff.

ance by the other picnickers: "The rest are eating and drink-
ing. / The big guy / in the black hat is too full to move" (II, i,
73). He then coldly compares the picnickers with a Mexican
peon in an Eisenstein film and the satyrs of classical mythology.
Paterson even more ruthlessly rejects an evangelist, Klaus
Ehrens, and his pathetic "congregation" by depicting their poverty, discomfort, and mechanical enthusiasm, and by contrasting
Ehrens with St. Francis and "The gentle Christ / child of
Pericles / and femina practa" (II, ii, 89).

The poet Paterson's fastidious disgust and erudite contempt
for his townspeople makes true, poetic communication with
them impossible for him. He cannot comprehend the "roar" of
the life being lived around him. Like Patch, Mrs. Cumming,
and the Falls, the life of his environment crashes upon his deaf,
"stone ear" and is lost:

> beside the water he looks down, listens!
> But discovers, still, no syllable in the confused
> uproar: missing the sense (though he tries)
> untaught but listening, shakes with the intensity
> of his listening   .
>   (II, iii, 100)

This failure to communicate with his material causes the poet to
become impotent, unable to impregnate his "female" world
with meaning or significance or form. He cannot

> .   .   accomplish the inevitable
> poor, the invisible, thrashing, breeding
> .   debased city
>   (II, iii, 99)

so that it may escape its debased condition. "Though he sweat
for all his worth / no poet has come."

He becomes angry, "chilled," and so confused that "he all but
falls," like Mrs. Cumming. He nearly loses consciousness and
turns into the unconscious nature around him—unable to comprehend, invent, or even think clearly. "From his eyes sparrows
start and / sing. His ears are toadstools, his fingers have / begun
to sprout leaves (his voice is drowned / under the falls)   ." (II,
iii, 102). He is now among those "divorced from knowledge and
learning" and therefore unable to save or realize themselves.

> Invent (if you can) discover or
> nothing is clear—will surmount
> the drumming in your head. There will be
> nothing clear, nothing clear   .
>   (II, iii, 103)

He flees ignominiously, complaining that "the language is worn out," and "pursued by the roar" of life which he cannot comprehend. He knows, intellectually, that what he confronts "is the new, uninterpreted, that / remoulds the old, pouring down" (II, iii, 101); however, like the conquistadors in *In the American Grain* he can only be deafened and violently confused by the "recreative New."

The breakdown of the poet's communication with his world is a disaster for others than himself. This is revealed in excruciating detail by a series of letters from a poetess who signs herself "C." and claims that Paterson betrayed her. C. is apparently some kind of "new Woman"; in her letters she alludes to her pioneer efforts to live and write in a way that will enable the American woman to have a new position in society and "sail free in her own element." But to achieve this, she badly needed considerable love and financial aid. Living, she informs "Dr. P," "requires the cooperation and the understanding and the humanity of others in order to bring out what is best and most real in one's self" (II, iii, 106-107).

Because of the power of Paterson's sensitivity and his skill as a poet, she turned to him for the emotional and material aid she desperately needed in order to fulfill herself. He, however, was deaf to her, ignored her real needs, and sent her a small money order and offered to introduce her to his literary friends. When C. persisted in her covert pleas for help and love, Paterson refused to answer her letters, then sent a note asking her not to communicate with him further. She could not comprehend his indifference to her. "How were you," she demands, "a man of letters, to have realized it when the imagination, so quick to assert itself most powerfully in the creation of a piece of literature, seems to have no power at all in enabling writers in your circumstances to fully understand the maladjustment and impotencies of a woman in my position?" (II, iii, 108). As a result of Paterson's failure to understand and help her, C. is emotionally sterilized. She is far lonelier and poorer than she was before she met him. She cannot even afford to rent a typewriter, and as for her emotional condition—"I have been feeling . . . that I shall never again be able to recapture any sense of my own personal identity (without which I cannot write, of course—but

in itself far more important than the writing) until I can recapture some faith in the reality of my own thoughts and ideas
and problems which were turned into dry sand by your attitude
. . ." (II, ii, 94).

Paterson II is the most complex expression of a conflict which
exists throughout Williams' writing—particularly in *In the
American Grain, White Mule,* and his Objectivist poems of the
1930's. It is the conflict between two kinds of mind which he
described in a 1951 letter about the poetry of Eli Siegel. The
immediate effect of "everything truly new," Williams wrote, was
one of complete surprise because it was "powerful evidence of a
new track," the product of a mind "different . . . from ours,"
that was "following different incentives." A person can react to
the shock of this new identity, Williams went on, with either
fear or pleasure: "The evidence [of the newness] is technical but
it comes out at the non-technical level as either great pleasure to
the beholder, a deeper taking of the breath, a feeling of cleanliness, which is the sign of the truly new . . . [or as] the extreme
resentment that a fixed, sclerotic mind feels confronting this
new [being]."[18]

Williams presents this conflict as an external, historical drama
in *In the American Grain.* He contrasts the baby Flossie's open-
ness to the world to her parents' resentment of America in
White Mule, and in his Objectivist poems he portrays how these
two kinds of mind may suddenly and inexplicably succeed one
another in the same consciousness. But in *Paterson* Williams
completely internalizes the conflict to show how a man may
"invent" himself (II, i, 65), make himself new to escape being
the Puritanical "scurvy mind" he describes in his poem "The
Observer":

> unable or unwilling
> to own the common
> things which we must
> do to live again
> and be in love and
> all its quickening
> pleasures prove—
> *(CLP,* 20)

[18]"A Letter by William Carlos Williams" used as an introduction to Eli
Siegel's *Hot Afternoons Have Been in Montana* (New York, 1957), pp. xvi-
xvii.

In *Paterson III* and *IV* Williams presents the destructive consequences of his indifference to the "common / things" of life; for
"Not until I have made of it a replica / will my sins be forgiven
and my / disease cured . . ." (III, iii, 172). But at the same
time he also presents the process by which the mind creates itself
anew. Creation and destruction are inextricably mixed as they
are in so many of Williams' poems of the late 1930's and the
1940's—"Catastrophic Birth," "Burning the Christmas Greens,"
"To All Gentleness." The process is the rebirth-through-death
cycle which fascinated Williams as early as "The Wanderer"
when he described himself as reborn through immersion in the
Passaic. It is the "Descent" which he described in *Paterson* Book
II and *In the American Grain*. "However hopeless it may seem,
we have no other choice: we must go back to the beginning; it
must all be done over; everything that is must be destroyed"
(*IAG*, 215). It is the "make new" process which Williams himself experienced during his composition of *Paterson*. "Just yesterday," he wrote to Horace Gregory in 1945, "I learned one of
the causes of my inability to proceed: I MUST BEGIN COM-
POSING again. I thought [that] all I had to do was to arrange
the material but that's ridiculous. Much that I have collected is
antique now. The old approach is outdated, and I shall have to
work like a fiend to make myself new again. But there is no
escape. Either I remake myself or I am done" (*SL*, 234-235).

But even though regeneration has begun, the sense of death,
or powerlessness and impotence, is no less real in Books III and
IV. It is late summer, and the power of the Falls will soon be
ended. The waters of the river whirl and eddy "below the cata-
ract / soon to be dry." The indifference, ignorance, and brutality of the previous Books culminate in the barren harvest of

> .   .   .   a world of corrupt cities,
> nothing else, that death stares in the eye,
> lacking love: no palaces, no secluded gardens,
> no water among the stones; the stone rails
> of the balustrades, scooped out, running with
> clear water, no peace   .
>
>   The waters
> are dry. It is summer, it is   .   ended[19]

[19]III, i, 130. Cf. T. S. Eliot's "Unreal City" image of sterility in *The Waste Land*, II, 372-377.

The poet's mind is similarly sterile; his "brain is weak. It fails mastery."

The poet has lost the poetic purity and power which were the bases of his creation of Books I and II; but, according to the poem's headnote, Paterson is still capable of devising "*a plan for action to supplant a plan for action.*" Since he cannot create or invent through composition, he will do it by destruction.

In Book III the poet sets out to "fall," to descend from the erudition and fastidiousness that made him impotent in Book II. The action of the book takes place in his mind as he reads in a library. As he reads, Paterson deliberately destroys his own erudition by contemplating prose passages and personal memories which drain all *meaning* from the images or "words" which he discovered in Book I and saw diminished in Book II. The wilderness is destroyed: "The last wolf was killed near the Weisse Huis in the year 1723" (III, i, 119), and Indians are sadistically tortured to death by Kieft, an early Dutch governor, and his soldiers. Patch is more subtly destroyed. His "art" and daring are degraded, until they can no longer be taken seriously, by the antics of tightrope walkers over the Passaic Falls. One named Leslie "did the Washerwoman's Frolic, in female attire, staggering drunkenly across the chasm, going backward, hopping on one foot and at the rope's center lay down on his side. He retired after that having 'busted' his tights— . . ." (III, i, 127).

The poet's own pretensions to being the culture-hero and "conceiver" of his society are similarly destroyed by one of his own townspeople's reaction to his work: "Geeze, Doc, I guess it's all right / but what the hell does it mean?" (III, ii, 138). Even the poem's major theme, the concept of the sterile marriage, is debased by being drained of dignity and significance. A grimy, fiftyish man with a Volunteers of America cap asks a doctor: "I got / a woman outside I want to marry, will / you give her a blood test?" (III, i, 126).

Reality assails him, as it did in Book II, with degradations of the vision which he proclaimed in Book I. But now Paterson accepts this destructive process; he even improves upon it. He portrays himself in Book III, Part 2, as a heroic, self-destroying seeker of the truth—only to destroy this new pretension with puns and ridicule:

> The night was made day by the flames, flames
> on which he fed—grubbing the page
>   (the burning page)
> like a worm—for enlightenment
>   (III, ii, 141)

He describes how "An old bottle, mauled by the fire / gets a new glaze, the glass warped / to a new distinction," and then he quickly destroys any temptation to identify with the bottle and share its "distinction." "Hell's fire. Fire. Sit your horny ass / down. What's your game? Beat you / at your own game, Fire. Outlast you: / Poet Beats Fire at Its Own Game!" (III, ii, 142-143).

As Book III continues, the poet does more than destroy his own "words." By reading a "leaden flood" of "rubbish" he drives himself to revolt against the entire principle of books, the entire humanistic tradition of relating the living to the past. By forcing himself to read meaningless, dead books, Paterson's mind is driven to reveries about their antithesis: the "Beautiful Thing," the young woman he worships at the end of Part 2 of Book III. She lives in the squalor of the totally immediate, illiterate present. He sees her "drunk and bedraggled" as she and her companions "slum away the bars," sick in bed "under the mud plashed windows among the scabrous / dirt of the holy sheets," and at a brawl and party at which

> . . . the guys from Paterson
>   beat up
> the guys from Newark and told
> them to stay the hell out
> of their territory . . .
> . . . .
> Then back to the party!
>   and they maled
> and femaled you jealously
>   Beautiful Thing
>   (III, ii, 153)

Paterson's reveries about the Beautiful Thing cause him to decry "all books / that enfeeble the mind's intent." Her "vulgarity of beauty surpasses" all the books' "perfections" (III, ii, 145). He rejects the entire library as worthless because it contains nothing of her and, in his mind, consigns it to flames of destruction like those that destroyed Paterson in 1902. Thus, when Paterson rejects his erudition, the "library is muffled and dead" and the reign of the dead over the living is ended (III, ii, 140).

Now he is able to appreciate the drunken, totally immediate lives of the Beautiful Thing and persons like her. Her epithet is taken from the climax of Columbus' journal, as Williams presented it in *In the American Grain* and quoted it in *Paterson IV.* For she does reveal a New World to Paterson: the world around him which is beautiful and vital even though it is without precedent. He describes the Beautiful Thing's adventures and quotes from a young Negress' letter without eruditely "explaining" them as he explained his townspeople in Book II. Instead he appreciates and savors their freedom and generosity—much as Rasles appreciated the Indians in *In the American Grain.* Paterson's cold indifference has melted, and, for the first time in the poem, he is capable of silent, tender devotion: "I can't be half gentle enough, / half tender enough / toward you, toward you, / inarticulate, not half loving enough" (III, ii, 154).

Destruction by fire in Parts 1 and 2 of *Paterson III* is followed by destruction by flood in Part 3. Having "destroyed" the cold, erudite indifference which enfeebled him, Paterson next attacks his fastidiousness. Deliberately he "floods" himself with the most inane details of life in his historic and immediate environment: a dreary account of colonial witchcraft and a long, embarrassing quarrel over a dog who was killed by the police. He immerses himself in the trivial, much as the Wanderer was immersed in the filthy Passaic. "The stream / grows leaden within him, his lilies drag. So / be it. Texts mount and complicate them- / selves, lead to further texts and those / to synopses, digests and emendations. So be it."[20]

In the park the poet was confused and feared the anarchy of the life around him, the absence of coherent relations between its parts. As Book III nears its climax he allows this leaden flood of unrelated and therefore meaningless facts to fill his mind. Clarity and purity are lost, and the poem and his mind become confused and incoherent. Fragmentary patches of prose and po-

---

[20]III, ii, 156. These lines may refer to the stage in Williams' development when he believed that sheer "reading" could overcome the deficiencies in American culture. *IAG,* p. 109.

etry interrupt one another, but a rush of images and anecdotes depicting all types of violence in society and nature creates an immense tension which is broken by the appearance of Williams' poetic representation of the Falls: pages 164, 165, and 166 of *Paterson III*, each of which is a "torrent" of crude facts.

Because it is still summer, the Falls, the natural torrent of indifferent power, are still reduced to a rivulet. But they are re-created within Paterson's mind. The first torrent, page 164, is the torrent of the irresponsible imagination: a surrealistic downpour of incoherent phrases. The second torrent is of irresponsible erudition, a semi-coherent letter from Ezra Pound at St. Elizabeth's Hospital. The third torrent, page 166, represents totally local, ignorant materialism in the form of a "tabular account" of rock specimens found during the drilling of a well at the Paterson Falls. All of these torrents are powerful but essentially sterile, because they are "divorced" from one another.

Yet each torrential page contains a "seed." The surrealistic nonsense on page 164 has many hints that the deadly routine of "natural" time can be amended to a process more favorable to life, through the playful operation of the imagination. "All manner of particularizations" can "stay the pocky moon," i.e., slow nature's decay. Pound's garbled reading list on page 165 suggests that erudition can be controlled so that it usefully serves the present, rather than ignores it: "don't / go rushin to *read* a book / just cause it is mentioned eng / passang." Finally, the "tabular account" of the geological specimens concludes that "The fact that the rock salt of England, and of some of the other salt mines of Europe, is found in rocks of the same age as this, raises the question whether it may not also be found here." In other words, if one reached the "bed rock" of material American reality by drilling deeply enough, he may reach a universally significant reality.

These seeds have only fallen. Another season is needed for their gestation before they can re-create life. A winter of "death" must come before spring. Williams shows this negatively in Book III by bitterly arguing that the "fall" is not a magical rejuvenation of life or the poem. He points out that the mud left after a flood is not fertile but "a sort of muck, a detritus, / . . . a pustular scum, a decay, a choking / lifelessness." Its "stench—fouls the mind," and rocks covered by it can be used for decoration only if "scoured three times." He also ridicules T. S. Eliot and women who believe that death leads immediately to new life for what has been destroyed.

> Who is it spoke of April? Some
> insane engineer. There is no recurrence.
> The past is dead. Women are
> legalists, they want to rescue
> a framework of laws, a skeleton of
> practices. . . .
>
> (III, iii, 169)

Book IV is winter, the dead season. The Passaic River is totally polluted and loses itself in Newark Bay. Human life, both male and female, is lost in the "perverse confusions" engendered by the abuses of power described in the previous Books. "I was getting up closer to the city," Williams said of *Paterson IV*, ". . . the Passaic enters into Newark Bay. If you are going to write realistically of the conception of the filth in the world, it can't be pretty. What goes on with people isn't pretty. With the approach to the city, international character began to enter the innocent river and pervert it; sexual perversions, such things that every metropolis . . . houses. Certain human elements can't take the gaff, have to become perverts to satisfy certain longings" (*IWW*, 79). The "words" of the poem are not merely diminished or destroyed as they were in *Paterson II* and *III*. In Book IV they are perverted like the river. The most prominent "poet" of the Book is an old Lesbian who tries to seduce a young nurse with a "Pastoral" cribbed from Eliot and Yeats. The male daring of Patch and Paterson is reduced to the futile adulteries of a suburban Prufrock:

> Oh Paterson!   Oh married man!
> He is the city of cheap hotels and private
> entrances   .   of taxis at the door, the car
> standing in the rain hour after hour by
> the roadhouse entrance   .[21]

Even as sorry a figure as the evangelist of Book II is, Williams shows, capable of perversion.

> And Billy Sunday evangel
> and ex-rightfielder sets himself
> to take one off the wall   .

[21]IV, i, 183. See the famous opening lines of Eliot's "The Love Song of J. Alfred Prufrock," and also *The Waste Land*, II, 131-138; III, 215-217.

. . . .
  . to "break" the strike
and put those S.O.Bs in their places, be
Geezus, by calling them to God!
                   (III, ii, 203)

Yet even as these images decay through their living deaths, new images of the forces they represented are in the process of being reborn. There is, Williams wrote in 1939, "the salutary mutation in the expression of all truths, the continual change without which no symbol remains permanent. It must change, it must reappear in another form, to remain permanent. It is the image of the Phoenix. To stop the flames that destroy the old nest prevents the rebirth of the bird itself. All things rot and stink, nothing stinks more than an old nest, if not recreated" (*SE*, 208). In a work-note Williams called Book IV ". . . Winter [,] the conserver of life, solver—forgetfulness—conserver and progenitor."[22] The image which best recapitulates the Book's meaning and structure is that of seeds afloat in the cold, confused currents of the "sea of blood."

float wrack, float words, snaring the
seeds   .
. . . .
—though seeds float in with the scum
and wrack   .   among brown fronds
and limp starfish   .
              (IV, iii, 234-235)

In Part 1 of this Book the seed which saves itself, or at least stays afloat, is the young nurse. She is the "young female phase" of Paterson from a "primitive, provincial environment" (*SL*, 305). Her strength and virginity attract the weak and corrupt Paterson and the Lesbian who attempt to seduce her by offering warped, debased substitutes for marriage. One of the dominant images of her experience is an obscene feeding of the old upon the young. Paterson "took her nipples / gently in his lips." The Lesbian's "pastoral" features a Hindu princess, about the nurse's age, who committed suicide in the East River, where the gulls now feed upon her corpse.

The nurse coldly endures Paterson's and the Lesbian's advances, and then repels both of them. Unlike the young women

---

[22]Yale Collection, ZA 188. See also note 6 above.

in the earlier Books, she is not completely divorced from knowledge. Her knowledge, like the vocabulary which embodies it, is crude but effective. "Be careful . / I've got an awful cold," she warns Paterson when he grows too persistent. And when the Lesbian asks her if she likes almonds, the nurse replies, "Nope. I hate all kinds of / nuts. They get in your hair . your / teeth I mean ." Unlike Mrs. Cumming, C., and even the Beautiful Thing, she is not lost or corrupted in the life around her; she preserves her virginity and waits for marriage.

The young nurse seems to represent the renewal, in a new form, of conservative, traditionally feminine values: the preservation of integrity (virginity) amidst temptation. In Part 2 of *Paterson IV* Williams' emphasis is upon the seeds of new forms for such traditionally male virtues as discovery and invention: achievement despite adversity. A new poet from Paterson, Allen Ginsberg, writes a letter in which he says that though he will not slavishly imitate Paterson he will carry on Paterson's example of localism and give it new meaning. "This place is as I say my natural habitat by memory, and I am not following in your traces to be poetic: though I know you will be pleased to realize that at least one actual citizen of your community has inherited your experience in his struggle to love and know his own world-city, through your work, which is an accomplishment you almost cannot have hoped to achieve" (IV, ii, 205). Ginsberg's significance for Williams is not fully apparent in *Paterson*. In his introduction for *Howl* Williams emphasized that Ginsberg had managed to survive in the sordidness of the modern world without becoming cold or indifferent.

I never thought he'd live to grow up and write a book of poems. His ability to survive, travel, and go on writing astonishes me. That he has gone on developing and perfecting his art is no less amazing to me.

The wonder of the thing is not that he has survived but that he, from the very depths, has found a fellow whom he can love. . . . Say what you will, he proves to us, in spite of the most debasing experiences that life can offer a man, the spirit of love survives to ennoble our lives if we have the wit and the courage and the faith—and the art! to persist.[23]

In this respect Williams must have considered Ginsberg an im-

[23]Introduction to Allen Ginsberg's *Howl and Other Poems* (San Francisco, 1956). See also Williams' comments on the French poet René Char in *SL*, pp. 321-322.

provement over the artists of earlier generations, symbolized by Paterson in Book II, whom Williams considered cold, indifferent, and evasive toward a world which harmed them. All literature, Williams claimed in 1949, *"is* escape—from the herd. . . . Hemingway assumes a cloak of vulgarity, let us say, to protect a Jamesian sensitivity to detail. Just when you think you have a good man, he's not there. . . . Is not Shakespeare . . . really the escaped man? He is a man who from indifference has escaped to the sun itself by the gift of words alone" (*SL,* 273).

As a complement to Ginsberg in Part 2 of *Paterson IV,* there is Madam Curie. Unlike C. in Book II, Madam Curie is the real "new woman." She is divorced from neither the male nor knowledge. Impregnated by both, "—with ponderous belly, full / of thought," she discovers radium (IV, ii, 208). Her presence in the poem indicates that invention and discovery will no longer be purely male prerogatives; and men like Curie and St. Joseph may "buttress" the woman so she may create more than infants. Moreover, the manner of her discovery implies that invention will become more "female," more a creation of patience and work, and less a matter of "male" daring like Patch's or Paterson's leaps.[24]

Finally Part 2 ends with a description of a social-credit economy that would reward all creative work, no matter how obscure the worker, or how new his work. Everyone will be given "credit" for his achievements. "Credit" will cure the cancer of usury which feeds on and destroys economic life. Therefore, no power will be wasted as the Falls were. "Credit makes solid / is related directly to the effort, / work: value created and received, / 'the radiant gist' against all that / scants our lives" (IV, iii, 218).

Parts 1 and 2 of *Paterson IV* are concerned with the recreation of the male and female forces of creation. Part 3 seems to be about the renewal of the poet himself. The nature of the death that threatens him in the "sea of blood" is particularly invidious.

Love, the creative act, has itself changed. It is no longer the "leap" Patch performed, the creative act described in *Many*

---

[24]For Williams' theory of the differences between male and female creativity, see his "Men...Have No Tenderness," *New Directions* 7 (Norfolk, Conn., 1942), pp. 429-436. Also see Chapter Eight below.

Loves as "That anguish, / that insistence, that mad fatalistic / plunge! The arrow . . . insistent, / unrelenting, an arrow / that seeks its mark through all / obstructions" (*ML*, 88-89). Instead the good, creative act is represented by Madam Curie stirring pitchblende in cauldrons.

> . . . with coarsened hands
> by the hour, the day, the week
> to get, after months of labor   .
>
> a stain at the bottom of the retort
> without weight, a failure, a
> nothing. And then, returning in the
> night, to find it   .
>   LUMINOUS!
>   (IV, ii, 209)

Virtue, the poet realizes, is no longer a "mad fatalistic plunge"; it is "achieved slowly," "takes connivance, / takes convoluted forms, takes / time!" (IV, iii, 221).

But this creative process, like the previous one, has a danger. What shall the artist do while he waits?

>   not half asleep
> waiting for the sun to part the labia
> of shabby clouds . but a man (or
> a woman) achieved
>
>   flagrant!
> adept at thought, playing the words
> following a table which is the synthesis
> of thought, a symbol that is to him,
> sun up!
>   (IV, iii, 210)

In Book IV Paterson is exhausted: "The brain is weak. It fails mastery, / never a fact." "Weakness, / weakness dogs him, fulfillment only / a dream or in a dream" (IV, iii, 223, 224). He is tempted to wait comfortably in the poem rather than in the world, to remain asleep amid his symbols of power (the sun) rather than in the world while he waits for a spring of new power and creation. The fact that *Paterson* is a long poem makes this temptation entirely natural for its poet. Wordsworth spent some fifty years revising *The Prelude;* Pound has spent nearly that long on the *Cantos.*

In Part 3 Paterson languidly examines previous images, quotes more documentary prose, and has reveries about women he has known. He begins to write long, placid lines about the bucolic amenities of early nineteenth-century Paterson. "At the top was Fyfield's tavern—watching / the birds flutter and bathe in the little / pools in the rocks formed by the falling / mist—of the Falls . . ." (IV, iii, 232). This thought of the Falls suddenly reminds him this nostalgic use of the poem as a womb is merely another version of the indifference and ignorance toward the world which breeds death. Hastily, he thinks of a murder in 1850 by a man named Johnson which was particularly brutal, senseless, and ignorant. He recognizes that the womb-sea of blood is a sea of violent, random impulses as well as nostalgic bliss, and he struggles to "Waken from a dream, this dream of / the whole poem . sea-bound, / rises, a sea of blood" (IV, iii, 234). He cries out, "the sea is not our home," and struggles like Odysseus to resist its siren attraction, the attraction of unearthly beauty and peace: "immaculata: our home, our nostalgic / mother in whom the dead, enwombed again / cry out to us to return . " (IV, iii, 236).

The poem ends with a deliberately plain account of a man who has waded ashore after a long swim, slept, dressed, and "then headed inland." It is the action of Odysseus and also of Poe, of whom Williams wrote: "His greatness is in that he turned his back and faced inland, to originality, with the identical gesture of a Boone" (*IAG*, 226). It is the artist returning once again to the earth, where he must continue to work and create. "In the end," Williams wrote of *Paterson*, "the man rises from the sea where the river appears to have lost its identity . . . turns inland toward Camden where Walt Whitman, much traduced, lived the latter years of his life and died. He always said that his poems, which had broken the dominance of the iambic pentameter in English prosody, had only begun his theme. I agree. It is up to us, in the new dialect, to continue it by a new construction upon the syllables" (*Autobiography*, 392). This is, of course, Williams himself beginning the "new measure" which he discovered in *Paterson* and developed in his poetry of the 1950's.

However, this beginning is accompanied by an entirely necessary ending. The lines immediately below the one which states that Paterson "headed inland" are a prose account of the execution of the murderer Johnson. It is finally the end of "that / tied man, that cold blooded / murderer" with whom Paterson identified himself in Book II (II, ii, 89). The coldly destructive user of human power is dead; a new poet and measure are born.

In terms of Williams' development, *Paterson* seems to have formalized his adoption for his poetry of the same creative process which underlay his short stories. Before *Paterson,* there was little change in one aspect of Williams' theory and practice of poetry—his determination to begin his poems with an extraordinary clarity of vision achieved by the exclusion of all inessentials. This can be seen by his practice of *ordering* his poems almost entirely by cutting them.[25] Or it can be seen in many of his critical statements, for example, those on Laforgue and Sheeler in 1922 and 1939 (*SE*, 36, 231). In this type of creative process, the artist begins with a vision of the essential, real, or valuable; he uses order in the work of art to communicate this vision by eliminating everything else.

In contrast, Williams' short stories begin with only an apprehension of value, a sense that something within the subject is essential. The vision of the valuable is the end, not the beginning, of the creative act. This creative process is strongly implied in stories like "Life Along the Passaic River," and explicitly stated in "Comedy Entombed." Near the end of the latter story, as he stands in a patient's kitchen, everything about Williams suddenly ceases to be a senseless disorder.

I took my time to look around a bit. . . . The whole place had a curious excitement about it for me, resembling in that the woman herself, I couldn't precisely tell why. There was nothing properly recognizable, nothing straight, nothing in what ordinarily might have been called its predictable relationships. Complete disorder. . . .

I have seldom seen such disorder and brokenness—such a mass of unrelated parts of things lying about. That's it! I concluded to myself. An unrecognizable order! Actually—the new! . . . And so compact. Excellent. And with such patina of use. Everything definitely "painty." Even the table, that way, pushed off from the center of the room.[26]

Similarly in *Paterson* and his later poetry, Williams showed greater patience with his materials and less tendency to prune

[25]Linda W. Wagner, *The Poems of William Carlos Williams* (Middletown, Conn., 1964), p. 48.
[26]*FD,* p. 327. Recently certain scientists have similarly asserted that the attitudes men bring to the unknown influence the nature of their discov-

them in the interests of an immediate clarity. Writing about *Paterson* in 1951, he remarked that

one fault in modern compositions . . . is that the irrational has no place. Yet in life (you show it by your tolerance of things which you feel no loss at not understanding) there is much that men exclude because they do not understand. The truly great heart *includes* what it does not at once grasp, just as the great artist includes things which go beyond him. . . . The irrational enters the poem in those letters [in *Paterson*], included in the text, which do not seem to refer to anything in the "story" yet do belong somehow to the poem—how, it is not easy to say (*SL, 309*).

The artist engaged in such a creative process must have faith in his materials. He must trust that an "order" or excellence is present in them and will appear. In the poet's case, Williams argued in his 1937 dialogue "The Basis of Faith in Art," this meant that he must have faith in the people and their language which were his materials. He cannot react to his surroundings, as Williams claimed Poe did, by abhorring "the contamination of the UNFORMED LUMP" of humanity around him (*IAG*, 228). Instead he must have "no principles in matters of the imagination . . . save the rediscovery in people of the elements of order" (*SE*, 189). For only by having faith in the emergence of order and clarity could men escape the deadly disappointment caused by the decay of the existing order, clarity, and beauty. If we live in the world, but lack faith in it and its people, "we are confused, embittered," Williams claimed, "we lose our sense of order and are likely to cling to death because we fear the apparent disorderliness of our lives. We have no faith so we accuse everyone else of breaking his vows."[27]

---

eries. Michael Polanyi, for example, uses the instance of the pupil's relationship to his teacher to show how a "tacit dimension" of faith must precede discovery: "tacit knowledge dwells in our awareness of particulars while bearing on an entity which the particulars jointly constitute. In order to share this indwelling, the pupil must presume that a teaching which appears meaningless to start with has in fact a meaning which can be discovered by hitting on the same kind of indwelling as the teacher is practicing. Such an effort is based on accepting the teacher's authority." *The Tacit Dimension* (Garden City, N.Y., 1966), p. 61. The revolutionary element in Williams' work—particularly in *Paterson* and his short stories—is his insistence that the poor and the "anti-poetic" are our best teachers and that they should receive the faithful "authority" which has previously been accorded only to the past and tradition (see Chapter Five above).

[27]*SE*, p. 189. See also Williams, "Symposium on Writing," *The Golden Goose*, Series 3, No. 2 (Autumn, 1951), p. 92.

CHAPTER | EIGHT

When he finished *Paterson* in 1951 Williams was sixty-eight years old and seriously troubled by increasing ill health. But he had always believed that art was needed most when and where it was most difficult to achieve, and the last decade of his life was no exception. In a letter to Louis Martz, written in 1951, he rededicated himself to his "task as a poet." He no longer felt that his first duty was to be a poetic revolutionary and innovator. The "crude fight" which he and other modern writers had had to wage to gain acceptance of their work was over, and Williams looked forward to the "enforced idleness" caused by his strokes as an opportunity to refine and clarify what he had already achieved. He now believed that some of his basic themes had been expressed too obscurely and that he had used his techniques too crudely in his earlier work. "I realize fully," he wrote,

that I have not been able to state clearly enough, articulately enough, what I have to say and that it is a duty which everyone (who reads me) has a right to expect of me.

I have been brought hard down on the facts of a situation which can no longer be delayed. . . . I must now . . . make myself clear. I must gather together the stray ends of what I have been thinking and make my full statement as to their meaning or quit.

I begin to see what I have been after. . . . Verse form, the actual shape of the line itself, must be as it is the first visible thing. I'm finally getting to understand what I want to do.

For there is not only a rightness in what must be done toward a new understanding (and practice) of the metric, but there is a new sensitivity that is required (*SL*, 298-299).

Fortunately, as Williams predicted in 1951, his technical skills were not impaired by his age;[1] however, as Linda W. Wagner has noted, the subject matter of his poems was affected by his increasing confinement. As he grew older and weaker because of heart attacks and strokes "the boundaries of his physical world became" more narrow, and, "to compensate, he turned at times to the realms of imagination and memory."[2] For some forty years Williams' writing had been the embodiment of Wallace Stevens' early praise:

> One has to keep looking for poetry as Renoir
> looked for colors in old walls, woodwork and so on.
>   Your place is
>   —among children
>   Leaping around a dead dog.
> A book of that would feed the hungry (SE, 13).

When old age and illness limited his capacity for finding poetry in his immediate environment, he changed the realm of his poetry to a "region of the mind" and showed the same skill at feeding a hungry age with what he found there.

He proclaimed in his late poem "Shadows" that "Memory / is liver than sight," since men inhabit two worlds, day and night, immediate experience and memory,

> one of which we share with the
> rose in bloom
>   and one,
>   by far the greater,
>   with the past,
>   the world of memory,
>   the silly world of history,
>   the world
>   of the imagination.
>   (Pictures, 151)

In his poems about this "world of the imagination" Williams once again revealed his ability to make poetry out of whatever life was available to him. Moreover, it was within this "world of the imagination" that he discovered the grounds for the faith in

---

[1]"If your interest is in theory . . . and your mind is alive and you're trying to improve your poems technically, you will produce the work, and will never cease to produce it." Williams, "Symposium on Writing," *The Golden Goose*, Series 3, No. 2 (Autumn, 1951), p. 91.

[2]Linda W. Wagner, *The Poems of William Carlos Williams* (Middletown, Conn., 1964), pp. 129-130.

his materials which he affirmed in the composition of *Paterson I-IV*. Both the thematic and prosodic qualities of Williams' late poetry are derived from his "new sensitivity" to the ways in which even the rawest materials of human experience may respond favorably to the imagination which respects them. His prosodic "new measure"—the "variable foot"—affirms that the ordered music of verse can be found in common language and that therefore there is no need to disdain our speech and seek to impose beauty or clarity upon it. His treatment of the themes of marriage and the "anti-poetic" in his late poems shows a similar faith. Men need not fear "divorce" and artists need not fear the presence of deformity in their works, Williams believed; for within both art and marriage—no matter how chaotic these things may become—they are always seasons, a dynamic, self-creating order, a "music" which men may possess imaginatively and live by. "And I could not help thinking," he concluded in *The Desert Music,* "of the wonders of the brain that / hears that music and of our / skill sometimes to record it" (*Pictures,* 120).

Love—"the he and the she of it" which underlay all creative activity[3] was the subject which most concerned Williams in his late poems. As in *Paterson I-IV,* he presented this theme in terms of marriage and the conflict between the male's need for renewal of love and the woman's need for constancy.

Williams gave the male's side of the argument in "The Basis of Faith in Art" when he suggested that "a marriage might be invigorated by deliberately breaking the vows," because mere constancy could not renew love (*SE,* 188). In *Paterson,* the poetess C. gives the woman's viewpoint. Because she was so dependent upon Paterson for fulfillment, she argues, it was his duty to be devoted to her—no matter how emotionally unsatisfactory their relationship might have been. "I didn't need the *publication* of my poetry . . . half as much as I needed your friendship in other ways (the very ways you ignored) in order to write it. I couldn't, for that reason, have brought the kind of responsiveness and appreciation that you expected of me (not with any real honesty) to the kind of help from you which I

[3]"How to Write" in *ibid.,* p. 147.

needed so much less than the kind you withheld" (II, iii, 107-108).

Williams' play *A Dream of Love* is largely a dramatization of this conflict between the male's need for emotional renewal in love and the female's need for constancy in love. Dr. Thurber, the hero of the play, believes that his marriage is being eroded by the routines of middle-aged married life. Therefore, he deliberately commits adultery to renew his imagination and save his marriage from boredom. "I was getting bored," he tells his wife, Myra, ". . . I never wanted to go far. . . . I knew that if we were to keep on loving each other something had to be done about it. This opportunity offered itself and I took it" (*ML*, 208). The "best moments" in their lives, he says, were when he was "saying hello, my darling, and good-bye to you—the anodic opening and the cathodic schluss. . . . The most intense in the current of our lives" (*ML* 213). Therefore, on the very day that he took his "opportunity" to commit adultery, love was uppermost in the Doctor's mind since he desired "to renew our love, burn the old nest and emerge transcendent, aflame—for you!"[4]

Myra is not impressed by her husband's theory. She considers him entirely responsible for their lives and believes it was callous and irresponsible of him to risk their marriage. She considers "the anodic opening and the cathodic schluss" which he desires nothing more than a search for cheap thrills "with this woman or that woman—or man or boy or little girl or anyone your mind will lead you to" (*ML*, 212).

But beyond Doc and Myra's quarrel there is a conflict between the male and female phases of creativity which concerned Williams throughout his long career as a writer. "The male scatters his element recklessly," he wrote in 1942, "as if there were to be no end to it. . . . That profusion you do not find in the female but the equal infinity of the single cell. This at her best she harbors, warms and implants that it may proliferate."[5] The conflict between the sexes in many of Williams' works may be traced to this distinction. Men, in Williams' works, usually seek the freedom to scatter "their element recklessly." Like art-

---

[4] *ML*, p. 207. At one time during the composition of *Paterson I-IV*, Williams may have considered using the plot of *A Dream of Love* as the structural basis of the poem. See *ND 17*, pp. 266-267, 306.

[5] "Men...Have No Tenderness," *New Directions 7* (Norfolk, Conn., 1942), p. 432.

ists, they feel themselves free to respond to any promising new material, to possess sexually and impregnate any vital, attractive female. Women, on the other hand, need the male's sustained devotion if they are to be creative. Only then, like artists, they nurture and harbor the "infinity of the single cell" which fulfills and preserves their lives: children, the home, the garden.

Because of his "recklessness," the male must be continually renewed. There was, Williams believed, "really nothing much to [a] man aside from what he does, what he knows, what he desires or makes."[6] A man exists entirely within his own mind, where he is "consumed and turned, simultaneously, into ideas *in his own head*."[7] If a man is to be "made new" the impetus must be external. He must discover new lands and new women who will renew his mind or imagination by giving him new desires, new knowledge, and new materials for his arts. Thus in *In the American Grain* Williams' heroes are either "great wench lovers" (*IAG*, 143) or else, like Boone, their whole souls are entirely given to the perpetually virgin wilderness which is their "land of heart's desire." Either way, they are not constant husbands or lovers.

In contrast to the male, the woman exists in the full cycle of natural, material life. If she is to "harbor" the creative force within her, the woman herself must be nurtured. The male must be constant to her if she is "to lift herself from a minor key of tenderness and affection to a major love in which all her potentials will find employment."[8] This concept is stated obliquely in Williams' essay "Woman as Operator" and in C.'s letters in *Paterson;*[9] it is expressed most fully and eloquently in the image of the woman's mutability which occurs in *Many Loves* and "The Comic Life of Elia Brobitza," a one-act play which Williams wrote in 1919.

"Age in age is united— / Indifferent, out of sequence, marvelously!" in the being of the old woman who appears in "The Wanderer." She is able to drag "a blunt boat on the yielding river—" and fly with the young poet over the New Jersey mountains. She appears as a gull, a repulsive old prostitute, and the

[6]"Woman as Operator," Buffalo Collection, tape 25.
[7]*Ibid.*
[8]"Men...Have No Tenderness," p. 430.
[9]II, ii, 93-94; II, iii, 105-113.

"old queen" or priestess who baptizes the poet in the "filthy
Passaic." Williams identified her, at various times, with the goddess Demeter, his Grandmother Wellcome, the Baroness von
Freytag Loringhoven, and Elia Brobitza, the heroine of his
poem "Portrait of a Woman in Bed."[10]

In "The Comic Life of Elia Brobitza" female mutability possesses a definite and significant form. The play's heroine and
only main character is Elia Brobitza, the speaker of Williams'
poem "Portrait of a Woman in Bed" (*CEP*, 150-151). Elia first
appears as a "solitary girl" standing before a "lighted hotel
window" through which can be seen the happiness and pleasure
of life which she will never possess. She then begs a man named
Jim, who is her husband or lover, to return to her. He brutally
shakes her loose, strikes her, and then runs off stage. After a few
moments the girl sits up on the stage where she has fallen
*"without much ado and seems to readjust her hat and clothing.
In doing so she begins to laugh."*[11] Somehow—perhaps through
a lighting change—the girl has been magically transformed into
a woman who is the product of the man's brutality. Her *"hair is
now seen to be grey. Her walk and bearing have changed, her
dress hangs loosely about her. She is a sturdy old woman."*

Elia is now the cynical old woman of "Portrait of a Woman
in Bed." She has moved into a deserted house and defies the
County Poor Master and County Physician with vulgar mockery.
As soon as the Poor Master leaves Elia receives an unexpected
visitor. *"A young man in a glittering peasant costume leans in
and looks at her."* It is the ghost or spirit of Flavi, her first lover,
who deserted her when she was a beautiful young girl before she
came to America. Elia is ashamed of her degradation and cowers
from Flavi when he enters the room, but *"he draws her forward.
At his touch her old clothes fall off, she straightens herself. She
is in peasant's dress—and Young!"* But the time of Elia's dream
is measured; for a few minutes she possesses the *proper* time of

[10]"To her kind only could his mind go to be kindled. It had always been
so. (See, Portrait of a Woman in Bed, in Al Que Quiere.) In the same manner
he had cried out, I love you, in the direction of his own unbelievable
grandmother, the wolf of the family. (See, Dedication of a Plot of Ground,
Al Que Quiere.)" Williams, "The Three Letters," *Contact III* (1921), 11. See
Chapter One above.

[11]"The Comic Life of Elia Brobitza," *Others*, V, 3 (April-May, 1919), 3. All
italics in the quotations from the play's stage directions are Williams'.

her life: a happy romance with the man she loved. Flavi explains his long absence with a tale of how he was forced to hire himself out for a month to a miller,[12] but then the clock strikes twelve. The Cinderella dream is over, Flavi's spirit disappears, Elia *"gets up and goes slowly into bed, an old woman."* The real time of Elia's life has returned, and she is once again old and abused and pathetic beneath her defiant mockery. The Poor Master enters with police officers to evict her—a final male brutality—but she dies, and the play ends.

Williams gave an extremely significant casting direction in his production notes for *Many Loves: "The roles of Alise, Serafina, Agnes Breen and Clara are to be played by the same actress. Other roles in the playlets may be doubled at the discretion of the director"* (ML, 2). All of these woman, like Elia Brobitza, are denied the proper fruition of their femininity because of some sort of male failure. Williams' direction that they all be played by the same actress implies that she is the same essential woman betrayed by a succession of males—all of whose responses are tragically or absurdly inadequate to their responsibilities. Elia Brobitza's metamorphoses indicate that all the ages of womanhood are scarred by male inconstancy and brutality— Flavi's, Jim's, and finally the Poor Master's. Alise's metamorphosis into Agnes Breen in the second playlet of *Many Loves* is therefore logical. Agnes is a lesbian, a stylish, sophisticated career woman. She "looks like a man," but she offers the younger woman, Ann, a sympathy and sensitivity that none of the men around her have ever given her. Since marriage doesn't work, Williams implies, women will seek fulfillment where they can find it—from one another.

The conflict between the male's need for the new and the female's need for constancy and responsibility culminates in the tragic "divorce" which underlies *Paterson I-IV*. There Williams discovered that the divorce between men's and women's creative needs, which he first expounded in *In the American Grain,* exists throughout American history and can be applied to all of men's relationships to their material (female) environments. Denied "marriage," both Paterson's and the poetess C.'s powers become destructive inversions of their creative energies. He uses his male "freedom" to clamber mechanically over the "female"

[12]Flavi's story is a synopsis of Chaucer's "The Reeve's Tale."

park (I, i, 57-64). He possesses everything he sees; but because he is truly faithful to none of it, he destroys its integrity in the process. C. "harbors, warms and implants" the memory of her aborted relationship with Paterson and nurtures all the cruel details of their failure in her letters—to destroy him.

The solution to this impasse, Williams believed, lay not in the "nature" or "facts" of love itself, but in "the imagination [which] / across the sorry facts / lifts us / to make roses / stand before" the thorns of love (*Pictures,* 126). In the midst of a book review, written in 1946, Williams suddenly exclaimed: "How foolish to seek new worlds, sometimes, when we must know that any world warmed by the arts will surpass the very Elysian Fields if the imagination reaches its end there."[13] This statement, in context, applies to art and poetry, but its basic meaning applies to love and marriage as well.[14] For the imagination, when aroused, may make marriage as constant as the woman may desire and yet as perpetually "new" as the man may wish. Constancy in love best persists when it is a process, when it is based upon emotional renewal—and not upon static, legalistic "vows."

The renewal of love, Williams emphasizes in *Asphodel* and *Paterson V,* is an imaginative challenge for both the man and the woman. At the beginning of their marriage, he wrote to his wife in "Asphodel,"

> There had come to me
> a challenge,
> your dear self,
> mortal as I was,
> the lily's throat
> to the hummingbird!
> (*Pictures,* 155)

"Mortal as I was, / the lily's throat"—these two phrases imply the challenges which love must surmount. There is first the challenge of the woman's mutability.

---

[13]"Preface," *Quarterly Review of Literature,* II, 4 (1946), 348.

[14]In fact, Williams used the vocabulary of marriage to describe poetic techniques in another review: "But I find little if any verbal invention in Rexroth—there is no . . . wedding figure of verbal design. The wedding he speaks of is not *in* the words, his words merely carry it about." "In Praise of Marriage," *Quarterly Review of Literature,* II, 2 (1945), 149.

> . . . you were a woman
> and no flower
> and had to face
> the problems which confront a woman.
> But you were for all that
> flowerlike
> *(Pictures,* 177)

If women are "flowerlike" they share the defects as well as the virtues of flowers. Flowers wither and grow ugly; they may be uprooted or be abused. Similarly the woman's condition changes. If she grows old, or is "whored" by use and familiarity, men may no longer love her. Her great enemy is time, symbolized by the clock in "Elia Brobitza," which ages her and causes the male's vision of her value to decay.

The wives of the African chief, described in *Paterson I,* may let their husband love them "in a descending scale of freshness," (I, i, 22); but a civilized woman demands more individual fidelity after she loses her "freshness." She can receive it, Williams suggests in *Paterson V,* if her man can use his imagination to keep his love vital despite the material loss of her virginity, novelty, beauty, and youth. To do this, the male must be able to identify imaginatively "the virgin and the whore," that is, to know the woman's natural fate (to be "whored") and yet respond to her with the same love that he devoted to her when she was a virgin.[15]

As in the other books of *Paterson,* the virgin is the *desired* woman. She represents pure and untainted beauty; and, therefore, the male—particularly the poet-unicorn—must love her, heed her beauty, and desire to possess her. But the virgin becomes a "whore" in men's eyes when she is possessed by the male. True recognition of her beauty, like that in Toulouse Lautrec's paintings, is excluded by all religions (III, i, 134). She is treated like the "Beautiful Thing" in *Paterson III;* her beauty is abused, ignored, or feared (III, i, 129).

Williams suggests in *Paterson V*—which is dedicated to Toulouse Lautrec—that a woman's "corruption" may actually be her means for living fully, and that a virgin is often rightfully a whore in her own mind. In Lorca's *The Love of Don*

[15]See *CLP,* p. 31; *Paterson* IV, iii, 223-224.

Perlimplin, "Love's whole gamut, the wedding night's promiscuity [exists] in the girl's mind, her determination not to be left out of the party, as a moral gesture, if ever there was one" (V, i, 242). The virgin and the whore are "an identity." Both are "for sale / to the highest bidder! / and who bids higher / than a lover?" (V, iii, 276). Therefore a woman should not ignore her own sexuality and deny the physical pleasures of love to herself and her lover. For "no woman is virtuous / who does not give herself to her lover / —forthwith" (V, iii, 266).

Nor can any man's husbandry be so perfect that he can avoid somehow "prostituting his woman." Even the most honorable of husbands "whores" his wife; and so, instead of being guilty, he should continue to love and cherish her in his imagination.

>   —shall we speak of love
>   seen only in a mirror
>   —no replica?
>   reflecting only her impalpable spirit?
>   which is she whom I see
>   and not touch her flesh?
>
>   —every married man carries in his head
>   the beloved and sacred image
>   of a virgin
>   whom he has whored   .
>   (V, iii, 272)

Similarly, a man should not cease to love a woman because she has aged. For age fulfills and enriches the woman's life even though it diminishes beauty. In "For Eleanor and Bill Monahan," another late poem, Williams wrote to his wife:

>   You have no lovers now
>   in the bare skies
>   to bring you flowers,
>   to whisper to you
>   under a hedge
>   howbeit
>   you are young
>   and fit to be loved.
>   I declare it boldly. . . .
>   (*Pictures,* 84-85)

The physical mutability of the woman becomes irrelevant, for the male renews his love for her in his imagination rather than through adulterous actions. Instead of seeking to renew his love by possessing "fresh" women, he remains constant to his wife and renews his love for her by continuing to respond to "the beloved and sacred image / of a virgin" which he "carries in his head" (V, iii, 272).

The process through which the male renews this "image" constitutes the second challenge to love in Williams' late love poems: the challenge of human mortality, particularly the male's ("Mortal as I was"). At the beginning of his marriage, Williams wrote in "Asphodel," his love was a clear vision or communication of his creative responsibility to his wife and the world.

> For our wedding, too,
>   the light was wakened
>   and shone. The light!
> the light stood before us
>   waiting!
>   I thought the world
> stood still.
>   At the altar
>   so intent was I
> before my vows,
>   so moved by your presence
>   a girl so pale
> and ready to faint
>   that I pitied
>   and wanted to protect you.
>   (*Pictures,* 181)
>
> Endless wealth,
>   I thought,
>   held out its arms to me.
> A thousand topics
>   in an apple blossom.
>   The generous earth itself
> gave us lief.
>   The whole world
>   became my garden!
>   (*Pictures,* 155-156)

But because men are mortal, their visions of love are finite and inconstant. "Love and the imagination / are of a piece," and therefore, the greatest evil that can befall a man, Williams wrote in "Asphodel," is the "death of love," for "then indeed / for him / the light has gone out" (*Pictures,* 179). When the "light" of a man's vision "goes out," when his loving communication with his wife or world ends, he lives in darkness and his responses are destructive. Without the "poem" of communication, life becomes worthless and men waste and abuse it accordingly. "It is our inability to communicate to another," Williams wrote in his *Autobiography*, ". . . unable to say the simplest thing of importance to one another . . . even the most valuable, that makes our lives like those of a litter of kittens in a wood-pile" (p. 361).

Williams gave several examples of the "dark" or destructive responses which particularly concerned him in Book II of "Asphodel." All involve failures of communication. Above all there is "the bomb," which, as in *Paterson III-IV*, signifies a power totally unresponsive to life and therefore totally destructive.

> We come to our deaths
> in silence.
> The bomb speaks.
> All suppressions,
> from the witchcraft trials at Salem
> to the latest
> book burnings
> are confessions
> that the bomb
> has entered our lives
> to destroy us.
>
> (*Pictures*, 168)

He also refers to the theme of *In the American Grain*—the death and destruction caused by men's failures to respond creatively to the new and beautiful (*Pictures*, 167). Finally he speaks obliquely of his failures as a poet and husband when he too could not communicate with what he loved, when he "failed" the poem or "risked what I had to do, / therefore to prove / that we love each other / while my very bones sweated / that I could not cry to you / in the act."[16]

Williams was still hopeful about the nature of love despite his pessimism about the mortality of human vision and communication. He believed that the "light" of men's visions of their responsibilities in love preceded and were greater than the "darkness" of their destructive responses. Light is "inseparable from the fire" and "takes precedence over it" (*Pictures*, 178).

---

[16]*Pictures*, p. 161. Cf. *Paterson* IV, i, 196 and the conclusion to Eliot's *Ash-Wednesday*.

> But love and the imagination
>   are of a piece,
>   swift as the light
> to avoid destruction.
>   So we come to watch time's flight
>   as we might watch
> summer lightning
>   or fireflies, secure,
>   by grace of the imagination,
> safe in its care.
>   (*Pictures,* 179-180)

Men's destructive responses, no matter how blindly "cruel / and selfish / and totally obtuse," are therefore only seasons of love "for and against, / whatever the heart / fumbles in the dark / to assert" (*Pictures,* 126, 125). They are the winter seasons of love, and, like winter, they may be transformed to spring. Like the rose or the asphodel, love is a hardy perennial.

> With daisies pied
>   and violets blue,
> we say, the spring of the year
>   comes in!
>   So may it be
> with the spring of love's year
>   also
>   if we can but find
> the secret word
>   to transform it.
>   (*Pictures,* 170)

This "secret word," Williams implies, is forgiveness—woman's forgiveness of the man for his failures in love. "What power has love but forgiveness? / In other words / by its intervention / what has been done / can be undone" (*Pictures,* 169). Through forgiveness love can come again springlike "to delect us" "after winter's harshness."

Forgiveness is the woman's responsibility and contribution to the renewal of love. But to achieve it, she too must possess "the grace of the imagination."

Before *Asphodel* Williams usually presented the woman's role in love as a relatively passive one. She exists, in works like "Elia Brobitza," *Many Loves,* and *Paterson I-IV,* to be fulfilled by the male when his vision of love is pure and to be betrayed by him when it wanes. When the marriage of her femininity to the male's masculinity fails, there is little that she can do about it. She may, like Helen in "The Farmers' Daughters," lead a life of mute desperation, seeking emotional satisfaction in wine and the friendship of older men and other women. Or, she may pursue a series of equally worthless, insensitive, and treacherous men, like Margaret in the same story. At most the dissatisfied woman may rebel against heterosexuality and seek love from other women—as she does in "The Knife of the Times" and *Paterson IV*. What she does not do, in these works, is make any creative, imaginative contribution to the male-female relationship, for this element of love is presented as a male responsibility. "Just as a woman must produce out of her female belly to complete herself—a son—" says the Doctor in *A Dream of Love*, "so a man must produce a woman, in full beauty out of the shell of his imagination and possess her, to complete himself also . . ." (*ML*, 200). In other words, the woman creates life biologically, materially, whereas the male creates it imaginatively and mentally.

Williams presents the woman as an imaginative being in her own right in *Asphodel* and other later poems. His wife understands the seasons of life in *Asphodel* as she waters and pities her plants. When he addresses her and requests her forgiveness, Williams assumes that she will be able to understand, imaginatively, the correspondence between the mortality of natural and human life. Finally, the very opacity of the "steps" which he gives her in *Asphodel* reveals that he believes she will be able to decipher his images and meditations and understand him and their life together from them. Williams develops this theme through an oblique, very personal parable in Book III of *Asphodel*. First, he tells his wife that he will "give the steps . . . by which you shall mount, / again to think well" of him and forgive him. These "steps" are a series of meditations and images.

The first image is "Colleoni's horse / with the thickset little man / on top / in armor / presenting a naked sword" and "with him / the horse rampant / roused by the mare in / the Venus and Adonis" (*Pictures*, 171). These images, says Williams, are "pictures of crude force." Both represent an insensitive use of masculine power. The "horse rampant" is the natural symbol for brutal masculinity. Colleoni—a ruthless Renaissance *condotiere*—is a social and historical symbol for this type of brutality. He is the classic "man on horseback," ruthless, aggressive, and insensitive ("in armor").

Williams then describes two autobiographical incidents. While waiting at a railroad station, he and a friend see a fast freight go by.

> a distinguished artist,
> turned with me
> to protect his eyes:
> That's what we'd all like to be, Bill,
> he said. . . .
> *(Pictures,* 171)

This brief anecdote is followed by a long description of a bearded Negro man whom Williams once saw in a subway. This man possesses no "crude force." His eyes are mild and evasive, and he carried not a "naked sword" but only a "worn knobbed stick . . . suitable / to keep off dogs." He is immersed, a passenger, in the life around him and dirtied by it. Yet he is obviously intelligent, alert, and sensitive. Williams concludes his portrait of the bearded man with a long series of comparisons in which he associates this man with his own father, a flower, and the prehistoric cave painters. The bearded man, Williams suggests, is the creative being, the father, the true man: "all men / and all women too" are in his loins.

Williams first "step" toward receiving his wife's forgiveness, the description of Colleoni and his horse, is to recognize the winter, dark side of his masculine nature, the temptation to be nothing more than a brutal, "crude force."

In the second "step," the incident at the railroad station, the "distinguished artist" is Marsden Hartley (*Autobiography,* 172). Hartley was a pathetically lonely, frustrated man. Though an excellent painter he never received any adequate financial reward or critical appreciation, and his personal life was even less satisfactory. A bisexual, he was unable to achieve a lasting, satisfactory relationship with any of the men and women he pursued. "I felt sorry for him, growing old," Williams recalled. "That was the moment he took for his approaches. I, too, had to reject him. Everyone rejected him. I was no better than the others. One of our finest painters . . . and he didn't have any-

thing much as far as I could tell" (*Autobiography,* 173). This is
the sort of man, Williams implies, who wishes to be a "crude
force," a locomotive, a conqueror. He suggests to his wife in this
way that the winter, dark element of masculinity is a product
not of an evil potency but of loneliness, disappointment, and
emotional and sexual frustration. Thus women should pity as
well as fear the man who is insensitive and brutal.

Williams' description of the bearded man is the third "step"
toward forgiveness. By praising this man so lovingly and sensitively and at so much length, Williams reveals his commitment
to a gentle, sensitive masculine potency. He is not this man
himself and he knows it, but he reveres and cherishes the element of his masculinity which the bearded Negro represents.
Therefore his wife should "think well" of him despite his faults,
and forgive him for the winters of their marriage. He watches
her water her plants in the winter. They, like the poet's love, do
not flower, yet she cares for them. "Poor things! you say / as you
compassionately / pour at their roots / the reviving water. . . . I
say to myself / kindness moves her / shall she not be kind / also
to me?" (*Pictures,* 175). In effect, she builds up and possesses an
image of her husband which will sustain her during the winter
seasons of love and then motivate her to be "kind" to him so
that the spring of their love may be renewed.

If the woman can surmount the challenge of forgiving the
male his mortality, she may also achieve her own triumph over
mortality. This triumph will be imaginative and not physical;
she will still age and die, but this physical death will be irrelevant. Individual flowers die and rot, Williams wrote in *Paterson
V,* but "there is a hole / in the bottom of the bag," the imagination, and life can escape from death through this hole (V, i,
247). Similarly, the beauty of individual women lives and dies
but the beauty of art lives on. "—the virgin and the whore,
which / most endures? the world / of the imagination most
endures" (V, i, 248).

If a man is a poet, as Williams is, his verses are "destined / to
live forever" (*Pictures,* 166).

> The rose fades
> and is renewed again
> by its seed, naturally
> but where

> save in the poem
> shall it go
> to suffer no diminution
> of its splendor
> (Pictures, 39)

Similarly, the woman celebrated in a work of art shall "suffer no diminution" in the world of the imagination. Therefore, Williams promises his wife in "Asphodel,"

> You have forgiven me
> making me new again.
> So that here [in the poem]
> in the place
> dedicated in the imagination
> to memory
>
> . . . .
>
> you will be my queen,
> my queen of love
> forever more.
> (Pictures, 177-178)

Williams began his poetic career in "The Wanderer" deeply concerned about the fate of the world and the women he loved. Nearly forty years later, in "Asphodel" and *Paterson V*, this concern was still uppermost in his mind, but his experience as a poet gave him a much greater and finer awareness of men's and women's creative powers to preserve what they love from the destructive effects of time and mortality.

A second major theme of Williams' later poetry is his concern with the artist's relationship to deformity, pain, and disease—the forces which warp or diminish human life. For Williams the artist's responsibility to what is beautiful and desirable was always clear: he possesses their splendours in life and preserves them in the "world of the imagination" so they will survive decay and death. In turn, beauty—the flower in nature or the woman in humanity—will nourish and revive the artist, renew his interest in life, and "startle" his imagination so that he can escape the drab cycle of mechanical, unimaginative life (*Paterson V,* iii, 278). Obversely, Williams was also concerned with the artist's relationship to the aspects of life which are repellent or damaging to human life and imagination. He was convinced that the existence of such things was inevitable (*FD,* 208), and that they should be present in works of art because art had to deal with the totality of life. "The traumas of today," he wrote in 1952, ". . . are plain enough upon our minds. Then how shall our poems escape? They should be horrible things, those poems. To the classic muse their bodies should appear to be covered with sores. They should be hunchbacked, limping. And yet our poems must show how we have struggled with them to measure and control them" (*SL*, 315-316).

Williams was deeply concerned with this problem throughout his life, and he devised several significantly different ways of integrating deformed or ugly subjects into his art. The young poet of "The Wanderer" is immersed in the "filthy Passaic" of squalid life around him, and he benefits from it. However, this immersion is traumatic and not volitional; literally the poet is seized by the scruff of his neck and dunked into the river by the "old queen."[17]

During the 1930's Williams exhibited two complementary attitudes toward the deformity of life. He argues in his prose, particularly in *In the American Grain,* that a great deal of deformity is accidental for it is imposed upon American reality by persons like the Puritans who hate and fear life as they find it in the New World. In other works of this period—*A Voyage to Pagany* and his poems which resemble Demuth's paintings— Williams' hero is the artist or scientist who fearlessly animates or cleanses drabness, deformity, and disease by masterfully forcing them into the imaginative, "pure" order and clarity of scientific and artistic works.

Williams remained convinced that a great deal of deformity and ugliness are avoidable and that the greatest evil was the maiming of life. In 1947, for example, he wrote that writers like Proust and Rousseau had warped their lives because they had been concerned with surviving rather than loving life. "Both men are moralists, they tell you, don't let it happen as it happened to me or to Swann or to Thal. They are saying as any sensible man must say: Stop maiming the times! Fear deformed us and we reveal to you the depths of our deformity" (*SE*, 271). During the 1930's and 1940's Williams added a new dimension to his understanding of his "anti-poetic" subjects and their place

[17]*CEP*, pp. 11-12. In an early poem Williams addressed the old woman, his grandmother Wellcome, as "you who / with an iron head, first, / fiercest and with strongest love / brutalized me into strength. . . ." *ND 16,* p. 19.

in his art. He acknowledged that some sordid, deformed things were organic parts of life, particularly of modern life. They are, he told Marianne Moore, the "dirt" of reality from which rare, fine things grow, and therefore there is no "incompatability" in their existing side by side with the beautiful (*SL,* 156). They are harsh complements to the "poetic," desirable elements of life, and the modern artist has to deal with them if he wishes to be true to an age which is more deformed than beautiful.

Consequently in his poems Williams generally presents the relationship between his beautiful and his deformed subjects as one of harsh but necessary alternation. After visiting the painter Tchelitchew in 1942, he wrote that "any [one] who would know and profit by his knowledge of the great must lead a life of violent opposites" (*SE,* 250). And he sympathetically described Tchelitchew's obsessive alternation between paintings filled with the most monstrous realities and other paintings composed according to fairly conventional standards of beauty and desirability.

> Our life is horrible, he [Tchelitchew] said. We are monsters. We hate each other and we try to destroy everything that is lovely . . . we are disgusting. And when I show them how disgusting they are they say, He only wants to paint monsters!
>
> I don't want to paint monsters. Pretty soon I will be tired of monsters. I want to communicate with people. That is painting. The ancients knew what painting was. It is to say something. It is to communicate. It is to use beautiful colors because we love them. We enjoy what is lovely and we paint to speak of it (*SE,* 252-253).

Williams made the same sort of violent alternations in *Paterson I-IV, Many Loves,* and many of his poems of the 1940's: the beauty of the rose and the violence of war, the well-made counterplot of *Many Loves* and its "crude" prose playlets, the poetic Mr. Paterson and his prosaic, sordid environment.

Williams often asserts in these works that there is a cyclical or seasonal connection between these extremes. "Catastrophic Birth," for example, concludes:

> Rain will fall. The wind and the birds
> will bring seeds, the river changes
> its channel and fish re-enter it.
> The seawind will come in from the east.
> The broken cone breathes softly on
> the edge of the sky, violence revives and
>   regathers.
>
>   (*CLP,* 9)

Violence, ugliness, the "anti-poetic"—all must exist in the poem and in life so that the beautiful, loving, and gentle may exist. Like life, Williams wrote, poetry must be composed of "that gentleness that harbors all violence, / the valid juxtaposition, one / by the other, alternates, the cosine, the / cylinder and the rose" (CLP, 29). But in the construction of these works Williams often treats these extremes as opposites rather than as phases or "seasons" of the same process. The juxtapositions are so sudden, the alternations are so violent, contracted, and unexpected that the action of these poems, Paterson I-IV and Many Loves, is frequently as traumatic as it is in "The Wanderer."

In his poems of the 1950's that deal with "anti-poetic" or deformed subjects, Williams presents these subjects as possessing a more positive value than that of being harsh prerequisites to the presentation of the beautiful or pleasant. He now believed that the presence of such subjects in works of art could heal the effects of an age's deformities as well as record their existence. At the same time Williams also treats these subjects less violently. His construction of his later poems juxtaposes the extremes of reality to one another more gently and meditatively so that they become seasons of the same process in the pattern as well as the theory of his poems.

In his late poem "The Yellow Flower," Williams compares Michelangelo's Slaves to his own "crooked / and obscure" flower, "a single spray / topping the deformed stem / of fleshy leaves / in this freezing weather" (Pictures, 89). Even if he sees that the destructive "weather" of life will ruin him and all that he loves, he also sees

> through the eyes
> and through the lips
> and tongue the power
> to free myself
> and speak of it, as
> Michelangelo through his hands
> had the same, if greater,
> power.
>
> (Pictures, 91)

Williams contrasts the human condition with that of animals in another late poem. "The pitiful dumb beasts" are trapped in the agony that life inflicts upon them. But with courage and invention men may "surpass" the animals and find relief by singing beautifully of the very afflictions that harm them (*Pictures*, 86-88).

He did not believe that art could cure life's pain, ugliness, or deformities; but in these poems Williams affirms that art can heal the effects these things have upon men's minds. In "Tribute to the Painters" he implies that centaurs, satyrs, and other monstrous beings have "danced" in art throughout history so that the images of their deformity would not tyrannize over men's imaginations.[18] "Men in their designs / have learned / to shatter" the tyranny of the image, "that the trouble / in their minds / shall be quieted, / put to bed / again" (*Pictures*, 137).

In "The Orchestra," another late poem, Williams suggests the reason that art gives relief from pain.

> The purpose of an orchestra
>   is to organize those sounds
>   and hold them
>   to an assembled order
>   in spite of the
>   "wrong note."
>   (*Pictures*, 80-81)

Life is bound to have its "wrong notes," its moral and aesthetic deformities, but in works of art they exist as part of a design. They are held "to an assembled order" which forces men to experience them in relation to other, less terrible, "notes" of existence. Therefore they cannot dominate or obsess the mind and paralyze it with dread and repugnance.

In his long poem "The Desert Music," Williams made the fullest presentation of the process through which art brings men relief from the deformities of their lives. The poem begins with an image of total human inertia and deformity: "a form / propped motionless—on the bridge / between Juárez and El Paso" (*Pictures*, 108). The sight of this "inhuman shapelessness" makes Williams poetically impotent. "The poem" sticks in his throat, and he cannot "vomit it up." But instead of fleeing or abhorring the lump, Williams treats it as a challenge. He defines the poem as a "dance," the full, free use of the human faculties. And then he affirms that it must begin with and include the monstrous lump upon the bridge, the deformed, the "anti-poetic." It must

---

[18]Williams incorporated this poem, in slightly different form, into *Paterson* V, ii, 258-261.

"dance / two and two with him— / sequestered there asleep" (*Pictures*, 109).

In the 1940's Williams would have probably ended the poem at this point by harshly juxtaposing the dance and the lump and asserting that they were connected. In "The Desert Music" he plunges further into his experience in Juárez to discover a clearer connection between these two extremes.

At first he finds only further deformity—tales of vice and violence, begging children, vulgar tourists "loaded with loot." Then in a bar he discovers the answer to the question of how men can be monstrous lumps and yet compose poems that are dances.

> What in the form of an old whore in
> a cheap Mexican joint in Juárez, her bare
> can waggling crazily can be
> so refreshing to me, raise to my ear
> so sweet a tune, built of such slime?
>
> (*Pictures*, 116)

Williams presents his answer obliquely. The "music" of the bar's Mexican band radically limits experience because of its absurd sentimentality. The stripteaser's dance completes reality because its "music" counterpoints the Mexicans'.

> Why don't these Indians get over this nauseating
> prattle about their souls and their loves and sing
> us something else for a change?
>
> This place is rank
> with it. She
> at least knows she's
> part of another tune,
> knows her customers,
> has the same
> opinion of them as I
> have.   That gives her
> one up   .   one up
> following the lying
> music   .
>
> (*Pictures*, 115)

It is this completion of experience through the expression of "another tune" that refreshes Williams. From the stripteaser's example he learns how the desert's music may be composed so that the mind may find relief. In his description of the next bar he implicitly imitates the process. He sees drunken American tourists behaving in an asinine way, but finds "another tune" of life expressed by the bar's Mexican patrons and cook.

> A foursome, two oversize Americans, no
> longer young, got up as cowboys,
> hats and all, are drunk and carrying on
> with their gals, drunk also,
>
> . . . quiet family groups, some with
> children, eating. Rather a better
> class than you notice
> on the streets. So here we are. You
>
> can see through into the kitchen
> where one of the cooks, his shirt sleeves
> rolled up, an apron over
> the well pressed pants. . . .
>
> (*Pictures,* 116-117)

Williams is now aware that all of life or poetry is a "dance" from one "tune" to another. Fortified by this awareness, he again sees the formless lump of humanity on the bridge which defeated his poetic powers at the beginning of "The Desert Music." He discovers that he is now able to integrate it successfully into his poem by recognizing its place in the dance of life. The lump represents the necessary, ultimate relief from all the musics of existence. He is the bass note of life, "the / *music!* as when Casals struck / and held a deep cello tone."

> headless, packed like the pit of a fruit into
> that obscure corner—or
> a fish to swim against the stream—or
> a child in the womb prepared to imitate life,
> warding its life against
> a birth of awful promise.   The music
> guards it, a mucus, a film that surrounds it,
> a benumbing ink that stains the
> sea of our minds—to hold us off—shed
> of a shape close as it can get to no shape,
> a music! a protecting music   .
>
> (*Pictures,* 119-120)

"The Desert Music"—and Williams' long concern with the "anti-poetic"—concludes with this assertion that even the worst deformities cease to be repellent and may even become objects of wonder if properly seen as part of the "music" of life rather than negations of it.

Williams believed that his "task as a poet" during the 1950's applied to the technique as well as the content of his poems. "I hope," he said in 1951, "that with my last breath I shall make an addition to my technical equipment."[19] And when an interviewer asked him in 1962 what he had left to younger poets that was of special value, Williams replied: "The variable foot—the division of the line according to a new method that would be satisfactory to an American."[20]

At an age when most poets become publishers, philosophers, or professors, Williams decided to invent a prosody. During the 1920's and 1930's he had complained about the poor condition of the "words" of American poetry, and in *Paterson* he wrote of the American failure to achieve a valid "language" (I, i, 20-21). But during the 1940's he became more and more convinced that "it is in the structure of the line that the stasis of the *thought* is lodged."[21] Having decided that American poetry needed a new "line" or "measure," Williams attempted to contribute all that he could to its establishment. "There will be other experiments," he wrote about his own work in 1953, "but all will be directed toward the discovery of a new measure" (*SE*, 340).

Conventional metrical systems are based upon the principle of paradigms, lines which are structured so exactly upon an abstract sound pattern that they enforce that pattern throughout the poem. The presence of these lines in the poem causes the poet, consciously or unconsciously, to use their "pattern as a basis of selection so that he may choose out of the infinite number of sentences of natural language those which qualify for inclusion in the poem."[22] The presence of these paradigms also causes the reader to expect the repetition of the pattern and read the lines in terms of how well they conform or deviate from it.

Williams' long search for a "new measure" was based on the fact that he never accepted the principles which underlie con-

[19]"Symposium on Writing," p. 91.

[20]Stanley Koehler, "The Art of Poetry VI: William Carlos Williams," *Paris Review*, 32 (Summer-Fall, 1964), p. 148.

[21]"An Approach to the Poem," *English Institute Essays, 1947* (New York, 1948), p. 64.

[22]Morris Halle, Samuel Jay Keyser, "Chaucer and the Study of Prosody," *College English*, XXVIII (Dec., 1966), 187. See also Harvey Gross, *Sound and Form in Modern Poetry* (Ann Arbor, 1965), pp. 3-8.

ventional, metric poetry. He believed that a poet was bound to "deform" language if he selected his word order or line divisions on the basis of conformity to any abstract pattern. "When a man makes a poem," he argued, ". . . he takes words as he finds them interrelated about him and composes them—without distortion which would mar their exact significances—into an intense expression of his perceptions and ardors that they may constitute a revelation in the speech that he uses" (*SE*, 257). Because he believed poets must be true to their immediate, native language, Williams was particularly and violently opposed to American poets using traditional, English meters. "Five beats to the line here," he complained in a review of a book by Wallace Stevens, "and that's where the trouble is let in. . . . The result is turgidity, dullness and a language, God knows what it is! certainly nothing anybody alive today could ever recognize. . . . The language is constrained by the meter instead of there being—an impossible peak it may be—a meter discovering itself in the language."[23]

The bad influence of English meters upon American poets was so insidious, Williams believed, that the development of a truly American prosody had to be an iconoclastic as well as constructive process. The first objective of American poets, he wrote in 1953, was to invent a prosody of their own, and the first step in this process was for them to realize that "English prosody is not, finally, an inevitable deterministic dispensation from the gods; it is an historical development growing from English conditions. . . . Its forms are the form of empire. The first thing we must do as poets . . . is to throw it out, body and soul."[24]

Very early in his career, about 1913, Williams gave up most of the devices of conventional prosody along with rhyme and capital letters at the beginning of his lines (*IWW*, 15). He then briefly used Whitman's "nonmetrical prosody," which is based upon speech rhythms and syntax.[25]

As early as 1917 Williams became dissatisfied with this Whit-

[23]"Poet's Corner," review of Wallace Stevens' *The Man with the Blue Guitar and Other Poems, New Republic*, XCIII (Nov. 17, 1937), 50.

[24]"Experimental and Formal Verse," *Quarterly Review of Literature*, VII, 3 (1953), 174.

[25]For an excellent study of Whitman's prosody see Gross, *Sound and Form in Modern Poetry*, pp. 83 ff.

manesque form of free verse and agreed with Pound's and
Eliot's contention that it was too loose and undisciplined. "Having gained a certain devil-may-care disregard for poetry's long
used forms by abusing them as best we know how," he wrote,
". . . let it be stated with finality that 'free verse' is a misnomer.
. . . It has been the proper turn for us to take. But because we
have worked in a careless mood along hidden channels would be
a poor excuse for any declaration of freedom. The only freedom
a poet can have is to be conscious of his manoevres [sic], to recognize whither he is trending [sic] and to govern his sensibilities
. . . so that it [the poem] accord delicately with his emotions."[26]

Unlike Pound and Eliot, however, Williams did not compromise between freedom and tradition by adopting a prosody
which was flexible enough to approximate a live voice yet contained enough traditional—though often unorthodox—meters
to reveal a recognizable metrical pattern. Pound, for example,
condemned iambic pentameter but he also ordered the modern
poet to "fill his mind with the finest cadences he can discover,
preferably in a foreign language . . . e.g., Saxon charms, Hebridean Folk Songs, the verse of Dante, and the lyrics of Shakespeare."[27] Williams, on the other hand, would accept no pattern which was not derived from his own speech. A poem should
have a pattern because its meter was "intrinsic" to the character
of the poet's speech (SE, 256)—not because it echoed the
rhythms, i.e., paradigms, of Hebridean folk songs. In his earlier
poetry he compromised between freedom and order by arranging his poems in "rhythmic units" which would achieve some
"formal arrangement of the lines" without deforming the
spoken language. "The rhythmic unit decided the form of my
poetry," he recalled later. "When I came to the end of a
rhythmic unit (not necessarily a sentence) I ended the line. The
rhythmic unit was not measured by capitals at the beginning of
a line or periods within the lines. . . . The rhythmic unit usually came to me in a lyrical outburst. . . . The rhythmic pace
was the pace of speech, an excited pace because I was excited
when I wrote. I was discovering, pressed by some violent mood.
The lines were short, *not* studied" (IWW, 15, 22-23). But since

[26]"America, Whitman, and the Art of Poetry," *The Poetry Journal*, VIII
(Nov., 1917), 28. For Pound's description of his and Eliot's rejection of *vers
libre*, see "A Retrospect," *Pavannes and Divisions* (New York, 1918), p. 108.
[27]Pound, "A Retrospect," p. 98.

the forms of these "rhythmic units" are particular to the individual poems in which they appear, Williams' early poetry possesses no recognizable, over-all prosodic pattern or "line." Consequently while critics have often praised the formal arrangements of these poems, they also have been forced to assert that Williams' poetry lacks a formal prosodic base. For example, when Karl Shapiro tries to define Williams' prosodic methods in conventional terms, he can only describe them negatively as "not a prosodic line at all."

By prosody Williams does not mean versification. If you examine his own poems or his own remarks about what he calls mysteriously "the line," you will see the following things: He neither preaches nor practices "foot" prosody; he does not preach or practice meters; nor syllabic versification . . . nor is his prosody accentual; nor is it "typographical" . . . nor does he base versification on rhyme nor on the internal figurations which rhyme may produce.[28]

Williams never seems to have been much troubled by this type of criticism. As long as a poem's form was right to his own ear, he did not worry about whether or not it seemed formless to his critics. During the 1940's, however, he began to take his responsibilities to American poetry more seriously. In a 1942 letter to his son William Eric he doubted whether his "technical influence" upon other poets had been "good or even adequate," because his poems were so intensely personal. There was nothing in them that could be copied, and this disturbed Williams for he wished to make a contribution to "the true evolving tradition" of poetry—as well as develop individually as a poet (SL, 202). He frequently asserted in his lectures and criticism of this period that American poetry had to have its own line or measure, its own recognizable metric pattern. After one of these demands for American poets to "break away from the confining British tradition," Williams told Parker Tyler in 1946:

Someone in the audience . . . asked me if I thought I had given any evidence of the "new way of measuring" in anything I had read that night or in anything that I myself had written at any time. It was a fair question but one I shall have to postpone answering indefinitely.

It may be that I am no genius in the use of the new measure I find inevitable; it may be that as a poet I have not had the genius to do the things I set up as essential if our verse is to blossom (SL, 243).

[28]"The True Contemporary," Start with the Sun (Lincoln, Neb., 1963), p. 211.

Williams' humility about his own experiments was needless. Actually, as Linda W. Wagner has pointed out, he had begun to experiment intensively with the length and form of his lines in the early 1940's, and his search for a "final solution in [poetic] structure led him through more prosodic experimentation in the coming fifteen years than he had attempted in the previous thirty-five."[29]

At first, in the early 1940's, Williams experimented chiefly with line length and an assortment of typographical devices— some of which were mannered. The following passage from *Paterson* is a good example of his early prosodic experiments.

<blockquote>
The poem moves them or
it does not move them. Faitoute, his ears
ringing   .   no sound   .   no great city,
as he seems to read—
     a roar of books
from the wadded library oppresses him
        until
his mind begins to drift   .
       (III, i, 122-123)
</blockquote>

Williams achieves a good many of the effects of prosody in these lines without establishing a conventional prosodic line. For example, speech rhythms are established by the varied line lengths and the splitting of lines as if they were dramatic dialogue. The placement of words on the margins of the page gives them the same emphasis that they would receive at the end of conventional, rhymed lines. Duration and hesitations are enforced by the use of extra spaces and periods between words.[30] However, these typographical devices in *Paterson* are sometimes distracting and draw more attention to themselves than they do to the language which they are supposed to be measuring. Some seem improvised on a line-by-line or stanza-by-stanza basis; and many of them deserve the criticism Williams made of poetry that tried to adapt English meters to idiomatic American speech: "some pulling and padding, some skimping and stretching, which is no real break, an expedient no sooner mastered than discarded dejectedly."[31]

Williams prosodic experiments became less erratic during the

[29]Wagner, *The Poems of William Carlos Williams*, p. 85.
[30]*Ibid.*, pp. 85 ff.
[31]"Preface," 348-349.

early 1950's. Then he discovered his "variable foot," a rather long, Whitmanesque natural speech line which is broken into three steps or segments.

Williams first used this triadic line at the beginning of *Paterson II* (iii, 96-97). He did not then consider this form of line arrangement very special, but he later decided that it was his "final conception" of what his poetry should be (*IWW,* 80). Writing about a roughly similar form of line arrangement used by Byron Vazakas, Williams claimed that it "is a *line* that will allow us room in which to develop the opportunities of a new language, a line loose as Whitman's, but *measured* as his was not." Williams particularly admired the way Vazakas' device ordered language entirely by duration and thus functioned like a bar in music: "A bar, definitely, since it is not related to grammar, but to *time*. . . . The clause, the sentence, and the paragraph are ignored, and the progression goes over into the next bar as much as the musical necessity requires...a sequence of musical bars . . . capable of infinite modulation."[32]

There is a key difference between Vazakas' typography and Williams' triadic line. Vazakas' poetry is constructed in four-line units with the first line extending slightly to the left because the remaining lines of the "bar" are indented. These units can be read as lines or "bars"; but it is equally easy to read them as small verse paragraphs or even, though Williams denies this, as short, free verse stanzas. Williams' triadic line, on the other hand, is more definitely a line, and it is harder to read it as prose poetry or free verse because the "steps" enforce pauses more strongly than Vazakas' indentations do.

Despite this difference, Williams' triadic line has a good deal in common with Vazakas' indented "bars," and many of the advantages which he found in Vazakas' device also characterize his own "new measure." In particular, the triadic line is a good compromise between the regularity which Williams considered necessary in poetry and the "looseness" of free verse which makes complete fidelity to spoken language possible. "The foot not being fixed," he explained, "is only to be described as variable. If the foot itself is variable it allows order in so-called free verse. Thus the verse becomes not free at all but just simply variable, as all things in life properly are" (*IWW,* 82). Because

[32]*Ibid.,* 349. The second ellipsis in this passage is Williams'.

the "feet" of Williams' measure are not counted accent-by-accent, it is unnecessary for the poet to invert phrases or otherwise distort speech in order to make the meter come out right.

Yet the energy of the spoken language in Williams' "variable foot" poetry never becomes the "senseless / unarrangement of wild things—" which he accused Whitman of creating, the meaningless "torrent" of language which he depicted in *Paterson*. Because Williams himself "breaks" his lines into three-step segments, so that they have a faint but persistent musical regularity, it is impossible for them to "break" chaotically according to whatever way they may be read—as free verse frequently does.

However, these breaks are determined by the qualities of each individual line. They do not conform to an abstract pattern. Each line is, so to speak, the democratic equal of the others and has its own intrinsic "music" or measure which is revealed by the steps that form it. All the lines in Williams' late poems in this measure must be understood in their own right; each is its own paradigm.

Another advantage of Williams' "variable foot" is that its regularity, like Vazakas', is capable of considerable, if not "infinite," modulation. With it Williams was able to express the "music" or "time" of many kinds of experience in his late poetry. For example, there is the precise sound of exact thought in "The Gift."

> The rich gifts
> so unsuitable for a child
> though devoutly proffered,
> stood for all that love can bring.
>
> *(Pictures,* 61)

Or in "The Turtle," there is the light humor with which the old savor the intensity of children.

> When we are together
> you talk of nothing else
> ascribing all sorts
> of murderous motives
> to his least action.
> You ask me
> to write a poem,
> should I have poems to write,
> about a turtle.
>
> *(Pictures,* 63)

Often, Williams uses the "variable foot" to express the harsh, driving, elliptical rhythms of the mind—

> Without the quirks
>   and oddnesses of invention
>   the paralytic is confirmed
>   in his paralysis,
>   it is from a northern
>   and half-savage country
>   where the religion
>   is hate.
>
> *(Pictures,* 95)

and the harsh, sordid realities of life:

> The man
>   heavy-set
>   about my own age
>   seventy
>   was talking privately
>   with a sailor.
> He had an ugly jaw on him.
>
> *(Pictures,* 146)

Yet in "Asphodel" Williams uses his triadic line equally successfully to express the subtle "musics" of revery, meditation, and satisfaction.

> As I think of it now,
>   after a lifetime,
>   it is as if
>   a sweet-scented flower
>   were poised
>   and for me did open.
>
> *(Pictures,* 182)

And at times he achieves the great richness of strong but subdued emotional and intellectual experience.

>   Yet it is
>   that which made El Greco
>   paint his green and distorted saints
>   and live
>   lean.
>   It is what in life drives us
>   to praise music
>   and the old
>   or sit by a friend
>   in his last hours.
>
> *(Pictures,* 95)

> the tortured body of my flower
> which is not a mustard flower at all
> but some unrecognized
> and unearthly flower
> for me to naturalize
> and acclimate
> and choose it for my own.
>
> (*Pictures*, 91)

But even though Williams used his "variable foot" to express a broad spectrum of experience, he often seems to have preferred to use it to discover unexpected distinctions in the most commonplace and even mundane language. A new kind of poetic line exists, Williams wrote in 1952, "omitting memories of trees and watercourses and clouds and pleasant glades—as empty of them as Dante Allegiere's [*sic*] *Inferno* is empty of them—exists today. It is measured by the passage of time without accent, monotonous, useless—unless you are drawn as Dante was to see the truth undressed." Such a line might not express "the beat of dancing feet," but it would be able to permeate and express every facet of even the most mundane life. It would find "the mystical measure" of men's and women's passions "in the shuffling of human beings in all the stages of their day, the trip to the bath-room, to the stairs of the subway, the steps of the office or factory routine." "It is indeed a human pilgrimage," Williams concluded, "like Geoffrey Chaucer's; poets had better be aware of it and speak of it—and speak of it in plain terms, such as men will recognize."[33]

Williams' late poems like "The Pink Locust" are like the Shaker furniture Charles Sheeler collected—masterpieces in the use of plain materials. Yet for all its plainness, the language of Williams' late poems often seems surprising rather than monotonous. In *Many Loves* Hubert states his ideal of poetry that would have

> . . . a similarity
> to daily speech, the miracle being it
> sounds so, but by the awakening experienced
> is proven otherwise, charged to raise the
> spirit to a full enjoyment.
>
> (*ML*, 9)

[33]Introduction to Allen Ginsberg's *Empty Mirror* (New York, 1961), pp. 5-6.

And Williams himself stated the same ideal in greater detail in his review of Vazakas' *Transfigured Night*. "What an unimaginable pleasure it would be," he wrote, "to read or to hear lines that remain unpredictable, hold the ear in suspense, conceal all the elements of surprise to the end, and yet remain orderly, retain a perfect order, a meter to reassure us. This combination of order *with* discovery, with exploration and revelation . . . is of the essence of art."[34]

In his late poetry, particularly "Asphodel," Williams frequently attains this ideal of a common speech which is poetry not because it follows the beat of the metronome, but because the poem suddenly, surprisingly "awakens" us to the unexpected distinctions of our language's commonest phrases.

> The storm bursts
> 　　　　　　or fades! it is not
> the end of the world.
> 　　　　Love is something else,
> 　　　　　　　　or so I thought it. . . .
> 　　　　　　　　　　　(*Pictures,* 160)

> 　　　　The mere picture
> 　　　　　　　　of the exploding bomb
> fascinates us
> 　　　　so that we cannot wait
> 　　　　　　　　to prostrate ourselves
> before it. We do not believe
> 　　　　that love
> 　　　　　　　　can so wreck our lives.
> 　　The end
> 　　　　will come
> 　　　　　　in its time.
> 　　　　　　　　　　　(*Pictures,* 165)

In passages like these from "Asphodel" Williams presents the same kind of concern for the qualities of language that he urged writers to have for the qualities of "the people." He had argued in "The Basis of Faith in Art" that in times of social disorder the artist must have "no principles save the rediscovery in people of the elements of order" (*SE,* 189). And the function of short stories, he wrote in 1950, is to take "the materials of every day" and use "them to raise the consciousness of our lives to higher aesthetic and moral levels by the use of the art." The

---

[34]"Preface," 348.

form of a short story accomplishes this by taking a trait of some person and raising it "from the groveling, debasing as it is debased jargon . . . to the exquisite distinction of that particular man, woman, horse or child that is depicted" (*SE,* 297). In the same way Williams' triadic line discovers an order or measure within each phrase of even the most commonplace language. Moreover, this "variable foot" reveals how almost any spoken phrase contains qualities which can convey its unique identity and distinction when they are revealed by the form of the poetic line.

Or Williams' presentation of language in his late poems can be compared with his use of description in his early poetry. "I walk back streets," he wrote in 1916,

> admiring the houses
> of the very poor:
> roof out of line with sides
> the yards cluttered
> with old chicken wire, ashes,
> furniture gone wrong;
> the fences and outhouses
> built of barrel-staves
> (*CEP,* 121)

For throughout his career Williams was convinced that the America he knew possessed unexpected, even uncommon, riches of sight and sound which could be discovered if new forms and techniques could be invented to reveal them. "We are NOT poverty stricken," he wrote in 1950, "in the area of the New Language, that is, the area of literature which is all we should speak of. We are the richest in opportunity and, strangely enough, in accomplishment, in the making of poems, the richest area on earth. But we must know what our riches are and we must be single-minded and industrious in pushing our advantage...."[35]

CONCLUSION

Because of his awareness of these riches and his insistence in exploring them, Williams' development as a writer was consistently supported by several important elements which motivated the changes in his attitudes, theories, and techniques. Williams

[35]"Two Letters," *The Golden Goose,* VI, 5 (Oct., 1952), 30.

always had an unfailing commitment to the local and the commonplace. "Take anything," he advised his fellow poets in 1919, "take the land at your feet and use it. It is as good material as another."[36] "The American must work toward a present, a local necessity," he wrote. "This necessity is precisely the same as that which animated Athens, Rome or whatever other locality you may wish to name, present day London among the rest. Each man uses what he *has* for his constructions."[37]

This application of art to the environment was "a necessity" because only works of the imagination could "refresh" the world so men could possess it and live well in it. "How foolish to seek new worlds," Williams wrote in 1946, "sometimes, when we must know that any world warmed by the arts will surpass the very Elysian Fields if the imagination reaches its end there."[38] But a man's relationship to his environment, as Williams was aware, is not constant. The environment changes economically, socially, and culturally; and men change personally. "Certainly I am not a robin," Williams noted in *Paterson*,

> nor erudite,
> no Erasmus nor bird that returns to the same
> ground year by year. Or if I am   .   .
> the ground has undergone
> a subtle transformation, its identity altered.
>
> (I, ii, 29)

He therefore based his art upon not one but a number of subtly different relationships between himself and his "ground."

In his critical writings, Williams repeatedly argues that the artist must renew his art through experimentation or "invention" if it is to accomplish its task of renewing the world. Writing about his own "various phases" as a writer, he claimed that "the processes of art, to keep alive, must always challenge the unknown and go where the most uncertainty lies" (*SE*, xvii). The poem, he wrote in 1947, "needs continual redesigning in each period of the world so as to increase its capacity . . . to refresh the world (if possible) in each period by conceiving the world anew in terms of the arts."[39]

---

[36]"A Maker," *Little Review*, VI, 4 (Aug., 1919), 38.
[37]Untitled reply to "American and English Poetry: A Questionnaire" in *Modern American Poetry*, ed. B. Rajan (New York, 1952), pp. 189-190.
[38]"Preface," 348.
[39]"An Approach to the Poem," p. 53.

Seen in its broadest outlines, Williams' poetic career possesses a number of "peaks," a number of periods when he possessed extremely intense visions of his relationship to his American environment.[40] These peaks are the seminal moments of Williams' life as an artist, the times when "love and the imagination / are of a piece" for him (*Pictures*, 179), because he possessed that "streamlike human purity of purpose" which animated men like Columbus and Rasles (*IAG*, 11). Following these peaks are "descents," periods when he applied the themes and techniques of his seminal works to the phenomena of his environment. At the end of these descents are "depths," periods characterized by very chaotic or prosaic works when Williams could see no poetic alternatives to "classic imitation or tightness" and "a loose nothing, a rhythmical blur, a formlessness" which he considered equally abhorrent (*SL*, 132). But within these depths, Williams discovered the seeds for new artistic growth, for ascents back to new peaks, new "marriages" with his world. The over-all pattern of his development might be seen in this way.

The first peak occurs between 1914 and 1916 and is expressed in "The Wanderer" and Williams' adoption of the theories of Imagism. The second peak can be located in the mid-1920's, between the composition of *In the American Grain* and the *Dial* "Paterson" (*CEP*, 233-235). Another peak begins in the late 1930's; it includes his anti-poetic critical theories, *Many Loves,* and poems from *The Wedge* such as "Paterson: The Falls," "Catastrophic Birth," and "Writer's Prologue to a Play in Verse." The final peak of Williams' career was in the early 1950's when he wrote "The Desert Music" and formulated his theory of the variable foot.

Williams' depth periods of creativity are also fairly definite. During the early 1920's there is the phase marked by *The Great American Novel* and the prose passages of *Spring and All*. Next there is the rather long "prose" period of the early 1930's, described in his letter to Kay Boyle (*SL*, 129-136), during which he

[40]My usage of the term "descent" is derived from *Paterson* II, iii, 96-97, 104. An analysis of Williams' development, which is similar to mine, is that of Richard A. Macksey, " 'A Certainty of Music': Williams' Changes" in *William Carlos Williams: A Collection of Critical Essays,* ed. J. Hillis Miller (Englewood Cliffs, N.J., 1966), pp. 132-147.

wrote "Notes in Diary Form," *White Mule,* and his early short stories. The final depth occurs in the late 1940's during the composition of *Paterson III* and *IV*.

Most of Williams' other works can be considered "descent" works, domestications of the seminal theories, myths, and techniques of his peak periods. For example, the poems in *Al Que Quiere, Sour Grapes,* and *Spring and All* are animated by the myth expressed in "The Wanderer" and their techniques are derived from Imagism.

This is a rough sketch of a very complex process. Other works than those I have used could easily be added or substituted as representatives of the various stages. Some works, for example *Asphodel,* seem to fit two categories. Nevertheless, the pattern which emerges has certain significant features which are helpful in understanding Williams' creative development. First, the peaks of his career are characterized by eloquent, violently emotional works which are essentially creation myths, i.e., their main episodes are immersions which lead to some form of rebirth. These seminal works contain most of the themes and techniques of the "descent" works which follow them. Accompanying—and to some extent intellectualizing—these peaks are phases of intense theoretical activity during which Williams seems to have been very receptive to his own and others' ideas about art and life. In both his theories and the poetry of these peak periods, Williams expresses a great love for his material environment and a great faith in its virtues. He also expresses, in some works, a violent hatred for all who harm or disparage the American scene.

As he masters and possesses the feelings, theories, and techniques of his seminal works, Williams *domesticates* them by applying them to the concrete, local particulars of his environment. "In every man there must finally occur," he wrote in 1939, "a fusion between his dream which he dreamed when he was young and the phenomenal world of his later years if he is to be rated high as a master of his art" (*SE, 236*). His development as an artist is complex because he fused not one but several dreams with his immediate, "phenomenal world." "I've always wanted to fit poetry into the life around us," he said in 1956, "because I love poetry. I'm not the type of poet who looks only at the rare thing. I want to use the words we speak and to describe the things we see, as far as it can be done. . . . Poetry should be brought into the world where we live and not be so recondite, so removed from the people. To bring poetry out of the clouds and down to earth I still believe possible" (*ND 17,* 253).

But as Williams further domesticates the theories and techniques of his peak periods, his works lose their visionary or mythic qualities. Their original impetus becomes fainter and less obvious. Aesthetically these "descent" works are equal or even superior to his seminal works; they are calmer, more objective, and usually more carefully written, but they lack the great emotional intensity, and they are not so obviously guided by the original technical theory.

"At least we know," Williams wrote in 1929, "that a poem is a mechanism that has a function which is to say something as accurately and as clearly as possible, but that while we are even in the act of creating it, the words (the parts) are getting old and out of date just as would be the corresponding parts of a motor car."[41] When his poetic techniques and theories grow old, Williams does not try to prolong their existence. Instead he returns to the instinctual prosaic, chaotic reality which he considered the true basis of value. During these "depth" periods of his career he works mainly in prose and even resorts to automatic writing to overcome "blockages." He complains that he cannot discover any adequate poetic forms and doubts his ability as a writer. His emotional attitude toward his environment in these "depth" works is often destructive; he lacks faith in America, despises its language, and satirizes his subjects bitterly. But even though these "depths" are the most difficult periods of Williams' life as a writer, they are also the most valuable because they contain—in nascent form—seminal concepts and techniques for his new peaks of poetic activity. For example, *The Great American Novel* contains the concept of the New World which animates *In the American Grain; Paterson IV* possesses the creative method which underlies *Asphodel* and *Paterson V.*

[41]"For a New Magazine," *Blues,* I, 2 (March, 1929), 31. ". . . we are stopped in our tracks by the dead masquerading as life. We are stopped by the archaic lingering in our laboring forms of procedure . . . seeking to prevent the new life from generating in the decay of the old." *SE,* p. 204.

As he grew more experienced as an artist, Williams became more aware of the cyclical nature of his own imaginative processes. His use of seasonal and sexual metaphors, particularly in *Paterson,* often reveals his emotional awareness of the stages in his own and others' creativity. Certain poems written in the early 1940's—"The Clouds," "The Birth of Venus," "Burning the Christmas Greens," "Catastrophic Birth"—are structured upon this death-rebirth cycle. And, on a few occasions, Williams expresses a full intellectual awareness of this imaginative pattern in general, theoretical terms. "I have been working with prose, since I didn't know what to do with poetry," he wrote in 1932. "Perhaps I have been in error. Maybe I should be slaving at verse. But I don't think so. Prose can be a laboratory for metrics. It is lower in the literary scale. But it throws up jewels which may be cleaned and grouped" (*SL,* 130). And in 1946 he contrasted his own development with that of artists like Ezra Pound. Pound, wrote Williams, tried to renew his art through "reading," through returning to past excellence and attempting to apply it to the present. But, Williams argued, "there may be another literary source continuing the greatness of the past which does not develop androgynetically from the past itself mind to mind but from the present, from the hurley-burley" of modern life.[42] "I have written little poetry," he told Kay Boyle. "Form, the form has been lacking. Instead I have been watching speech in my own environment from which I continually expect to discover whatever of new [*sic*] is being reflected about the world. I have no interest . . . in the cosmic. I have been actively at work (if such sketchy trials as I employ can be called such) in the flesh, watching how words match the act, especially how they come together" (*SL,* 129-130).

Williams could not have achieved this "continual redesigning" of his own imaginative processes if he had been a primitive or "redskin" artist.[43] He criticized highly self-conscious or "aca-

---

[42]"Letter to an Australian Editor," *Briarcliff Quarterly,* III, 11 (Oct., 1946), 207. "How in the world are we to recognize the excellence of the classics other than in the conditions of our own lives? If they are not operative . . . in our own phase and conditions as they were in another phase and condition how can we have the vanity and silliness to believe them valuable. . . ." "The So-Called So-Called," *The Patroon,* I, 1 (May, 1937), 1.

[43]For my definition of the "primitive" or "redskin" writer I am indebted to Philip Rahv: "The redskin writer in America is . . . a crass materialist, a

demic" authors for "despising an essential part of the poetic process, the imaginative quota, the unbridled, mad—sound basis of all poems" (*SL*, 194). Yet Williams was not, as he himself protested, "a rough sort of blindman."[44] In a 1950 interview he emphasized that no matter how unconscious or spontaneous the sources of a man's poetry might be, "the better artist he is, the better he's able to recognize what is good and *why* it's good— and how to organize it into a satisfactory poem. He must have his theories, as Pasteur said, he must work to them, and so he becomes what has been termed in the past a master—a man who knows what everything means, knows why he put it down, can take it apart and put it together again and still have it spontaneous as ever. In fact, Yeats said you must labor to be beautiful."[45] Williams had his theories, and he did "work to them." Imagism, Objectivism, the "anti-poetic," the "variable foot," his conceptions of local cultures and American history—all of these ideas or theories guided his writings and are useful in understanding them.

Nor was Williams a primitive in the sense of being a careless writer. He was determined that American poetry should be equal or superior to that of other nations, and he knew that this goal could only be achieved through hard work and craftsmanship. When asked about the influence of Edith Sitwell's postwar poetry upon American poetry, Williams replied:

. . . influence or no influence, everyone who has read it is bowled over by Miss Edith Sitwell's recent work. . . . Should we do anything more, after our unstinted enjoyment, than marvel at the work of this woman? And when we have done that should we not look about to see whether or not we have anything comparable in excellence to present here? And seeing our lack what more is there for us to do than to

---

greedy consumer of experience, and . . . a sentimentalist, a half-baked mystic listening to inward voices and watching for signs and portents . . . [his] faults, however, are not so much literary as faults of raw life itself. Unable to relate himself in any significant manner to the cultural heritage, the redskin writer is always on his own; and since his personality resists growth and change, he must continually repeat himself." *Image and Idea* (Norfolk, Conn., 1949), p. 4.

[44]*SL*, p. 299. "I believe the mind is the dominant force in the world today—the most valuable possession with which to face the world. . . . I deny being anti-intellectual: I was always conscious of my mind." *ND 17*, p. 295.

[45]"Symposium on Writing," p. 94.

apply ourselves anew to our difficulties in order to try as we may to make of our own materials anything so successful and so fine.[46]

Above all, Williams was definitely not a primitive in his awareness of the emotional qualities which men needed to appreciate and develop properly "the new" in art and life. In his discussions of "the new," Williams emphasized that it could be an emotionally exhilarating experience that would renew men's lives only if they possessed the emotional and intellectual maturity, sensitivity, and tolerance to respond to it properly.

The great tragedy of America, Williams believed, was that most men had responded to its newness with feelings of fear, greed, and disappointment rather than with awe and wonder. Columbus' voyage, he wrote in "Asphodel," "promised so much / but due to the world's avarice / breeding hatred / through fear, / ended so disastrously" (Pictures, 167). It is the Puritans in In the American Grain who are the true "primitives," who fear and hate the New World because they are empty of any other emotional responses (IAG, 112). Indeed, no matter how talented men may be, Williams wrote about the conquistadors, they will destroy the world if they are "empty" of love for it. For any man whose imagination does not respond to life and serve it must serve death (Pictures, 179). "It was the evil of the whole world," he wrote of the destruction of Tenochtitlan, ". . . the perennial disappointment which follows, like smoke, the bursting of ideas. It was the spirit of malice which underlies men's lives and against which nothing offers resistance. And bitter as the thought may be that Tenochtitlan, the barbaric city, its people, its genius wherever found should have been crushed out because of the awkward names men give their emptiness, yet it was no man's fault. It was the force of the pack whom the dead drive" (IAG, 27).

Williams' life as a man and an artist is an answer to a single question: by whose virtues shall we live? The virtues of the living or those of the dead? Whose voices shall we hear and express in our art, those of the "illustrious" past or those of the "squalid" present?[47] No one lives more by the virtues of the

---

[46]Untitled reply to "American and English Poetry," p. 190.

[47]In what is perhaps his best analysis of his long hostility to Eliot, Williams wrote: "Our age is rich, not poor. It is rich in its inheritances for

past than the true primitive. "In the particulars of his conscious behavior," writes Mircea Eliade, "the 'primitive,' the archaic man, acknowledges no act which has not been previously posited and lived by someone else. . . . What he does has been done before. His life is the ceaseless repetition of gestures initiated by others."[48] Driven by "the dead," the primitive cannot acknowledge any other, any new virtue. He is forced endlessly to relive the virtues of the past.

William's great determination was to be driven by life, to pursue, acknowledge, and serve what he described as the "rare element" of life "which may appear at any time, at any place, at a glance . . . it is there, it is magnificent, it fills my thoughts, it reaches to the farthest limits of our lives" (Autobiography, 360). But it is neither simple nor easy to serve life. The moment we value any virtue of life it becomes fixed in the form—aesthetic, intellectual, religious—of our praise and recognition. This form becomes the virtue's monument, the icon becomes the idol, and life begins to decay within it. Then this form, created by life, begins to create death; for it will cause us to ignore newer, less formally excellent, living virtues. New manifestations of what is valuable in life will be sacrificed to the past, to death. "Formal patterns of all sorts," Williams wrote in 1939, "represent arrests of the truth in some particular phase of its mutations, and immediately thereafter, unless they change, become mutilations" (SE, 205-206).

We can only escape "the force of the pack whom the dead drive" if we are willing to sacrifice our allegiance to these "formal patterns," no matter how "beautiful," when they begin to falsify and deform life. "They found that they had not only left England," Williams wrote of the American colonists, but that they had arrived somewhere else: at a place whose pressing reality demanded not only a tremendous bodily devotion but as well, and more importately, great powers of adaptability, a complete reconstruction of their most intimate cultural make-

---

the mind, for the spirit. It isn't bare. That is why I have battled T. S. Eliot from the first. There's another [reason]. At the risk of making a fool of myself I have insisted that he has never known what the deepest knowledge of the world offers. It is NOT what he thinks it is; he has vitiated the good and emphasized the stereotype and the dead. . . ." "Two Letters," 30.

[48]Mircea Eliade, Cosmos and History: The Myth of the Eternal Return (New York, 1959), p. 5.

up, to accord with the new conditions. The most hesitated and turned back in their hearts at the first glance" (*SE*, 134). Williams' great heroes in *In the American Grain* are men like Columbus, Burr, Boone, and Rasles—who did not turn back. These men were able to possess and discover New Worlds only because they were able to value the virtues of American living no matter how raw and primeval. They were willing to "turn inland" and to ignore the "easier fortune" of allegiance to the past, dead virtues of European culture (*SE*, 140-142). In this sense, Williams' achievement was greater than that of his heroes. For he was willing to ignore not only the forms of European culture, but also those of his own creation when they became "dead." No matter how highly he valued his theories and discoveries, no matter how skillfully he used them, Williams was always willing to sacrifice them so that he could discover anew the "rare element" of life which he loved so faithfully.

BIBLIOGRAPHY

WORKS BY WILLIAM CARLOS WILLIAMS

Williams, William Carlos. "America, Whitman, and the Art of Poetry," *The Poetry Journal,* VIII (Nov., 1917), 27-36.

———. "The American Idiom," *New Directions 17.* Norfolk, Conn.: New Directions, 1961, pp. 250-251.

———. "An Approach to the Poem," *English Institute Essays, 1947.* New York: Columbia University Press, 1948, pp. 50-76.

———. *The Autobiography of William Carlos Williams.* New York: Random House, 1951.

———. *The Build-Up.* New York: Random House, 1952.

———. *The Collected Earlier Poems of William Carlos Williams.* Norfolk, Conn.: New Directions, 1951.

———. *The Collected Later Poems of William Carlos Williams.* Revised edition. Norfolk, Conn.: New Directions, 1963.

———. *Collected Poems 1921-1931.* Preface by Wallace Stevens. New York: The Objectivist Press, 1934.

———. "The Comic Life of Elia Brobitza," *Others,* V, 3 (April-May, 1919), 1-16.

———. *The Complete Collected Poems of William Carlos Williams 1906-1938.* Norfolk, Conn.: New Directions, 1938.

———. *Contact I-IV,* eds. William Carlos Williams and Robert McAlmon (1920-23).

———. *Contact* (second series), eds. William Carlos Williams and Nathanael West. I, 1-3 (Feb.-Oct., 1932).

———. "An Essay on *Leaves of Grass,*" *Leaves of Grass: One Hundred Years After,* ed. Milton Hindus. Stanford, Calif.: Stanford University Press, 1955, pp. 22-31.

———. "Experimental and Formal Verse," *Quarterly Review of Literature,* VII, 3 (1953), 171-175.

———. "An Extraordinary Sensitivity," *Poetry,* LX (Sept., 1942), 338-340.

———. "Faiths for a Complex World," *American Scholar,* XXVI (Fall, 1957), 453-457.

———. *The Farmers' Daughters.* Introduction by Van Wyck Brooks. Norfolk, Conn.: New Directions, 1961.

————. "The Fatal Blunder," *Quarterly Review of Literature*, II, 2 (1945), 125-126.

————. "5 to the Fifth Power," *New Republic*, CXXXVI (Jan. 21, 1957), 20.

————. "For a New Magazine," *Blues*, I, 2 (March, 1929), 30-32.

————. "Four Foreigners," *Little Review*, VI, 5 (Sept., 1919), 36-39.

————. "From: A Folded Skyscraper," *The American Caravan*, ed. Alfred Kreymborg *et al.* New York: The Macaulay Co., 1927, pp. 216-221.

————. Introduction to Allen Ginsberg's *Empty Mirror*. New York: Totem Press, 1961.

————. Introduction to Allen Ginsberg's *Howl and Other Poems*. San Francisco: City Lights Books, 1956.

————. *The Great American Novel* in *Great American Short Novels*, ed. R. P. Blackmur. New York: Thomas Y. Crowell Co., 1960, pp. 307-344. Originally published by The Three Mountains Press, Paris, 1923.

————. "Hart Crane (1899-1932)," *Contempo* (July 5, 1932), pp. 1, 4.

————. "Homage to Ford Madox Ford," *New Directions 7*. Norfolk, Conn.: New Directions, 1942, pp. 490-491.

————. "How to Write" in Linda W. Wagner, *The Poems of William Carlos Williams*. Middletown, Conn.: Wesleyan University Press, 1964, pp. 145-147. Originally published in *New Directions 1936*. Norfolk, Conn.: New Directions, 1936, n.p.

————. "Impasse and Imagery," *The Dial*, LXXXV (Nov., 1928), 431-433.

————. *In the American Grain*. Introduction by Horace Gregory. Norfolk, Conn.: New Directions, 1956. Originally published by Albert and Charles Boni, New York, 1925.

————. *In the Money*. Norfolk, Conn.: New Directions, 1940.

————. "In Praise of Marriage," *Quarterly Review of Literature*, II, 2 (1945), 145-149.

————. *I Wanted to Write a Poem*, ed. Edith Heal. Boston: Beacon Press, 1958.

————. "Jefferson and/or Mussolini," *New Democracy*, V, 4 (Oct. 15, 1935), 61-62.

————. *Kora in Hell: Improvisations*. San Francisco: City Lights Books, 1957. Originally published by The Four Seas Co., Boston, 1920.

————. "A Note on Layton," introduction to Irving Layton's *The Improved Binoculars*. Highlands, N.C.: Jonathan Williams, 1956.

————. "Letter on Pound," *Quarterly Review of Literature*, V, 3 (1950), 301.

————. "Letter to an Australian Editor," *Briarcliff Quarterly*, III, 11 (Oct., 1946), 205-208.

————. "A Maker," *Little Review*, VI, 4 (Aug., 1919), 36-39.

————. "A Man Versus the Law," *The Freeman*, I, 15 (June 23, 1920), 348-349.

————. *Many Loves and Other Plays*. Norfolk, Conn.: New Directions, 1961.

————. "Measure," *Spectrum,* III, 3 (Fall, 1959), 131-157.

————. "Men...Have No Tenderness," *New Directions 7.* Norfolk, Conn.: New Directions, 1942, pp. 429-436.

————. Microfilm tapes of Dr. Williams' manuscripts, tapes 21-26. Lockwood Memorial Library Poetry Collection, State University of New York at Buffalo, Buffalo, New York.

————. Microfilm tape of Dr. Williams' notes and manuscripts for *Paterson.* Lockwood Memorial Library Poetry Collection, State University of New York at Buffalo, Buffalo, New York.

————. Untitled reply to "American and English Poetry: A Questionnaire" in *Modern American Poetry,* ed. B. Rajan. New York: Roy Publishers, 1952, pp. 187-190.

————. Preface to Merrill Moore's *The Dance of Death.* Brooklyn: I. E. Rubin, 1957.

————. "More Swill," *Little Review,* VI, 6 (Oct., 1919), 29-30.

————. "Muriel Rukeyser's 'US 1,'" *New Republic,* XCIV (March 9, 1938), 141-142.

————. "New Directions in the Novel," *New Democracy,* V, 5 (Nov. 1, 1935), 81-83.

————. "The New Poetical Economy," *Poetry,* XLIV (July, 1934), 220-225.

————. "A Note on Poetry" in *The Oxford Anthology of American Literature,* eds. W. R. Benet and N. H. Pearson. New York: Oxford University Press, 1938, pp. 1313-14.

————. "A Note on the Art of Poetry," *Blues,* I, 4 (May, 1929), 77-79.

————. "Notes from a Talk on Poetry," *Poetry,* XIV (July, 1919), 211-216.

————. "Notes on Norman Macleod," *Mosaic,* I, 1 (Nov.-Dec., 1934), 27-28.

————. *A Novelette and Other Prose, 1921-1931.* Toulon: TO, Publishers, 1932.

————. "Objectivism" in the *Encyclopedia of Poetry and Poetics,* ed. Alex Preminger. Princeton: Princeton University Press, 1965, p. 582.

————. "An Objectivists' Anthology," *The Symposium,* IV, 1 (Jan., 1933), 114-117.

————. *Paterson* I-V. Norfolk, Conn.: New Directions, 1963. Originally published in single volumes by New Directions, 1946, 1948, 1949, 1951, and 1958.

————. *Pictures from Brueghel and Other Poems.* New York: New Directions, 1962. This edition also contains the complete texts of *The Desert Music and Other Poems* and *Journey to Love* which were originally published by Random House, New York, 1954, 1955.

————. *Poems.* Rutherford: privately printed, 1909.

————. "A Poet Remembers" in *Paul Rosenfeld: Voyager in the Arts,* eds. J. Mellquist and L. Wiese. New York: Creative Age Press, Inc., 1948, pp. 154-157.

————. "Poets' Corner," review of Wallace Stevens' *The Man with the Blue Guitar and Other Poems, New Republic,* XCIII (Nov. 17, 1937), 50.

————. "Preface," *Quarterly Review of Literature,* II, 4 (1946), 346-349.

————. "Introduction" to Sidney Salt's *Christopher Columbus and Other Poems.* Boston: Bruce Humphries, 1937.

————. *Selected Essays.* New York: Random House, 1954.

————. *The Selected Letters of William Carlos Williams,* ed. John C. Thirlwall. New York: McDowell, Obolensky, 1957.

————. *Selected Poems.* Introduction by Randall Jarrell. Norfolk, Conn.: New Directions, 1949.

————. "Sermon with a Camera," *New Republic,* XCVI (Oct. 12, 1938), 282-283.

————. "Seventy Years Deep," *Holiday,* XVI (Nov., 1954), 54-55, 78.

————. Foreword to *Charles Sheeler, a Retrospective Exhibition.* Los Angeles: University of California Art Galleries, 1954.

————. Letter to Martha Baird, November 3, 1951, used as an introduction to Eli Siegel's *Hot Afternoons Have Been in Montana: Poems by Eli Siegel.* New York: Definition Press, 1957.

————. "The So-Called So-Called," *The Patroon,* Bergen College, N.J., I, 1 (May, 1937), 1-2, 36-40.

————. "A Social Diagnosis for Surgery," *New Democracy,* VI, 2 (April, 1936), 26-27.

————. Williams' introduction to "Some Flower Studies" in *This Is My Best,* ed. Whit Burnett. Cleveland: World Publishing Co., 1945, p. 641.

————. *Spring and All.* Dijon: Contact Publishing Co., 1923.

————. "Symposium on Writing," *The Golden Goose,* Series 3, No. 2 (Autumn, 1951), 89-96.

————. "The Three Letters," *Contact III* (1921), 10-13.

————. "A Tribute," *John Marin.* Berkeley: University of California Press, 1956.

————. "A Twentieth-Century American," *Poetry,* XLVII (Jan., 1936), 227-229.

————. "Two Letters," *The Golden Goose,* VI, 5 (Oct., 1952), 30-32.

————. Unpublished manuscripts and notes. Lockwood Memorial Library Poetry Collection, State University of New York at Buffalo, Buffalo, New York.

————. *A Voyage to Pagany.* New York: The Macaulay Co., 1928.

————. "What Every Artist Knows," *The Freeman,* II, 45 (Jan. 19, 1921), 449.

————. *White Mule.* Norfolk, Conn.: New Directions, 1937.

————. " 'White Mule' Versus Poetry," *The Writer,* L (Aug., 1937), 243-245.

————. William Carlos Williams' manuscripts, notes, and letters. Collection of American Literature, Yale University Library, New Haven, Conn.

————. *Yes, Mrs. Williams: A Personal Record of My Mother.* New York: McDowell, Obolensky, 1959.

————. "Zukofsky," closing note to Louis Zukofsky's *"A" 1-12*. Ashland, Mass.: Origin Press, 1959, pp. 291-296.

OTHER WORKS CONSULTED

Anon. "Focus on William Carlos Williams, M.D.," *Roche Medical Image* (Dec., 1963), pp. 10-13.

Baur, John I. H. *Revolution and Tradition in Modern American Art.* Cambridge, Mass.: Harvard University Press, 1951.

Bourne, Randolph. *The History of a Literary Radical.* New York: B. W. Huebsch, 1920.

————. *War and the Intellectuals: Collected Essays, 1915-1919*, ed. C. Resek. New York: Harper & Row, 1964. Among the essays included in this collection are "Twilight of Idols," "The Puritan's Will to Power," and "The History of a Literary Radical."

Brinnin, John Malcolm. *William Carlos Williams.* Minneapolis: University of Minnesota Press, 1963.

Brooks, Van Wyck. *America's Coming-of-Age.* Revised edition. Garden City, N.Y.: Doubleday & Co., Inc., 1958.

Brown, Milton W. *American Painting from the Armory Show to the Depression.* Princeton: Princeton University Press, 1955.

Burke, Kenneth. "Heaven's First Law," *The Dial*, LXXII (Feb., 1922), 197-200.

————. "The Methods of William Carlos Williams," *The Dial*, LXXXII (Feb., 1927), 94-98.

————. "Subjective History," *Books* (March 14, 1926), p. 7.

————. "William Carlos Williams, 1883-1963," *The New York Review of Books*, I (Spring-Summer, 1963), 45-47.

Campbell, Joseph. *The Masks of God: Primitive Mythology.* New York: Viking Press, 1959.

Dewey, John. "Americanism and Localism," *The Dial*, LXVIII (June, 1920), 684-688.

————. *Democracy and Education.* New York: Macmillan, 1916.

Dochterman, Lillian. *The Quest of Charles Sheeler.* Iowa City: The University of Iowa, 1963.

Eliade, Mircea. *Cosmos and History: The Myth of the Eternal Return*, trans. Willard R. Trask. New York: Harper & Row, 1959.

Eliot, T. S. *Collected Poems, 1909-1962.* New York: Harcourt, Brace & World, Inc., 1963.

Ford, Ford Madox. *Portraits from Life.* Chicago: Henry Regnery, 1960. Originally published in America by Houghton Mifflin Co., Cambridge, Mass., 1937.

Frank, Waldo. *Our America.* New York: Boni and Liveright, 1919.

————. *The Re-discovery of America.* New York: Charles Scribner's Sons, 1929.

Friedman, Martin L. *The Precisionist View in American Art.* Minneapolis: Walker Art Center, 1960.

Frye, Northrop. *Anatomy of Criticism.* Princeton: Princeton University Press, 1957.

Fuchs, Daniel, *The Comic Spirit of Wallace Stevens*. Durham, N.C.: Duke University Press, 1963.

Gross, Harvey. *Sound and Form in Modern Poetry*. Ann Arbor: University of Michigan Press, 1965.

Halle, Morris, and Samuel Jay Keyser. "Chaucer and the Study of Prosody," *College English*, XXVIII (Dec., 1966), 187-219.

Hoffman, Frederick J., *et al*. *The Little Magazine: A History and a Bibliography*. Princeton: Princeton University Press, 1946.

The Homeric Hymns: A New Prose Translation, trans. Andrew Lang. New York: Longmans, Green, and Co., 1900.

Huber, Richard M., and Wheaton J. Lane, eds. *The Literary Heritage of New Jersey*. Princeton, N.J.: D. Van Nostrand Company, Inc., 1964.

Ignatow, David, ed. *William Carlos Williams: A Memorial Chapbook*, *The Beloit Poetry Journal*, XIV, 1 (Fall, 1963).

Johns, Orrick. *The Time of Our Lives*. New York: Stackpole Sons, 1937.

Jung, C. G., and C. Kerényi. *Essays on a Science of Mythology*, trans. R. F. C. Hull. New York: Harper & Row, 1963.

Kazin, Alfred. "White Mule," *The New York Times Book Review* (June 20, 1937), p. 7.

Kermode, Frank. "Disassociation of Sensibility" in *Modern Criticism: Theory and Practice*, eds. W. Sutton and R. Foster. New York: Odyssey Press, 1963.

Keyserling, Count Hermann. *America Set Free*. New York: Harper, 1929.

Koch, Vivienne. "All the Differences," *Voices*, 96 (Winter, 1939), pp. 47-49.

————. *William Carlos Williams*. Norfolk, Conn.: New Directions, 1950.

Koehler, Stanley. "The Art of Poetry VI: William Carlos Williams," *Paris Review*, 32 (Summer-Fall, 1964), pp. 110-151.

Kreymborg, Alfred. *Troubadour: An Autobiography*. New York: Boni and Liveright, 1925.

Lawrence, D. H. "America, Listen to Your Own," *New Republic*, XXV (Dec. 15, 1920), 68-70.

————. "American Heroes," *The Nation*, CXII (April 14, 1926), 413-414.

————. *Studies in Classic American Literature*. New York: Viking Press, 1964. Originally published by Thomas Seltzer, New York, 1923.

————. *The Symbolic Meaning: The Uncollected Versions of Studies in Classic American Literature*, ed. Armin Arnold. New York: Viking Press, 1964.

Lowell, Robert. "Paterson II," *The Nation*, CLXVI (June 19, 1948), 692-694.

Maas, Willard. "A Novel in the American Grain," *Books* (July 11, 1937), p. 4.

Martz, Louis. "The Unicorn in Paterson," *Thought*, XXXV (Winter, 1960), 537-554.

Miller, Fred B. "*The New Masses* and Who Else?" *The Blue Pencil*, II, 2 (Feb., 1935), 4-5.

Miller, J. Hillis. *Poets of Reality*. Cambridge, Mass.: Harvard University Press, 1965.

———, ed. *William Carlos Williams: A Collection of Critical Essays*. Englewood Cliffs, N.J.: Prentice-Hall, 1966.

Nelson, William. *History of the City of Paterson and the County of Passaic*. Paterson, N.J.: The Press Printing and Publishing Co., 1901.

The Northmen, Columbus, and Cabot: 985-1503, eds. J. E. Olson and E. G. Bourne. New York: Charles Scribner's Sons, 1906.

Oppenheim, James. "Editorials," *The Seven Arts*, I (Nov., 1916), 52-56; (Dec., 1916), 152-156; (March, 1917), 504-506.

Ostrum, Alan. *The Poetic World of William Carlos Williams*. Carbondale: Southern Illinois University Press, 1966.

Pearce, Roy Harvey. *The Continuity of American Poetry*. Princeton: Princeton University Press, 1961.

Polanyi, Michael. *The Tacit Dimension*. Garden City, N.Y.: Doubleday & Co., Inc., 1966.

Pound, Ezra, ed. *The Catholic Anthology, 1914-1915*. London: E. Mathews, 1915.

———. *Pavannes and Divisions*. New York: Alfred Knopf, 1918.

Pratt, William, ed. *The Imagist Poem*. New York: E. P. Dutton, 1963.

Quinn, Sister Mary Bernetta. *The Metamorphic Tradition in Modern Poetry*. New York: Gordian Press, Inc., 1966. Originally published by Rutgers University Press, New Brunswick, 1955.

Rahv, Philip. *Image and Idea*. Norfolk, Conn.: New Directions, 1949.

———. "Torrents of Spring," *The Nation*, CXLIV (June 26, 1937), 733.

Rakosi, Carl. "William Carlos Williams," *The Symposium*, IV, 4 (Oct., 1933), 439-447.

Rexroth, Kenneth. "A Letter to William Carlos Williams," *The Signature of All Things*. New York: New Directions, n.d., pp. 47-50.

———. *Assays*. Norfolk, Conn.: New Directions, 1961.

Ritchie, Andrew C. *Charles Demuth*. New York: Museum of Modern Art, 1950.

Rolland, Romain. "America and the Arts," *The Seven Arts*, I (Nov., 1916), 47-51.

Rosenfeld, Paul. *By Way of Art*. New York: Coward-McCann, Inc., 1928.

———. "Charles Demuth," *The Nation*, CXXXIII (Oct. 7, 1931), 371-373.

———. *Port of New York*. Urbana: University of Illinois Press, 1961. Originally published by Harcourt, Brace and Company, New York, 1924.

Rourke, Constance. *Charles Sheeler: Artist in the American Tradition*. New York: Harcourt, Brace and Company, 1938.

Shapiro, Karl. "The True Contemporary," *Start with the Sun*. Lincoln: University of Nebraska Press, 1963.

Slate, Joseph Evans. "William Carlos Williams, Hart Crane and 'The Virtue of History,'" *Texas Studies in Literature and Language,* VI (Winter, 1965), 486-511.

———. "William Carlos Williams' Image of America," unpublished dissertation, University of Wisconsin, 1957.

Spencer, Benjamin T. "Doctor Williams' American Grain," *Tennessee Studies in Literature,* VIII (1963), 1-16.

Suzuki, D. T. "Lectures on Zen Buddhism" in *Zen Buddhism and Psychoanalysis.* New York: Harper & Brothers, 1960.

Synge, John M. *Poems and Translations.* Dublin: Maunsel & Company, Ltd., 1911.

Thirlwall, John C., ed. "The Lost Poems of William Carlos Williams," *New Directions 16.* New York: New Directions, 1957.

——— "William Carlos Williams' 'Paterson,'" *New Directions 17.* Norfolk, Conn.: New Directions, 1961.

Wagner, Linda W. *The Poems of William Carlos Williams.* Middletown, Conn.: Wesleyan University Press, 1964.

Zukofsky, Louis. "American Poetry 1920-1930," *The Symposium,* II, 1 (Jan., 1931), 60-84.

———, ed. *An "Objectivists" Anthology.* Var, France and New York: TO, Publishers, 1932.

———, ed. " 'Objectivists' 1931," *Poetry,* XXXVII (Feb., 1931), 237-296.

INDEX

A. GENERAL

American culture: W.C.W.'s conception of, 75-77, 85-86, 89, 95, 133, 142, 162, 167

American heroes, 82, 109, 121, 125, 205. *See also* Boone, Daniel; Columbus, Christopher; Rasles, Père Sebastian

American history: W.C.W.'s attitude toward, 69-71, 78-79, 90, 137. *See also* "Usable past"

American idealists, 82-83, 86, 89, 90, 109-110, 120. *See also* Columbus, Christopher; Poe, Edgar Allen

American Indian, 26, 69, 90

American painting: revolt against Genteel Tradition, 12; W.C.W.'s relationship to, 31, 41-42

American poetry: W.C.W.'s opinion of, 25, 225, 234

"Anti-poetic," 49-50, 127-134, 146, 147-148, 152, 217-223, 240. *See also* Poetry, subject matter of; Totality

Art: W.C.W.'s conception of its relationship to nature and reality, 9-10, 30, 37, 46-47, 48-49, 52, 58-62, 74, 103-104, 146, 158, 237-238. *See also* Contact; Totality

"Beautiful Thing": heroine of *Paterson* III, 81n, 190, 191, 209

Boone, Daniel, 65-66, 82, 85, 103, 125, 198, 205, 243. *See also* American heroes

Bourne, Randolph, 66-67, 68-69

Brooks, Van Wyck, 12, 67, 69-70

Carnevali, Emanuel, 29

Chaucer, Daniel, 159, 207n, 232

"Classical" art: W.C.W.'s conception of, 40-41, 54, 100-101, 105, 239n

Columbus, Christopher, 2, 80, 85-86, 109, 110, 161, 162, 164, 191, 236, 241, 243. *See also* American heroes; American idealists

Contact: W.C.W.'s conception of the artist's connection with the world, 21-22, 29-30, 46, 62, 78-79, 82, 85-86, 90-91, 115. *See also* Art

Creative process: in W.C.W.'s writings, 9-10, 25, 196-200, 204, 236-237, 238-240

Curie, Marie, 3, 161, 196, 197

Dante Alighieri, 232

Demeter: myth of, 16-17, 22, 206

Demuth, Charles, 7n, 31, 41-53, 101, 218

Dewey, John, 55, 162

Diagnosis: as a technique in W.C.W.'s writings, 137-138, 140

Divorce: as a theme in W.C.W.'s writings, 165-173, 196, 203, 207

Eliade, Mircea, 23, 242
Eliot, T. S., 17-18, 37, 53, 73, 184, 193, 226, 241n
English poetry: W.C.W.'s objections to, 225

Faith: W.C.W.'s conception of, 8-9, 200, 233-234
Ford, Ford Madox, 155
Frank, Waldo, 66, 68
Franklin, Benjamin, 82, 84
Freud, Sigmund, 156
Freytag Loringhoven, Elsa von, 17, 206
Frye, Northrop, 125

Genteel Tradition: W.C.W.'s break with, 11, 41-42
Ginsberg, Allen, 164, 195

H.D. (Hilda Doolittle), 31
Haiku: compared with W.C.W.'s poetic techniques, 35
Hamilton, Alexander, 82, 84, 162, 164
Hartley, Marsden, 13, 31, 65, 215-216

Imagination: W.C.W.'s theories of, 9, 19, 30, 72, 92, 133, 156, 202, 208, 216, 217, 236
Imagism, 31-40, 41, 93-94, 96, 105n, 240
"Invention": W.C.W.'s conception of creativity, 38, 181-182
Irony: in W.C.W.'s writings, 50-53, 125

Johns, Orrick, 12, 13
Joyce, James, 63, 129

Keats, John, 15
Keyserling, Count Hermann, 55n, 162
Kora, myth of, 16
Kreymborg, Alfred, 12, 72n

Laforgue, Jules, 38, 132, 199

Language: in W.C.W.'s poetry, 3, 15, 33-34, 63, 224-225, 230, 232-234; relationship to society and environment, 6-7, 131, 150-151, 156-157; in In the American Grain, 78-81; in White Mule, 108; in Paterson, 156-157, 159-161, 162, 172, 186
Lawrence, D. H., 66-68, 82, 92n
Local environment: W.C.W.'s attitude toward, 5-6, 17-20, 37-38, 40, 47, 132, 142-143, 160; his use of it in Paterson, 163, 175-177, 180
Locality: W.C.W.'s theory of ("the local is the universal"), 21-22, 40, 54-64, 153-154, 162-173, 175-177, 235
Love: as a theme in W.C.W.'s works, 82, 121, 146-148, 203-217, 236
Lowell, Robert, 169

Male and female: the relationship of the sexes in W.C.W.'s writings, 6, 124-125, 147, 164-173, 193, 195, 203-217
"Money": as a subject of poetry, 157-158, 181, 196

New, the: men's reaction to, 2, 75-77, 81, 110, 111, 121-122, 184, 186, 212, 241-243; need for new forms in art, 3, 10, 26-27, 43, 74, 235, 243; conflict with the old, 46, 112, 184, 187, 238, 241-242
New World, 73, 90-91, 161, 162, 191

Objectivism, 36, 51, 63, 93-125, 136, 187, 240
Oppenheim, James, 13, 66, 69
Order: as a conscious concern in W.C.W.'s work, 200, 230, 233. See also Poetry, structure of

Patch, Sam, 163, 171-172, 177, 180, 185, 189

Poe, Edgar Allen, 38, 46-47, 73, 82-83, 88-90, 120, 156, 198, 200. *See also* American idealists

Poet: function, 2-3, 19, 175-176, 182; attitude toward life, 8, 20-21, 25, 39; qualities of, 49, 104-105, 124-125, 233-234, 240-243

Poetry
effect and function of, 10, 98, 133-134
origins of, 2, 8, 26, 91, 156-157
and painting, 41. *See also* Demuth, C h a r l e s ; Sheeler, Charles
and prose, 154-162, 239
relationship to language, 1, 232-234
structure of, 39-40, 101-104, 111-112. *See also* Order
stylistic qualities: "clarity," 43, 46; "austerity," 98, 100, 200
subject matter of, 1, 19, 40, 44-45, 127-130, 156-157, 203, 235. *See also* "Anti-poetic"; Totality
W.C.W.'s theories of, 94-95, 201, 235-237, 240

Polanyi, Michael, 199-200n

Poor: their role in art and society, 26, 134-137, 144, 146. *See also* Social responsibility

Possession, 30, 66, 70-71, 91-92

Pound, Ezra, 7, 16, 21, 31, 37, 53, 73, 94, 159, 164, 168, 173, 184, 192, 197, 226, 239

Prose style: W.C.W.'s conception of, 95, 107-109

Prosody, 32-34, 198, 201, 224-234, 240

Puritans: and Puritanism, 26, 68-69, 81-82, 83-84, 90, 118, 125, 218, 241

Radium, 161, 196

Rasles, Père Sebastian, 82, 85, 90-91, 125, 178, 191, 236, 243. *See also* American heroes

Rebirth and renewal, 9-10, 85, 91-92, 187-189, 194-200, 205, 208-217, 238

Rexroth, Kenneth, 39, 168

Rosenfeld, Paul, 67

Rukeyser, Muriel, 134, 158

Seasons: of life and reality, 176-177, 181, 188, 192-193, 203, 214, 219-220

Seven Arts, The, 12-13, 66-70

Shakespeare, William, 149, 154-155

Shapiro, Karl, 227

Sheeler, Charles, 2, 13, 41-44, 53-61, 92n, 101, 199, 232

Short stories: themes, 134-146; techniques, 136-138, 145-146; structure, 136, 139, 144, 199, 234

Siegel, Eli, 187

Social Credit: economic theory, 127n, 133, 196

Social responsibility of the artist: W.C.W.'s conception of, 27, 50, 127, 133-134, 140, 141-144. *See also* Poor

Stevens, Wallace, 125, 202, 225

Stieglitz, Alfred, 42, 92n

Totality, 25, 129, 131, 137, 153-154, 157, 158-159, 222-223. *See also* "Anti-poetic"; Art

"Usable past," 67, 70-71, 78, 83, 89. *See also* American history

"Variable foot." *See* Prosody

Wellcome, Mrs. Emily Dickenson (grandmother of W.C.W.), 15, 206

Whitman, Walt, 19, 33, 50, 67n, 198, 225-230 *passim*

Williams, Mrs. William Carlos (née Florence Herman), 3, 106, 214-217

Williams, William George (father of W.C.W.), 178

Williams, Mrs. William George (mother of W.C.W.), 7, 14-15
Wordsworth, William, 12, 157, 197

Vazakas, Byron, 229-230, 233

Zukofsky, Louis, 93-104 *passim*

B. WORKS BY WILLIAMS

"Accident, The," 144-145
Al Que Quiere, 34, 39, 42
"Apology," 38
"Asphodel," 5, 208-217, 231, 233, 237, 238
"At the Ball Game," 56-57

"Bastard Peace, A," 52
"Beer and Cold Cuts," 144
"Birth of Venus, The," 239
"Burning the Christmas Greens," 239
"By the Road to the Contagious Hospital," 74

"Catastrophic Birth," 219, 236, 239
"Clouds, The," 239
"Comedy Entombed: 1930," 145-146, 199
"Comic Life of Elia Brobitza, The," 205-207, 213
"Composition," 56

"Danse Pseudomacabre," 145
"Danse Russe," 33-34
"Death," 98
"Dedication for a Plot of Ground," 39
"Deep Religious Faith," 231
"Defective Record, The," 5
"Descent of Winter, The," 59-60
"Desert Music, The," 221-223, 236
Dream of Love, A, 204-205, 214
"Drunk and the Sailor, The," 231

"Early Martyr, An," 96-97

"Face of Stone, A," 139
"Farmers' Daughters, The," 138-139

First President, The, 63
"For Eleanor and Bill Monahan," 210

"Gift, The," 230
Great American Novel, The, 17, 71, 74-78, 106, 236, 238
"Great Figure, The," 44

In the American Grain, 26, 58, 71, 78-92, 95, 109-111, 118-125 *passim,* 137, 154, 155, 166-168, 170, 178, 184, 187, 191, 205, 207, 212, 218, 236, 238, 241
In the Money. See White Mule
"It Is a Living Coral," 51

"January Morning," 39, 132
"Jean Beicke," 140-141

Knife of the Times, The (collection of stories), 141-144
"Knife of the Times, The" (short story), 214
Kora in Hell, 17, 71-73, 106

"Life Along the Passaic River," 144, 176n, 199

Many Loves, 63, 146-152, 159-160, 171, 207, 212, 213, 219, 232, 236
"Mind's Games, The," 157-158, 178
"Morning," 8, 132-133
"Morning Imagination of Russia, A," 62

"Night in June, A," 165-166
"Notes in Diary Form," 63, 107, 155, 237
Novelette and Other Prose, A, 107

"Observer, The," 187
"Old Doc Rivers," 142-144
"Orchestra, The," 221
"Ordeal, The," 23
"Overture to a Dance of Locomotives," 47

"Paterson" (1927 poem), 25-26, 91, 179, 236
Paterson I-V, 4, 7, 15-19 passim, 63-64, 90, 150-151, 153-200, 201, 203-204, 207-211, 212, 213, 217, 219, 229, 237, 238
"Perpetuum Mobile: The City," 136
Pictures from Brueghel, 101
"Pink and Blue," 139-140
"Pink Locust, The," 232
"Poem, The," 216-217
Poems (1909), 11, 14, 42
"Portent," 23
"Portrait of a Woman in Bed," 206

"Raleigh Was Right," 157
"Romance Moderne," 47

"St. Francis Einstein of the Daffodils," 98-101
"Shadows," 202

"Source, The," 102-103
Sour Grapes, 35
Spring and All, 71, 73-74, 236
"Struggle of Wings," 44-45
"Sun, The," 103-104

Tempers, The, 14, 32-33, 42
"To a Dog Injured in the Street," 220-221
"To All Gentleness," 130-131
"To Elsie," 97
"To Waken an Old Lady," 35-36
"Tribute to the Painters," 221
"Turtle, The," 230

"Use of Force, The," 139
"View of a Lake," 97
Voyage to Pagany, A, 106-107, 218

"Wanderer, The," 14-25, 33, 61, 191, 218, 236
White Mule, 106-125, 146, 154, 187, 237
"Writer's Prologue to a Play in Verse," 151, 236

"Yachts, The," 28, 51, 97
"Yellow Flower, The," 220, 231, 232
"Young Love," 48